THE CUNARD
BOOK OF
CRUISING

David St John Thomas

DAVID & CHARLES
Newton Abbot London

Photographs by David St John and Georgette Zackey Thomas
unless credited otherwise

Frontispiece *The* QE2 (Tony Stone Photolibrary – London)
Page 6 *Queen Elizabeth and Princess Margaret after launching*
the QE2 (Glasgow Evening Herald)

British Library Cataloguing in Publication Data

Thomas, David St John
    The Cunard book of cruising.
    1. Cruises by liners, history
    I. Title
    910.45

    ISBN 0-7153-9074-0

Typeset by Typesetters (Birmingham) Ltd, Smethwick, West Midlands
and printed in Singapore
by C.S. Graphics Pte Ltd
for David & Charles plc
Brunel House   Newton Abbot   Devon

Distributed in the USA by Sterling Publishing Co. Inc.,
387 Park Avenue South, New York, NY10016-8810

CONTENTS

INTRODUCTION

THE tugs cut loose and the ship starts making her own way towards the narrows, coming vibratingly to life again after her long day at rest. She gathers speed quickly, and passengers anxious not to miss the passage past the castle stream out on deck. Three long blasts from the deep, throbbing whistle echo out to sea and are answered by the higher pitch of a ferry's whistle and acknowledged by a final short blast by the captain; some of the passengers on the observation deck smile at this friendly exchange, though one or two put their hands over their ears. Passengers are still coming out of half a dozen doorways to swell the crowd already on deck. Cameras are now at the ready for a final shot of the castle guarding the narrows, the mellow stone bathed in the fading sunset; a picture indeed.

An equal crowd, though by no means all the same passengers, had been up at daybreak to enjoy the sunrise over the ancient city and see the tugs take hold. Others had not woken until after the ship's arrival, half an hour earlier than scheduled. By the time they had left their cabins, she was already tied up at her berth, and the first coaches for the morning excursions were manoeuvring into position on the quay. By coach, taxi and on foot, most passengers had disembarked shortly after breakfast; many staff followed as soon as their duties were done. As the ship lay motionless all day, only a handful of people moved about her, though lunch and tea were available for those who stayed, a few sunbathed and read books and watched the painters continuing their everlasting round of re-whitening the superstructure. A handful of local dignitaries had been lunched by the captain and shown the amenities on board. They had expressed their amazement at the range and the quality, but with the ship so lifeless they cannot have gained a true impression of what it would be like normally.

But now, as we go back to sea, the ship is throbbing with life. It is not only those on deck who are enjoying a spectacular view of the narrows and of the old castle. Many dressing in their cabins have grabbed a camera for a shot through their porthole, while in the bars many turn with a drink in their hand to take a final glance.

As we pass the castle, the first gentle motion of the sea can be felt, a sensation thrilling to many regular cruisegoers signifying that once more we are on our way by the world's best form of transport. As we reach the open sea, the wind becomes much stronger. A few ladies are temporarily blinded by their own billowing dresses as they wait their turn to descend the steps from the observation deck. Soon only a handful of hardier passengers are left outdoors, and the half dozen determined walkers and joggers have an uninterrupted passage for their final mile. Yet the now almost horizontal rays of the setting sun on the western cliffs make a sight as pretty as any seen during the day – briefly enjoyed by a room stewardess who is waiting for her first passengers to leave for dinner so that she can clean their cabins, turn down the beds and change the towels for the second time today.

The occasional fishing vessels heading back to port are hardly noticed. Now everyone is concerned with social affairs, changing, refreshing their memory of the evening's entertainment, ordering drinks, comparing notes on the day ashore and the shopping. Bartenders are busy. Menus are handed round. Then come the trays of canapés. As the curtains are steadily drawn, the sea is forgotten. Then attention is focussed on the dining room as tables steadily come to life, food and wine orders are given, the special dishes ordered last night skilfully chaperoned from kitchen to the right waiters' station for serving at exactly the right moment. And there come the musicians who ceremoniously played us out of port the first night, ready to celebrate the birthday of one early eater.

After dinner, less than a score venture out onto the windy deck to pay homage to the silvery moon. The interesting thing is that though perhaps half of the total passengers enjoy the evening's main entertainment in the ballroom, there are literally dozens of minorities of around a score doing different things: reading in the library, playing cards, gambling in the casino, in the lobby consulting the purser's office, looking at the map of the ship's progress and details of the forthcoming world cruise, trying to recognise themselves in the rows of photographs taken the previous day, in the various bars, theatre (three or four score enjoying tonight's film here), and holding conversations outside the elevators or at the foot of stairways. It is almost as though a model-maker had put the people into position to show off the ship's spaciousness and variety.

It will be just the same for our day at sea tomorrow. If it is warm, as we expect, the largest single contingent of passengers mid morning or afternoon will be sunning themselves and reading in their chosen position on the acres of spacious deck. But the majority

will be made up of numerous minorities – in the pools (indoors and out), at the beauty salon, listening to the financial lecture or improving their photographic technique in the theatre or one of the bars, sipping their favourite drink in one of the other bars, writing letters or playing scrabble, working the slot machines or working out at the fitness centre, telephoning or telexing home, having private conversations with their spouses in their cabins, snoozing, contemplating, solving the world's problems, planning the next trip, pursuing new friendships.

But now to bed. We go down to our cabin while the ship is still agog with social life. Tomorrow's programme is under the door along with an invitation to a party. A piece of chocolate wishing us a good night's sleep is on the pillow together with a reminder that the clock goes back an hour, so we will have a good long night and surely sleep soundly after our bath with the water gently slopping over us with the ship's gentle motion.

People who have never done it have many different concepts of cruising, but nearly all miss two basic essentials: the thrill of the journey itself, and the enormous range of options, indoors and out, around the clock, that enable you to be truly yourself. 'I couldn't possibly enjoy that lifestyle', might be a remark fairly said of a few down-market ships processing passengers in a mass-production manner every few days, but has to be inaccurate for the vast majority of cruises since it is the passengers who decide their own style. Only prejudice dictates that cruising has to be this or that.

There can be no other type of holiday so viciously attacked by those unfamiliar with it and so loved by those partaking it as cruising! The author has to admit that at first he was caught up in the bias. A user only of *Queen Elizabeth 2*'s transatlantic scheduled services,

Though not frequent, Queen Mary's *cruises were splendid occasions* (Imagebank)

he explained to colleagues that 'of course' he would not wish to go cruising but that crossing the Atlantic with a typewriter in the cabin had practical advantages. 'Well, I certainly can't imagine you enjoying cruising', would come back the comment of a kind bound to affect one's own attitude.

When it was proposed that an international organisation of book publishers hold an anniversary convention on a cruise liner, there was near pandemonium. Delegate after delegate denounced 'that kind of thing', castigating too much social life, too much eating, too much drinking and above all too much luxury. You felt that the very act of stepping up the gangway of a cruise liner would sully your character. Yet as a group of prosperous, highly communicative people, they were almost all into socialising, good food and drink, and as a routine went to no end of trouble to ensure they stayed at the right hotels and were seen in the correct restaurants. Inevitably, those most closely associated with gracious living were the most appalled at the prospect of graciousness on board.

Part of the problem is that cruising has been served badly by the media with its own predetermined images. Of course films and television reports emphasise the extremes of lavish entertainment and behaviour. Ordinary people enjoying and fulfilling themselves in their own way do not make dramatic viewing. It might be recalled that one of the greatest culprits in misreporting cruising on television also looks at famous bridges more as a service for suicides than as engineering works in the transportation business! *Loveboat* is as exaggerated as any soap opera.

Such is the strength of the anti-cruising lobby that many people only take their first trip with extreme caution. Then the facts speak for themselves. An extremely high proportion of passengers return – often to the same ship. Some of Cunard's parties for repeaters attract over three-quarters of those on board. Many of the regulars know the staff better than they know their own families. And while everybody gasps at the fact that one passenger has spent a total of a year and a half on that self-same ship, the majority have more ordinarily done two, three or four cruises – and would love to do more.

Attitudes have mellowed, especially in the United States, now that millions give personal testimony of the pleasures of cruising. There is, however, still a substantial age bias: 'surely you're young for that kind of thing'. Most people with young children cannot afford cruising holidays, while to be able to take a round-the-world cruise of three months when you are in your forties suggests that you are not in a job where you are indispensable. What you cannot do because of money and time constraints, it is easy to rationalise into being undesirable.

Yet cruising has such varied advantages that it is indeed appropriate for people of all ages and walks of life. It is of course costly compared to camping or even touring with bed-and-breakfast accommodation, but few who have been on even a single cruise doubt its value for money. In a single sentence, cruising is exciting, carefree, offers enormous options, and is safe as well as good value.

Among the advantages, your bedroom moves with you. Once unpacked, you can forget about opening and closing cases and lugging them about, and also about checking in and out of hotels, ensuring there is indeed a vacant room with suitable facilities along the route ahead, and all the other details that are a perpetual tax on a conventional touring holiday. Unless air transport is also involved, there is virtually no restriction on the amount of baggage you can take along.

Your ship's layout may seem overwhelmingly complicated when you first board, but you will quickly understand it and not have to enquire where everything is, as is likely to be

the case when you spend a night here and a couple there. Usually you will have the same seat in the dining room throughout. There is no parking. The laundry is open seven days a week and there is a launderette down the corridor. You do not have to worry about banking hours, check-out times, standing in line to settle accounts.

Your itinerary will have been worked out through great and long experience, and just as much thought will have been given to all the on-shore entertainment and other options. You are thus able to do things most people on holiday could not possibly undertake for themselves, though the choice is entirely yours.

A cruiseliner is not only one of the world's most comfortable but also one of the safest places. There is overall safety and a safety net in a hundred and one ways. Thousands of single women have discovered that travelling by ship is the one holiday they can take without fear of being molested or shunted to one side. Singles are a nuisance to couple-orientated tourist hotels; most cruise liners encourage them as an essential part of their business and arrange parties for them. Medical attention is at hand. Special diets are routinely catered for. Rip a precious dress and it will be repaired as expertly as anywhere on land and usually much quicker. Need a telephone and the exchanges of the world are at your disposal by your bed. Cruising has an especial advantage when visiting less-developed or alien parts of the world. Many have first been behind the Iron Curtain with the security of Cunard. 'I

could have kissed the walls of my cabin it was so good to be back', said the American young lady after an adventurous expedition into Cairo.

Though a few sensational ones have naturally hit the headlines, shipboard robberies are rare. Unlike most hotels, your ship will usually automatically give you two keys to your room, and you can lock a drawer and maybe a safe box within it, though valuables go to the box allocated to your room in the purser's office or elsewhere. Requesting the box and selecting the jewellery for today will normally only take a moment. Nowhere else in the world is more genuine jewellery routinely worn than at sea.

The fare includes just about everything: transportation, often on the grand scale to exotic destinations and even free launch and shuttle buses in many ports; accommodation including an ever higher proportion of luxury rooms with a high level of personal service and cleanliness (never a worry about when the next fresh towels will be available); all food (which can be six or more meals daily usually of outstanding variety and quality) and soft drinks, teas and coffees; all entertainment including nightly live shows, live music around the ship much of the day, films, lectures and demonstrations, sporting facilities, daily newspaper and programme. Other than the advertised port charges, there is a wonderful freedom from taxes and other extras. Even drinks, though not normally included, are good tax-free value. You simply cannot compare a cruise fare with an hotel's daily rate.

QE2 pays a rare visit to dry dock in Southampton
(Ron Baker)

1

A DAY IN THE LIFE OF THE CAPTAIN OF THE *QE2*

THE alarm goes off at 7 and I have a cup of tea and do my ablutions. Then the international mailbox, checking any telexes from Cunard or from the agents of future ports. If we are arriving in port today I need to know how our approach is going, especially where the depth of water decreases such as at the entrance to Bombay or Mauritius. [This is Alan Bennell speaking.]

My first visit to the bridge is at 7.45 and I wait to see the changing of the watch at 8. The printouts of weather and the maps need to be checked. If we are at sea, we have to consider the most commercially viable course. We burn a lot of fuel, and getting it right can make a big difference to our costs, and also affect passenger comfort.

At 8.30 it's a glass of orange juice and another cup of tea. I read the news broadcast and the daily programme, especially noting any passenger news, and also listen to our Channel 4. Reading the daily programme means noting what looks good or bad.

I listen to the junior officer of the watch make the day's first announcement – giving his own name, the name of ships passing us, the nearest land, and anything of special interest like dolphins or flying fish. 'This is the officer of the watch speaking', has passengers very attentive, but sailors are not trained to communicate and have to be encouraged to work with their own peculiarity. We try to give them confidence and like to say 'that was nice'.

At 8.45 I ring the hotel manager, and around 9 have a conversation with the chief engineer who reports on how many engines we have

The photograph of Alan Bennell that appeared in the programmes of his popular cruises

running, fuel usage, any technical problems and freshwater conditions. Normally we make all our freshwater as we go, but we have to take it on in port because we're not making it then. About every four days I chair the shipboard meeting with the chief engineer, hotel manager, financial operations manager and the staff captain.

Then come reports about burst pipes causing flooding, banging noises, and it is time to see anyone who refuses to discuss a complaint with anyone else. It is always informal. I make tea for them and give an attentive ear. When something gets upsetting it is usually because an earlier complaint has not been properly addressed. The history of every case needs checking.

At 10 it's my first coffee and I answer telexes and passengers' letters. I share a secretary with the staff captain and up she comes. Every passenger's letter is answered, even if they write just to say it has been a 'delightful voyage' or what a pity it was we missed out a port. If there is a complaint that really touches them, the chief engineer, hotel manager or whoever will be telephoned to get the answer. Communications are most important. I can of course talk to the bridge at any time and am always in touch if anything out of the ordinary is happening, even when walking around the deck, which I usually do about now.

It might then be an inspection of the crew quarters and the kitchens. Public health is very important. And the walk might take in the Chinese laundry, the mechanical parts and crew areas, returning by the passengers' areas making mental images as well as records and notes of what needs to be done. Nearly always soon after 11 I sit down and prepare notes for my daily conversation with passengers over the ship's intercom. I try to make this a kind of fireside chat with details of what we're doing, the weather and even a punchline about a forthcoming cruise.

Then comes another session on the bridge. I like to be there as much as possible, and

usually make it seven times during the day: twenty minutes the first time and five minutes each of the others if we are at sea. As I'll tell you in a moment, it is quite different on port days, or even at sea in fog or something unusual. Then, maybe, there is a party for the Press or other VIP group. Nothing heavily social before lunch; indeed more often it is sorting out something to do with staff relations. Through the buffet areas and then have a light lunch with a beer. At 1.30 I make time for the afternoon visit to my quarters and get into the general paperwork on the desk. At 4 a selected passenger comes to tea. My wife or I make it ourselves. My wife is there two-thirds of the time, and she plays a major role and has made a big contribution to our style.

At 5 there's usually a telephone chat with the hotel manager, and the social hostess tells me about the parties. It's nice to drop in on any party, and then we have our own receptions in my quarters usually at 7.15. Getting the balance of people you invite right is very important. But for the first few nights of most cruises there are of course the passengers to be welcomed at the captain's cocktail parties in the Queen's Room, at 6.45.

I enjoy every minute of these occasions, which seem to have got more numerous as well as much longer than they used to be. You know, people are people, always so interesting. Being captain is very secondary to making people feel at home and telling the women, and I mean it, that they look and smell delightful. Spanish, Italians, French – a bash at all their languages at least makes them laugh. I used to have long lines waiting outside for a formal welcome but now we're doing it more informally inside the reception area. Taking time and enjoying it, and hearing what's happened to regulars since their last voyage is important – and we do have so many passengers coming back.

Dinner is at 8.30 or 8.45. I eat lightly, with fish or lamb. I'm not into heavy meats: salmon, escargots, frog legs, that kind of thing is best,

but not too elaborate. Many people come to the ship for the gourmet meals of their lives, but those who have really made it and can afford long times with us enjoy more simple fare. The great thing about the *Queen* is that you can do and have what you like. For dessert it is usually ice cream.

I have two tables, one in the Columbia and the other in the Mauretania restaurants, and alternate. There are eight on each table, which means four couples, or three if my wife is there. The fun is moulding them into a group and then we often get into talking ships. I look forward to every meal, and want to hear what people have been doing during the day.

I leave the table at around 10.15. I rarely have a nightcap, just occasionally a Campari and soda. If it is a gin and tonic, it will be before and never after dinner. Then to the bridge again and final rounds visiting the casino, yacht club, the cabaret and disco, and some fresh air on boat deck – the bleeper on of course. A last short visit to the bridge around midnight, and go to sleep with the television. Only one day in ten might I have a short catnap during the day.

There is never a boring day, but like many of the regular passengers I and my staff enjoy the rhythm of days at sea. Days in port are quite different from those afloat and vary greatly between themselves. Tomorrow, for example, I am hoping my wife will join me for a light lunch on shore in Madeira. If we are very lucky, we might get an hour or two to go shopping when we're in port, but even then the walkie-talkie is in the pocket. When back on the ship, there's usually the bottom of the pile of the in-tray to get down to. But some ports are very demanding.

Of course I take over the ship for all beginnings and endings, and whenever we're using tugs or have a pilot on board. Beginnings and endings are when the adrenaline flows. As you know, we had very strong winds coming into Tenerife a few days ago, and because the tugs didn't do what they should, we caught the quay and had to stay there an extra night for repairs. It shows the tensions, and in this case disappointed many people since we had to cut out the Cape Verde Islands.

New York is the most demanding port. It means taking over for two and a half to three hours coming in and going out, and with all that happens when we're tied up, including visits by the bosses, it makes a tiring day anyway. But it might be foggy all the way from Nantucket, and I could be on the bridge a total of twelve hours. When it is foggy I have a sea cabin, to be on immediate call by the bridge. It's still possible to make all the daily telephone calls, though the staff captain will do the inspections round the ship.

Though there is that delightful rhythm on a long voyage such as across the Atlantic when we speed, as only we now can in the whole world of ships, no two days are ever exactly the same, any more than any two passengers are identical. It's the variety that makes my life so fascinating.

I don't think I ever realised what being master of the *Queen* really entailed . . . you need public relations, marketing, technical skills, and much more. You're at the front of the house, so that when people walk across the gangway into a world called *QE2* they feel a real part of it and will want to come back. Yes, it's very exciting. Anywhere outside the civilised world the *Queen* creates an impression . . . wherever she goes. The crew love it, and it is a very young crew: like politicians they are getting younger all the time.

At the time of writing, when Alan Bennell is on leave his place is taken by the relief master, Robin Allen Woodall, as you would expect another great enthusiast: 'When I joined as a

Captain Woodhall's busy day includes a conference with senior colleagues in his office and (away from the paperwork) several visits to the bridge: being at the controls is always exhilarating

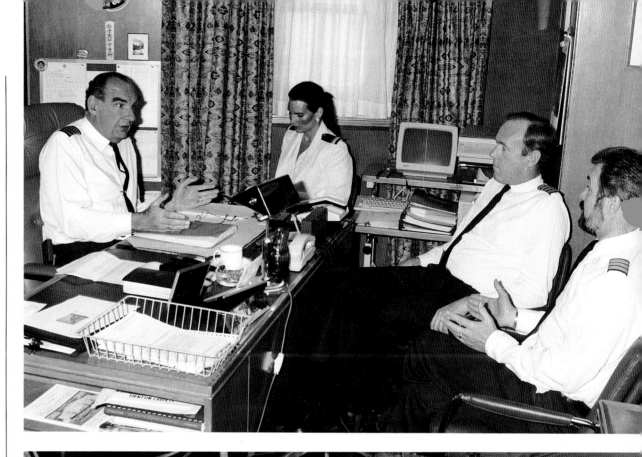

junior officer all those years ago I wouldn't have been able to comprehend the job satisfaction this job brings.' Since individuality is encouraged, there is naturally a difference of style when Captain Woodall is in charge. For one thing he still greets passengers with the traditional handshake at the door leading to the Queen's Lounge when holding his captain's welcome parties, normally three a cruise. 'At least I say a few words to everybody,' he says, regretting that many passengers see him as so exalted that they hardly like even to pass the time of day when meeting around the ship. Some ladies have even curtseyed to him!

'I really do like talking to people, but on a ship this size you can't hope to get to know everyone personally.' It is easier on *Cunard Countess* and *Princess*; he is relief master to them, too, these and the *QE2* forming one management unit, the two *Fjord* ships another, and the *Goddesses* a third so far as many staffing matters are concerned.

Captain Woodall also makes regular broadcasts to passengers, in rough weather even telling them he has experienced sea sickness many times himself. And there is a stiff round of formal entertaining keeping him busy even when the ship is in port. 'I enjoy it all . . . all except the paperwork, perhaps. I have to sit too long at my desk sorting through that, but then that is the price you have to pay for any really interesting job. But perhaps what surprises many people is the amount of time I spend actually driving the ship. She's a great ship to command, and I always enjoy my time on the bridge. Of course I am always there entering or leaving port, in storms or fog, sometimes for 24 or 36 hours at a time, but I also love it on an ordinary day as we cross an ordinary sea.'

Alan Charles Bennell was born on 26 September 1931 (Libra), educated in private schools,

The Master, Robin Allen Woodall, a 1987 photograph appearing on the cover of many daily programmes

HMS *Conway* and in the Merchant Marine and Royal Naval College, his final position being Chief Cadet Captain. He served on Shell tankers from 1948. He qualified as Master in 1957, and between then and 1982 was Third Officer to the Captain, Cunard Line, serving on *Sythia, Carinthia, Queen Elizabeth, Queen Mary, Caronia, Mauretania, Carmania, Franconia, QE2, Cunard Adventurer* and *Cunard Princess.* Between 1982 and 1987 he was general manager of *Cunard Princess.* His enthusiasm and outward-going personality were noticed by Cunard's hierarchy in New York and, much to his surprise (he had no idea why he had been summoned there) he was offered the post of Master of the *QE2* (also becoming assistant general manager) in 1987. His hobbies are sailing, fishing and gardening. He has been married to his wife, Sheila, for over thirty years and they live in Southampton, England.

Born in London in 1933, Robin Allen Woodall[1] continued his education at Birkenhead School when his family moved to the Wirral, near Liverpool, where he became a keen sailing enthusiast as he remains today, living in the same place ever since. He first joined Cunard as an apprentice officer in 1950 but worked for a merchant line before coming back to Cunard (serving as fourth officer on a cargo ship) in 1954. The 20,300 ton *Franconia* gave him his first taste of life on a luxury North Atlantic liner, but it was not until 1960 that he was permanently appointed to the Cunard passenger fleet, and even then he had several periods seconded to the Royal Navy.

In 1967–8 he served as first officer on the *Queen Mary, Queen Elizabeth, Carinthia* and *Franconia,* the latter being a much-loved cruising ship with an amazing record for rescuing people from other ships. He was on the maiden voyage of *QE2* and also working on her when tugs were on strike in New York and she had

[1]As this book went to press Robin Allen Woodall was promoted to Master of the *QE2,* Alan Bennell retiring on health grounds.

Back on the bridge: 'ever fascinating'

to be berthed without assistance, when there was a bomb scare in mid-Atlantic and four bomb-disposal experts were parachuted into the ocean, when speed was reduced to save fuel in the crisis of 1973–4, and when she broke down 250 miles off Bermuda and all passengers had to be taken off.

After periods as staff captain in various Cunard ships and further spells in the Royal Navy, he was promoted to relief master of the line in 1982 and since 1987 has been relief master on the *QE2* as well as the *Countess* and *Princess.* His first wife died after a short illness and he married Eileen his present wife (who plays an important part in his life at sea) in 1963. He greatly enjoys home life in the Wirral.

LATITUDE AND LONGITUDE

Latitude means distance north or south of the equator; longitude means distance east or west of the 0 degree at Greenwich, London. Both are recorded in degrees, minutes and seconds. At the equator a minute of longitude is equal to a nautical mile, but as the meridians converge away from the equator, meeting at the poles, the size of a degree becomes less.

2
ALASKA

WITH a thunderous roar echoing over the high mountains, a piece of the glacier, formed perhaps of snow that fell at the time of Christ, cracked. Apart from a few clustered round the picture windows in the lounges, everyone was on deck – alert, silent, cameras at the ready. 'There!' Slowly a large piece of the glacier detached itself, leant drunken fashion away from the rest, and then with a gentle rushing sound slipped into the water. Cameras snapped, videos whirled and a large cheer went up. For hundreds there had never been a closer encounter with nature. Half a minute later those holding a cup of the mulled wine thoughtfully provided on deck, had to steady themselves as the ship slowly rolled on the waves caused by the creation of an iceberg. The seals sunning themselves on a score or more smaller bergs ignored the waves, but slipped into the water when the voices of humans on the ship came too close.

Excitement on board had risen as the first glacier of the trip was approached. Already passengers had had a brown bear catching a salmon pointed out; indeed the ship had stopped and slewed to give a better view. The previous night some had spotted two kinds of whales as well as bald eagles, while many had enjoyed one of those splendid displays by friendly, cavorting dolphins enjoying the company of humans only feet away. The wildlife was endless. But the glacier! Some passengers had indeed come thousands of miles to see such wonders and had enhanced their experience by preparatory reading and listening to the ship's commentary. Hundreds of cameras were loaded with fresh film. And, yes, the sun was out. That would speed up the cracking or

'calving'. It remained warm on deck even when the ship nosed steadily through a sea packed with icebergs of various sizes and imaginative shapes – all that lovely blue caused by centuries of the snow's compression. Only when the end of the ½ mile (.8km) wide glacier was only ½ mile (.8km) away did the temperature drop as though one were going into a cold store.

The interest continued intense: the lighting, the reverberations of the cracking at times sounding like artillery attacks, the parallel lines of assorted rocks slowly being carried by the glacier to the sea and giving its sweeping curves something of the effect of freeway lane markings. It was indeed a good morning for calving. 'Congratulations, you have witnessed the birth of an iceberg, only an eighth of it now visible above the water', said the commentator. One of the ship's boats was lowered with a photographer so we could see what our position in the universe looked like from sea level, and crew to bring back part of a berg so our drinks could be cooled with the ice of ages that evening.

With increasing interest in the environment, Alaskan cruising has grown enormously in popularity, and deservedly so. For Americans it means visiting the 'last frontier' in comfort, without overseas travel, but steadily more Europeans fly out for the unique experience. Once you go to Alaska, they say, you never go all the way back. Its spacious timelessness, its grandeur and variety, its rich wildlife and scenic spectaculars of which glaciers are only one, perhaps above all its marvellous skies and lighting effects, especially on those long summer evenings when indeed it hardly gets

dark – lighting and colours totally unspoilt by pollution; they all contribute. Take a score of cruises and many may eventually blur in your memory; never the Alaskan one. It brings out the enthusiastic, wondering child in all of us. Who could not feel in awe of it all and much the better for that?

As you might expect, cruise lectures are better attended, casinos quieter, than on most itineraries. Most people come for what there is to see rather than shipboard life as such though long and, for many, energetic days make for hearty appetites. While the daytime temperature is usually at least in the upper sixties or even seventies, and often sunbathing is possible, even when the bow is pushing through ice-floes, clearly people do not choose Alaska especially for its climate. It therefore does not attract the cruising regulars who never tire of a round of Caribbean islands; conversely many newcomers who opt for cruising only as a way of unlocking Alaska's mysteries, are converted to the way of life.

So you don't choose an Alaskan cruise for the social life though passengers are quickly drawn together in a spirit of adventure that includes the main on-board events. Many of the ports, though not without historic and other attractions, have limited facilities especially for shopping. But the scenery, the sense of timelessness, photographic opportunities with up to twenty hours of daylight, the wildlife – if they switch you on, a cruise along the Alaskan coast is an experience of a lifetime. Pioneered by Cunard, itineraries have greatly improved in recent years. Most passengers now make a one-way journey between Vancouver and Whittier (port for Anchorage) or Anchorage

itself, or vice versa, and combine it with a few days' land sightseeing in Alaska. The better choice is to take the ship north into the last frontier, enjoying the sheltered water of the Inside Passage while you get accustomed to the sea; though you are in the open ocean for only a small proportion of time it can be rough, especially for ships going the whole way to Anchorage at the start or end of the short Alaskan cruising season. Most people want to go at the perfect time, July, when it has warmed up but the nights are still almost at their longest. Despite a dramatic growth in the number of ships offering Alaskan itineraries, the best cabins on the most popular dates quickly sell out. Alaska is unlikely to be a wise choice for a last-minute decision.

Vancouver makes an excellent starting point, perhaps after a trans-Canadian train journey or a ferry ride across the Puget Sound from Seattle with a stopover in the charming capital of Vancouver Island, Victoria. What better prelude to a sea journey to the forty-ninth state than a stay in Victoria's gracious Empress Hotel, taking tea perhaps after a visit to the famous Buchart Gardens. The ferry from the island to Vancouver is also full of interest; a civilised bus actually travels on it from Victoria's bus station at the back of the Empress to downtown Vancouver. But that is not to underestimate Vancouver's own many attractions, including Stanley Gardens and the oldtime Gastown. Cruise ships are served by one of the world's best sea terminals, with all kinds of facilities including shop for last-minute purchases, such as flowers for the cabin.

The whole of the first day is spent in the Inside Passage, surrounded by fir-covered hills, whether on the mainland or innumerable islands. Fog is not uncommon, but showers

The compressed snow falling off the end of the glacier might have fallen at the time of Christ . . . and you can hear, as well as feel the cold from the newly-formed icebergs passing by

mean the best possible lighting for photography between them, and indeed many of the most dramatic shots include fog banks or low cloud cutting off the tops of fir trees while their neighbours bask in sunshine. The passage varies greatly in width and cruise liners have to go around the islands rather than take the Wrangell Narrows, which is the most spectacular section for the ferries of the Alaska Marine Highway. But most of the route is common to both and you will see the vessels plying on the world's longest ferry route, plus a rich variety of cargo and fishing craft and yachts – a wonderful day to unwind and to marvel at the scale of it all and (apart from other vessls) the paucity of evidence of human habitation.

First port is usually Ketchikan, renowned for its 13ft (4m) of annual rainfall (most ports have nothing remotely like that), a city of 14,000 that absorbs many visitors but does not take too much notice of them as it goes about its daily business as salmon capital and running Alaska's oldest continuously operated manufacturing business, the spruce mills. Already we are in Alaska. For hundreds of miles the Canadian border is only miles inland, the coastal belt – now referred to as the 'panhandle' – having been first developed by the Russians who sold it to the United States along with the rest of Alaska for $7 million in 1867. Even at this first stop you will learn that Alaska (divide it in half and Texas would become the third largest state) is quite different from 'the lower forty-eight', as the other states are continuously referred to. Something of the friendliness of Alaska may be gauged from the fact that a group of women in Ketchikan, seeing the need and rising to the challenge, formed themselves into a cruise lecturer association. One of them, probably a mother enjoying a break from home, will be at the microphone at points of interest along the route and will give occasional lectures in the theatre or ballroom.

Next day probably includes a diversion up the Endicott or Tracey Arms, fjords of great drama and most likely the site of your first icebergs, and a call at Alaska's unlikely but civilised little capital Juneau, founded, like many of the small ports, in the gold rush. By bus or plane you can see your first glacier, Mendenhall, here and most who opt for the raft trip down from Mendenhall Lake are well pleased. Skagway, however, lives totally on its former glory as port and supply base for the prospectors, and it has to be admitted does so in style with its Wild West timber buildings, sidewalks and saloons – a bustling living museum. There could only be one Skagway. Though there are plans for reopening part of it, the famous Yukon & White Pass railway has long been closed; but even by coach the journey along the route of the Klondike gold rush across the Canadian border to Carcross is well worthwhile.

The guide-book's claim that Sitka is a little piece of Russia stretches the point, but it is a good place to learn of Alaska's Russian origin and indeed early American days, since the capital remained here until 1906. In the well-developed settlement including good shops, you can see icons in the Russian Orthodox church.

The next two days are the cruise's highlight – Hubbard Glacier and Columbia Glacier, with a short stop at Valdez at the Alaskan pipeline in between. The sheer scale of the glaciers is awesome, but you have to be a dull person not to become absorbed with the glacier lore that comes over in the ship's commentary and is the subject of much individual discussion and reading. Many passengers become glacier snobs! There are indeed great differences between them, those advancing healthily and those ailing and retreating. Some have periods of advance and retreat. Excitement on board any ship is never greater than when a great vessel is dwarfed by a wall of sheer ice over a mile wide, steadily carrying the pale-blue compressed snow of ages from the vast icefields to the sea. Calving, the cracking and falling off of sections to form icebergs, is but an added attraction.

The excitement can be gauged from the fact that the ship's personnel who, in a blasé fashion, ignore attractions such as the Panama Canal, now crowd on their own deck to get the best view and photographs. Even if you forget the rest of the magnificent scenery, that wonderful sunset long after most people back home are in bed while the ship rests in what seems a lake surrounded by untouched islands, the romance of the Russian age and the gold rush, the whole cruise would be rendered memorable by the glaciers. By plane and helicopter from various ports there are trips to see the icefields and glaciers, floatplanes even landing on one. The trips are expensive, noisy, sell out quickly; they leave everlasting memories. Valdez, the town that was moved after an earthquake, is one port for helicopter trips, and also for a visit to the Alaskan pipeline that terminates here; your ship might be followed out to sea by a giant tanker heading south. Valdez is the most northerly port open throughout the year.

Your cruise might terminate at Whittier, with an interesting train journey (there is no road) to Anchorage, or after days in Seward (more glacier possibilities) and Homer (an artists'

MIDNIGHT SUN

This is caused by three properties associated with the earth's own motion: first, that it rotates on a north-south axis once every 24 hours; second, that it circles the sun once every 365 days, moving in a flat plane which passes through the sun itself; thirdly, that its axis is *not* perpendicular to this plane but is tilted 23.5 degrees from the perpendicular. It is this slight tilt which brings nightless day to one pole and, simultaneously, dayless night to the other.

BOAT NO 12

colony with galleries and a bustling port) in Anchorage itself. A round trip would undoubtedly increase the chances of seeing the glaciers and other highlights in perfect or at least tolerable weather, but now that a one-way passage is possible, most people opt for a few days on land before returning home.

Despite the distance you will have come, for many Alaska only begins at Anchorage. Generally southern Alaska, including the whole panhandle, is not enjoying boom times, partly because traditional industries such as pulp have seen better days, partly because so many now view it from a cruise liner and do not patronise local accommodation. Several of the

ports are of course isolated as regards land transport and, like the capital Juneau, have only limited local road systems. The 'railbelt' on either side of Anchorage fares better, the city itself being worthy of at least a day, including time to admire the gardens with their huge flowers and ornamental vegetables thriving in summer mildness and almost continuous daylight. But Denali National Park is top attraction. One suggestion is to fly to the state's only major inland city, Fairbanks, and visit the park with an overnight stopover on the train journey back on the Alaskan Railroad. The train takes you through a kaleidoscope of Alaska, including Mount McKinley and a spectacular canyon,

Space is the most memorable feature of America's 'last frontier' and can frequently be found even on board

in old-fashioned comfort. A wide choice of land tours can be bought at value prices when you book your cruise.

Once you have been to Alaska and soaked in its spaciousness and friendliness, the rich vegetation of the coastal strip, the grandeur of the mountains, waterfalls and glaciers, not to mention the clean air, local fish and the wildlife, you will indeed never go all the way back. The Alaskan cruise will be with you for ever.

Dwarfed by the towering mountains and the glacier, the left-hand page shows Sagafjord in typical Alaskan scenery. On this page, clockwise: at Valdez a helicopter waits to take passengers over the glaciers; crew have the closest view of one of the larger glaciers; but passengers unwilling to venture outdoors are hardly deprived of outlook; and mulled wine is served to passengers feeling the chill thrown off by the ice of ages

3

PREPARATION

THE exciting moment is when you are offered an option (usually a week) on a cabin. If the cruise is to start within a couple of months, you will be expected to pay in full right away; otherwise you put down a deposit probably of 20 per cent plus insurance. Whatever you do, read the cancellation details in the small print carefully. It is generally foolish to decline cancellation insurance, but remember this is only activated by the bad health of those who are travelling or of close relatives. A sudden change in business plans might leave you still

First class passengers on Queen Mary *could choose an evening or morning boat train from London*

having to pay, or failing to get a refund, though if you are lucky you might get a voucher for the whole or part of the fare to use for travel by the same line within a stated period.

As stressed in Chapter 4, check up on any possibly difficult air-transport arrangements: unless you press for details, these may not be supplied until you have committed yourself to full payment.

On the booking form, or by separate letter, make sure you notify the shipping line of any health problem and special dietary need. Special diets rarely cause a problem, and in truth requests of most kinds can be handled more easily on a large ship than almost

anywhere else; but advance warning encourages co-operation and enterprise. Any physical disablement and request for special equipment should of course be made now.

The booking form is also the place to request the kind of table you prefer in the dining room. Failures of communication are not unknown, but each year tens of thousands of special requests get noted, passed through the machinery, and are smoothly granted. Obviously the clearer and sharper the request, the more seriously it will be taken. 'Must have table for two, please', is much stronger than ticking 2 (out of 2, 4 or 8). Most ships now have non-smoking areas in their dining rooms; indeed

Embarkation Arrangements   Southampton — New York Service

To conform to regulations governing embarkations it is essential that passengers, in each class, embark at the times shown, and if availing of the special trains travel by the trains arranged for the class for which they are booked.

STEAMER Date and Time of Sailing	SPECIAL TRAINS FROM LONDON (Waterloo Station) AND EMBARKATION TIMES					
	FIRST CLASS PASSENGERS		CABIN CLASS PASSENGERS		TOURIST CLASS PASSENGERS	
	Special Trains	Embarkation Times	Special Trains	Embarkation Times	Special Trains	Embarkation Times
*"QUEEN MARY" Tues. 2nd MAY 11 am	7.00 pm 1st May / 8.05 am 2nd May	8 pm - 10 pm 1st May / 9 am - 10 am 2nd May	4.49 pm 1st May	6 pm - 8 pm 1st May	4.07 pm 1st May	5 pm - 7 pm 1st May
‡"MAURETANIA" Tues. 9th MAY 1.15 pm	9.47 am	10.30 am - 12.30 pm	8.47 am	9 am - 11 am	8.47 am	9 am - 11 am
*"QUEEN ELIZABETH" Wed. 10th MAY 6.30 am	4.49 pm 9th May / 7.00 pm 9th May	6 pm - 10 pm 9th May	4.07 pm 9th May	5 pm - 7 pm 9th May	3.05 pm 9th May	4 pm - 6 pm 9th May
†"CARONIA" Sat. 13th MAY 1.15 pm	9.47 am	10.30 am - 12.30 pm	8.47 am	9.30 am - 11.30 am	—	—
*"QUEEN MARY" Wed. 17th MAY 11.30 am	7.00 pm 16th May / 8.20 am 17th May	8 pm - 10 pm 16th May / 9 am - 10.30 am 17th May	4.49 pm 16th May	6 pm - 8 pm 16th May	4.07 pm 16th May	5 pm - 7 pm 16th May
*"QUEEN ELIZABETH" Thurs. 25th MAY 5.00 am	4.49 pm 24th May / 7.00 pm 24th May	6 pm - 10 pm 24th May	4.07 pm 24th May	5 pm - 7 pm 24th May	3.05 pm 24th May	4 pm - 6 pm 24th May
‡"MAURETANIA" Sat. 27th MAY 1.15 pm	9.47 am	10.30 am - 12.30 pm	8.47 am	9 am - 11 am	8.47 am	9 am - 11 am

* Via CHERBOURG   † Via HAVRE
‡ Via HAVRE and COBH   REFRESHMENT CARS ARE AVAILABLE ON THE SPECIAL TRAINS

they often account for three-quarters of all tables. If you care, for or against, make it clear. If you are returning to a ship you have used before, remember your favourite table may now be unsuitable because of smoking/non-smoking.

The booking form may also ask if you require welcoming champagne and canapés served in your cabin on sailing – expensive but a nice way to start the cruise, provided of course you are not itching to be out on deck. Some ships also allow you to reserve a floral arrangement. Flowers add a civilising touch to any cabin, and greenery is especially welcome to garden lovers on days spent at sea.

It is worth remembering to take a copy of the booking form with you. It will help give authority should any of your requests not be honoured. It may also show that you had not made the special request on paper, only in your mind!

There is usually also the chance to reserve the organised shore excursions ahead of time. This is useful should you have some very definite objective in mind, and where space is strictly limited, as for example for helicopter rides over the glaciers on Alaskan cruises. But experience suggests that most people do not know what they really want to do until nearer the time and that advance booking across the board results in many later changes of mind. Read the section on ports of call before committing yourself to too ambitious a programme.

It is much more important to make advance arrangements for self-drive or chauffeur-driven cars. The tour office on the ship will not generally help with individual arrangements, being busy enough coping with all those who want to go on the organised excursions. Cars will not always be available locally once the ship has docked, and anyway (especially in the main European tourist countries such as Greece and Spain) will cost much more rented locally than in advance.

If you have friends at any of the ports,

obviously giving them advance notice is essential. Many ships will allow you to entertain them for lunch or dinner aboard while in port for a modest charge – but must know in advance.

At certain ports there are visa and health requirements. Remember that these are not always black and white. In Russia, for example, you will be allowed ashore without a visa but only if you go on an organised tour. Getting off the ship on your own even to buy a postcard within the terminal building may prove frustratingly impossible. You certainly need a visa to wander through the streets and shops alone.

As for health, even if you are allowed on shore without the recommended inoculations, you may not wish to run the hazard. Never take a chance so far as smallpox is concerned. Yellow fever is easily guarded against and the inoculation lasts many years. Cholera has to be renewed frequently and the inoculations upset many people (who might prefer to stay on board if, say, protection is recommended at just one port). Malaria still needs treating seriously; here there is the nuisance value of having to take pills before you arrive in a dangerous area and for weeks after.

You will probably be sent a checklist of all the things you should do before leaving home, such as cancelling the newspapers if you have a home delivery service. But your own checklist is more effective. Everybody is different; much heartache (and hard thinking) can be saved by writing out your own list of things to

For the privileged few

do and having it copied so that you can use a fresh sheet each time you go away.

Some things are of course absolutely essential. You will not even leave your own country without your passport, be allowed on the ship without your sailing passage ticket, or be able to drive a rented car without your driver's licence. (In some countries an international licence is still required.) A supply of your own medications and of money/travellers' cheques is hardly less vital.

Money is an important topic. All ships accept credit cards for payments of extras such as drinks and laundry. You normally sign a blanket authority at the start and charge items

TONNAGE OF SHIPS

The fact that there are at least three kinds of tonnage measurement for a vessel is apt to confuse the traveller who obtains his impression of the size of a vessel from the tonnage figure given in a brochure. Gross and net tonnage have legal recognition. The gross tonnage of a vessel is its internal capacity in 'tons' (a word derived from the days when a ship's capacity was measured by the number of *tuns* of wine carried) each of which represents 100cu ft. Net tonnage is calculated by subtracting, from the gross tonnage, all space used for the accommodation of officers and crew, for certain gear used in working the ship, engine room, boilers etc. Displacement tonnage means the weight of water displaced by the ship when fully laden. For example, MS *Vistafjord* has a gross tonnage of 24,492GRT (gross register tons) and displaces 19,500 tons.

Tortolla in the British Virgin Islands in the Caribbean

Sailing down the Elbe after departure from Hamburg

A group of passengers hear about the rainfall in the forest at Ketchikan

The tender ride back to the ship at Magdalena Bay in Spitzbergen

to your room, being sent a detailed account just before you disembark. It is not yet customary to pay tips by credit card. Major items such as car rental ashore can usually be paid for by credit card, but in some countries most garages, for example, still require cash for fuel. And the best bargains when you go shopping may only be available for cash: one has memories of being unable to buy the best port at what seemed incredibly low prices because most Lisbon wine shops did not take credit cards! Since many ships do not cash personal cheques (though they will, of course, travellers' cheques), you are forced into estimating how much cash you are likely to require, or making advance arrangements at a bank at a port of call if you are on a long trip. (The *QE2* has a full banking service and personal cheques can be cashed subject to the normal limitations ashore.)

There is also the question of which currency to take your money in. Most Cunard ships, even those operating in European waters (Southampton-based cruises of the *QE2* are different) stick with the American dollar. Certainly you will never go wrong with the American dollar, in cash or travellers' cheques, and a reasonable supply guards against those infrequent but highly inconvenient financial crises when rates jump around and the exchanges may even be temporarily closed. However, there is also a good case to be made for ordering from your home bank a small supply of the currency of all countries you will be visiting. A local bank usually comes on board to change money soon after the ship has docked at, say, breakfast time, but you do not go cruising for the privilege of having to queue.

Next, if you are going clothes shopping for yourself or friends, always make sure you know the correct British/American/Continental/whatever sizes. Being unable confidently to answer the inevitable question 'what size does she take?' possibly causes as much frustration and inconvenience as any other single instance of failure to plan ahead.

It is elementary, but many passengers are unable to take photographs because camera batteries have gone flat. Check your photographic and video equipment carefully. While the photo office on board may try to do their best to help, they will be very busy and mainly concerned with taking, processing, displaying and selling their own photographs. It is certainly worth taking all the film you are likely to use with you; it will probably save money as well as possible disappointment of what you want being out of stock.

Forgetting your address book so that you cannot send postcards to friends is another frequent cause of irritation, though some people prefer to write out a roll of address labels in advance. And if you want to know about the places you are visiting in detail, and require better maps than car-rental companies provide, make sure you get organised on that front too. Tourist information on board varies, but can be of the most elementary type.

The thing most people worry about unnecessarily is what clothes to take. It really matters little what you wear most of the time. Gone are the days when you felt positively awkward if you were not in formal attire for, say, the captain's welcoming cocktail party. Cunard ships certainly demand a minimum level of attire in the dining room, but the only practical problem might be persuading a teenage son to wear a tie! For most ladies the only practical consideration is to come prepared for a wide range of temperatures. It often feels colder on deck than it actually is, while even in Alaskan waters in high summer there is considerable strength in the sun. Beyond that do what you want to do. On *Princess* and *Countess* things are pretty informal. On the other Cunarders most people like dressing up for formal occasions and you will certainly see many ladies sporting spectacular dresses and jewellery. 'When else do you have a chance to show them off?' is an oft-stated comment.

So many cruisegoers hardly travel light. But experienced ones cut down on the number of everyday garments they carry because laundry is available seven days a week and replacement would anyway not be impossible. And while they may bring one personally chosen book along, they will also make use of the library. As for bringing food or drink along, forget it. If not illegal, it is quite unnecessary. You can buy spirits for your cabin duty free. Do keep your valuables, including passport, always with you, and if you are spending a night in an hotel before or after the cruise it makes sense to pack for that separately so that you do not have to disturb your main cases containing the cream of your wardrobe.

Finally, give clear instructions to those you do or do not want to communicate with you while you are on your voyage. Your ticket will come with details of how to get in touch with the ship. A telex delivered to your room is a painless means of business communication; some businessmen insist on there being a regular message as a means of knowing that a disaster has not occurred and the message describing it has got lost! Remember that it will not always be possible to get in touch with the ship when it is in port, and that having to take an inter-continental telephone call when you have ordered a special soufflé in the restaurant will have the chef, waiter, you and your family all getting ulcers. A useful tip: before you leave home, make a list of the days you will be at sea and quote your local time back home against each of those days for the period you will be in your cabin dressing before dinner.

The best cruises are undoubtedly those where everything goes smoothly because of proper preparation. And that means leaving space in the baggage (or better still carrying a stout fold-up bag) for the things you are bound to acquire en route: souvenirs of the ship itself, photographs, extra clothes, those items you simply could not resist in the local shops because they were so different or such bargains, the paperback you didn't quite finish reading. Your luggage will gain weight more inevitably than you do yourself.

4
CARIBBEAN

HERE we are once more at what is probably the world's most popular cruise port, Charlotte Amalie on St Thomas in the American Virgin Islands. There is no great thrill or excitement, and certainly not the feeling of pioneering since cruise ships arrive at breakfast time like commuter trains roll into city-centre railway stations; just the expectation of another leisurely day with a great choice of possibilities in a familiar, relaxing environment.

This morning we are parked at the farthest end of the long line of ships that have filled the long quay; better than last time when we had to anchor well outside the harbour and experienced one of the bumpiest tender-rides. We note that one of the *Sea Goddesses* is moored in mid harbour, adding her touch of dignity to a generally animated scene while no doubt giving her passengers a fine view of all of our less glamorous though larger vessels. Taxis immediately offer their services: not your conventional cars but open charabancs, many of them decorated in keeping with the character of their drivers, some with rows of benches to accommodate a couple of dozen passengers. It must be good business if you can charge for a bum on each seat, and we see a driver trying to persuade a large family that he has plenty of room. 'Sit down', he shouts to someone already on board who is disliking being even more huddled together. Anyway we had decided to walk into town, around the arc of the harbour, a rather noisy road but the weather perfect as always. St Thomas genuinely does have a better climate with fresher breezes, and blue skies almost unfailingly year round, than most of the Caribbean.

Some of the taxis slowly overtaking us along the congested road have their radios blasting out the news and Caribbean band music. And once more we enjoy that Virgin Islands' oddity of American-made vehicles for driving on the right keeping to the left British style, and remember how the car we rented last time had a large arrow across the dashboard pointing to the left. The view of the harbour is perpetually interesting as the angle changes with our gentle progress, many of the pedestrians wearing a hat or some other article of clothing telling us by what ship they have arrived.

To the shops! Who can possibly resist shopping in St Thomas? Just to watch people part with their money in the carnival atmosphere is fun enough, though not to fall into temptation oneself near impossible. The sheer scale of the displays, the bringing together of anything that could possibly attract the tourist from all over the Caribbean and most of the rest of the world, the originality of some of the packaging for carrying home, the matter-of-fact attitude of the salespeople who have seen everyone buy everything and are not going to be the least surprised even if you shock yourself with what seem outrageous purchases – these add up to one of the great experiences of a Caribbean cruise. The quality is good, and certainly the prices are keen, even if you had never heard of that liqueur in the funny-shaped bottle only five minutes ago and have no idea

whether you or your friends could tolerate, let alone actually enjoy it. Jewellery and a host of personal items, tablecloths and other linen, drink of every description, watches and clocks, tobacco goods, souvenirs, glass and china, 365 days a year the tills ring and passengers carry their loot back to their ships. There is surely always room for anything done well; St Thomas excels at taking your money and giving you the feeling you have parted with it wisely.

But while it is best known as the shopper's paradise, it in fact offers one of the widest ranges of attractions – the half-dozen organised tours including sailing to two nearby islands, a trip on a replica of the *Kon Tiki* as well as beach, scuba diving and Coral World Island tours. The range varies from time to time, but will always be among the greatest offered anywhere, giving those who come back on different cruises (some two-week cruises visit St Thomas both weeks) ample choice. Most people spend at least part of their day on a beach or beside a pool, a favourite destination of those making their own arrangements being Frenchman Reef Hotel on the promontory guarding the harbour entrance of which you have an excellent view arriving and departing. Some rent a car from the airport and enjoy the quite unexpectedly stunning panorama of cliffs and different islands that seems to open up at every turn. You certainly do not realise

VIRGIN ISLANDS
The US Virgin Islands belonged to Denmark from 1666 to 1917. Some street names and the fact that this is the only US territory with left-side traffic are reminders of this. The purchase of the islands by the USA for $25 million in 1917 is considered a bargain, although it would have been only a quarter of this sum about fifty years earlier.

THE CUNARD CARIBBEAN PORTS OF CALL

ANTIGUA A most beautiful island, Antigua boasts 365 beaches, an undulating coastline and countless hills sweeping majestically down to the sea. The island's best known sight is Nelson's Dockyard, the home of the Caribbean Fleet during the Napoleonic wars. The capital, St John's is noted for its colourful market place, old churches and good shopping.

BARBADOS Lord Nelson standing in Trafalgar Square, names such as Worthing, Windsor, Hastings and Brighton everywhere, it is no wonder that British visitors feel so at home in Barbados. The inhabitants of Barbados (Bajans) are very proud of their island and are keen that all visitors enjoy every moment of their stay.

GRENADA The scent of spices fills the air in this island of high mountains, waterfalls, superb sandy beaches and picturesque towns.

The welcome from the people is as warm as the climate, as friendly as the gentle sea which laps the fine beaches.

The state of Grenada proclaims the island the most beautiful in the Caribbean and few would argue. Whether it is the spectacular views or the charming pastel shades of the capital, St George's, there is much to enjoy.

GUADELOUPE This butterfly-shaped island was named Santa Maria de Guadeloupe de Estremadura by Columbus himself in honour of a Spanish monastery which had supported him in his exploration.

The two wings of the butterfly have profoundly different geographies. The main port of Pointe á Pitre – its shops filled with tempting French imports, native dolls, straw and wood craft – is on gently undulating Grande-Terre, with its sugar cane plantations and some wonderful beaches.

Look to the west and you can see Basse-Terre, one of the most craggy, mountainous parts of the whole Caribbean region, containing a spectacular 74,000 acre National Park. Here there are forests, waterfalls, even a volcano.

MARTINIQUE Just a few hours' sailing from Barbados, but what a contrast. Martinique is French. No, more than that, Martinique is France, as French as Paris or St Tropez. A taxi ride to the Bibliotheque, the brilliantly coloured library in Fort de France takes just a few minutes and is a good start to an exploration. Nearby is a statue to Napoleon's Josephine, who was born on the island.

SAN JUAN, PUERTO RICO Puerto Rico is one of the large islands of the Caribbean and has a population of around three million.

San Juan, its capital, has a reputation as the Las Vegas of the Caribbean, but here is far more to be found on the island than glitter and show business. Whilst the new city boasts skyscrapers, Old San Juan has some of the most charming and remarkable architecture in the western hemisphere, much of it lovingly restored.

ST LUCIA Such a beautiful island, it is no wonder that the British and French fought over it for so long. The port and main town of Castries reflects this mixed heritage and Fort Charlotte, the eighteenth-century fort behind the city, offers a spectacular view.

But take time to look at the rest of the island. There are the rain forests, the twin volcanic peaks of Les Pitons, and Soufriere known as the "drive-in" volcano.

ST MAARTEN/ST MARTIN An island with two names, at least three languages (English is the most commonly used) and three currencies. For over 300 years the island has been divided between French and Dutch jurisdictions and in all that time the two parts have lived in harmony,.

Phillipsburg, capital of the Southern Dutch half of the island, is a strikingly cosmopolitan town. A duty-free haven, there are busy shops along Front Street with bargains galore. Outside the town, there are 36 fine beaches, green hills, blue lakes and lagoons.

ST THOMAS Main St, the main street of the capital Charlotte Amalie, is reputedly the duty-free capital of the world. But St Thomas has a lot more to offer. One of the Caribbean's best-known beaches, the flawless Magen's Bay and the fantastic Coral World (an underwater observatory) are just two of the attractions. There is a spectacular view of the Virgin Islands, studded like precious jewels in the clear blue of the Caribbean, to be enjoyed from Drake's Seat.

TORTOLA This is the main island of 60 or more which make up the British Virgin Islands. Of the fourteen that are inhabited, it has the biggest population, but don't expect crowds. Only about 9000 people live here.

Around the coast are delightful beaches, coves, bays and tiny villages, whilst in the lush interior avocados, bananas and sugar cane are farmed.

TRINIDAD Geographically, Trinidad could be considered part of South America. It is after all just fifteen miles from the delta of the Orinoco. Culturally though, Trinidad is classic Caribbean, the home of the original calypso. Trinidad is thought the most exotic of the Caribbean islands with – thanks to oil – one of the strongest economies in the region. An island tour would not be complete without a visit to the Caroni Bird Sanctuary to see the scarlet ibis, Trinidad's national bird.

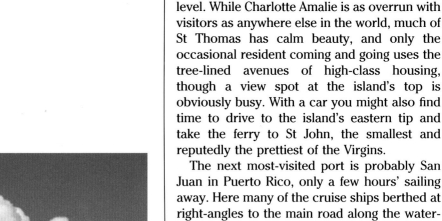

how star-studded these turquoise seas are without climbing a few hundred feet above sea level. While Charlotte Amalie is as overrun with visitors as anywhere else in the world, much of St Thomas has calm beauty, and only the occasional resident coming and going uses the tree-lined avenues of high-class housing, though a view spot at the island's top is obviously busy. With a car you might also find time to drive to the island's eastern tip and take the ferry to St John, the smallest and reputedly the prettiest of the Virgins.

The next most-visited port is probably San Juan in Puerto Rico, only a few hours' sailing away. Here many of the cruise ships berthed at right-angles to the main road along the waterfront are loading provisions and baggage and accepting new passengers at the start of their cruise, the airport being one of the region's busiest and best equipped. Whatever your reason for being in it, San Juan exudes a welcome and is ready to spoil you. Many retreat to El San Juan Hotel, 'Numero Uno' as the taxi driver assured us. No man-made resort offers more variety or greater style: here is the epitome of what many people dream about the Caribbean: the turquoise sea's noisy rollers breaking over a white beach pepper-potted with palms, the massive splendour of the hotel's main building, especially its casino, the restaurants indoors and out, and all human life around the massive pool.

But the old city of cobbled narrow streets and the fortress commanding the entrance to the splendid harbour (the approach to San Juan by sea is in the top world class) are great for exploring on foot. The Spanish colonial city that for many years was down on its luck has been steadily restored, every street having its buildings and vistas of interest. It is one of the surprises of a Caribbean cruise.

The round of ports Cunard Princess *makes every two weeks. The perennially popular San Juan and St Thomas are visited each week*

There are, of course, many such surprises: pieces of old England, Spain, France, Holland set among the generally more modern and enjoy-the-present ambiance of the carefree Caribbean. You will, for example, find markets as colourful as any and with poignant scents as the sun beats down on herbs and spices. You will find ample reminders of how wars were fought between the great European powers, and see splendid ancient churches, fortresses and civic buildings. In St Martin/Sint Maarten you can even drive from France to Holland since the island is divided. There are museums everywhere, and interesting relics of how people used to earn their living – voluntarily or as slaves in, for instance salt-pans – and of their Lilliputian slave houses. And always restaurants of great variety.

The classic St Thomas view with a Sea Goddess *anchored in mid-harbour*

Yet all these are bonuses, none of the things for which you actually go. What makes the Caribbean such a cruising paradise is its natural attractions sometimes enhanced by man. The climate, the beaches, the laid-back atmosphere, the close proximity of so many

mini-kingdoms of great physical charm, the tropical vegetation, landforms especially interesting where there has been volcanic activity, lack of industry, gentle pace (except on islands where the French influence comes through on quite unsuitable roads). Caribbean cruises are for unstructured time, casual clothing, long leisurely bathes, siestas, cocktails and dinners – and for balmy evenings when because you have been so gentle with yourself by day there is no rush to get to bed. Fascinating though it often is, few people bother to read up the local history. Gambling is far more popular than attending the lectures. Telexes to the office suddenly seem less pressing, business reading and worries cast aside.

Partly because of its very real attractions, partly because of its geographic convenience to Americans, the Caribbean probably draws in more cruises than operate in the whole of the rest of the world. They vary greatly. Nowhere else is the exact choice of ports perhaps less important, but picking the right ambiance of ship absolutely vital. Cheap-and-cheerful, mass-produced and often highly organised cruises abound, but are not Cunard's style. Cunard in fact has all four of its styles in the Caribbean: the yacht-like individuality of *Sea Goddess* slipping into ports larger ships cannot reach, the grandeur of the *QE2*, the five-star luxury of *Sagafjord* and *Vistafjord*, and the more informal, cheaper but still definitely Cunard *Countess*. At the time of writing *Countess* spends her whole year on the same two-week itinerary, and whether you take the whole two weeks or one of the shorter options combining a land stay, she gives an excellent introduction to the Caribbean. Her cruises, like most, of course provide a carefully balanced choice of ports, but will keep you busy. Only one day in fourteen is spent at sea.

While there may be a particular island you have always longed to visit, basically the Caribbean should be regarded as a single holiday playground, most of the islands lying in a great arc from the Bahamas off West Palm beach in Florida down to Trinidad and the Dutch Antilles close to the Venezuelan coast. Of the four largest islands, only Puerto Rico is a common calling place today. Cuba, by far the largest, is still generally off the tourist map, though you may catch glimpses of its coastline. The island mass divided between Haiti and the Dominican Republic does not figure much in the brochures either, while, of the islands lying away from the arc in the Caribbean Sea, Grand Cayman is a more popular stop for ships bound to or from the Panama Canal than larger Jamaica. The emphasis is thus very much on the diversity of smaller islands, technically in groups such as the Leewards and Windwards.

Few cruisegoers pay much heed to the atlas. Even those who, when in historic European ports conscientiously do their homework the night before and ensure they do not miss any of the top places of interest, simply relax when in the Caribbean. If the ship leapfrogs islands and calls at them out of order, who cares? In a sense, even to the most discerning one island is like another, an ingredient in the total Caribbean experience. Few of us can hope to visit the majority, even of those whose names are so familiar.

Yet it is an essential part of that experience that individually each island is so different. Most of them are volcanic, hilly if not positively mountainous, lush, owe much to their European connections (many changed hands, some several times, in the fight for supremacy between the great powers), are peopled by increasingly diverse ethnic mixtures generally moulded harmoniously together, and earn their livings somewhat precariously from primary agriculture (such as sugar cane) and tourism. Yet that only emphasises the differences: of language and political system, size (which varies greatly though you could see much of each in a long day), wealth and that less definable item, character. While most of them have that feel of being made late in geological history, with their hummocky green skylines and long stretches of white beaches, you begin to judge the character the moment the pattern of individual landscape becomes evident on your approach, usually before breakfast when the keenest passengers are already on deck. The buildings, what you can see of the road system and its traffic, the tidiness or otherwise of the dock area, the sounds, smells as you tie up – they are all part of the character, the image of individual islands that somehow stays with you even when you visit a dozen in a fortnight. Then the language, the shops, market stalls, public notices; whether you are in a piece of France, Britain, Spain, America or a highly independent Caribbean state, each mini-nation comes rapidly into focus, the scenery being an important but not necessarily the dominant factor. The islands are almost for devouring by the curious, especially those fascinated by the interplay of history and geography, yet you make your assessment without expending energy or deviating from the main purpose of a Caribbean cruise – relaxing and having fun.

With a succession of daily islands, you are mad to plan much. Go with the mood, exploring the old town and castle ruins if there is one, shopping when the opportunity occurs (which is distinctly not everywhere), buying the local newspaper if it is in a language you understand (you will not find the *Wall Street Journal* leave alone the *Financial Times* everywhere), and above all do not commit to too many organised tours. Remember that tours have a duty to discover 'things' of interest even when there really are not any, at least of top interest. The

chief attraction of some islands is, anyway, their port-cum-capital and nearby beaches, but ring the changes by going along the coast or up the mountains sometimes, by coach, taxi or rented car. Hill-, sea- and skyscapes seldom disappoint; from vantage points you frequently enjoy views of half a dozen or more islands at a time.

At first sight Tortola in the British Virgin Islands seemed a bit dull, the immediate environs of the dock extremely so, and we had heard that the nearby capital of Roadtown had little to offer apart from its floral displays. But the garage round the corner from the dock displayed the familiar Budget sign, and yes they had one car still free, other parties off the ship having already driven off in the others. The morning trip along the coastal road to East End round a great bay on which a Sunday yacht race was taking place, and then across a wooden toll bridge to Beef Island, was interesting enough; but after lunch on the ship we set out in the same direction again and then experienced sheer joy as we drove along the island's ridge road commanding breathtaking views of Tortola's northern coast (inaccessible by road) and of a score of other humpy, tree-topped Virgins of exotic shapes rising to different heights out of a now slightly misty sea. Then a hill-top café where, remarkably, one copy of that day's *New York Times*, the Sunday giant edition, waited to be bought in US dollars on a British island where of course again they drive on the left in right-hand drive cars, and where we were the only customers. As the crow flies we cannot have been more than 5 miles (8km) from the ship, glimpses of which we had occasionally caught on our drive, but wherever else the hundreds of passengers were, none intruded on our privacy here.

Every island has its great adherents, the French ones of course having a special appeal to Francophiles and all who love good food (though do not expect bargains). History exudes at every corner in Pointe-à-Pitre,

capital of Guadeloupe, with a marvellous market whose colour is a joy to the eye as the aromas of spices are to the smell only a few moments' walk from the dockside. There are two totally different terrains of the butterfly-shaped island to explore, and whatever your choice Guadeloupe will never give you a dull day, but the scale inland is quite sizeable and with so much of interest in the town many prefer not to be too ambitious.

Martinique, however, is an island to explore – an island of flowers and stunning green, volcanic landscapes, lush rain forests and dramatic coastline, often with picture-postcard views including other distant islands and also of points of special interest such as a replica of the Sacré Coeur of Paris and the ruins of the beach town of Saint-Pierre whose total population bar one was wiped out when the volcano at Mount Pelée (4,700ft; 1,430m) erupted in 1902. The sole survivor was in prison with thick walls. Martinique, which sounds so romantic to those longing to visit the Caribbean, is a jewel. It is proudly a department of France itself and some things including the noisy traffic in the capital are unmistakably French, but the Creole culture into which Africans, Asians, Indians and various whites have been absorbed is utterly individual. Here is an island really to get away from it.

As already mentioned, St Martin or Sint Maarten has a quite different, and split, personality. The capital of the French side, Le Marigot, lacks the exotic richness of Martinique, while the capital of the Dutch side, Philipsburg, is really only a glorified village catering for visitors in a quality way. But the roads between them, to the south encompassing a great lake, to the north through mountainous countryside with more of those picture-postcard views including glimpses of other islands in the Lesser Antilles chain, are unforgetable. If you ever rent a self-drive car, this is a place in which to do it. Your ship might land you at either of the capitals but here it is the experience of the total island that counts,

Above *All the scents and flavours of the Caribbean*

though as almost everywhere in the Caribbean there are plenty of beaches if all you want is a lazy day on the sand.

For their Dutch flavour, however, many cruises include a visit to one of the ABC islands of the Netherland Antilles, in fact quite close to the Venezuelan coast – as also are Trinidad and Tobago though very far to the east. The point has already been made that most people go to the Caribbean more for relaxation and to experience what comes along rather than with the feeling of making a journey of exploration; but it does not take much time to ensure you note which day's memories relate to which island! That the memories will be utterly different on each island is guaranteed, although you will not automatically remember whether you enjoyed that dance with the locals especially colourfully attired in Oranjestad on Auba, or Kralendijk on Bonaire. The capital of the island beginning with C, Curaçao, is Willemstad, often said to be the most photographed place in the whole Caribbean. With industry including oil refining, it absorbs its

Above left *Cunard's Paradise Beach, Barbados.* Left *Many small islands can be viewed from the ridge of Tortolla in the British Virgin Islands*

visitors without being overwhelmed by them. It displays its Dutch character vividly with its old buildings, canals and floating harbour as it goes about its daily business.

The other two ABCs are less showy and the fun is in getting more to grips with their totality (each is some score of miles long with an interesting but not overpowering capital) than in creaming off the main sites. This is specially true of Aruba where there is no single top tourist attraction but a fascinating, mainly arid mini-landscape bounded by a sea kept restless by the trade winds – a delightful spot in which gently to unwind especially if the day before was spent coping with the fast pace of Caracas (see the chapter on South America). Bonaire is noted for its coral reefs, crystal-clear water offering some of the best underwater activity in the Caribbean, its salt works with the remains of that slave village of mini-houses, and above all its natural history, especially its bird life, with one of the world's most famous

Cunard's La Toc resort in St Lucia

flamingo lakes. The ABC islands possibly offer the best Caribbean shopping after St Thomas.

And so one is in danger of producing yet another gazetteer of islands which this book has vowed not to do. There are plenty of excellent guides and, if you are lazy, Cunard will guide you adequately to each island's different character as indeed it provides an inspired sequence with daily changes of mood and likely level of activity. It has to be said that this is sometimes achieved by cheating on geography, giving you more miles and a better balance of ports than always going to the next nearest on the itinerary.

Though the overall stretch of the Caribbean from near Florida to near Venezuela is far greater than most people realise, many of the most popular destinations are well within a gentle, short night's voyage of each other, and leapfrogging makes it possible to enjoy more of those endlessly varied seascapes, and to arrive in style after sunrise. Undoubtedly one of the main attractions of cruising here is everlastingly watching the waves gently breaking over the coral, with glimpses of white beaches clearly designed for lazy days, and senuously shaped mountains towering overhead – perhaps belonging to that island or to a higher one whose top is visible beyond. Certainly on a clear day there is seldom a sea empty of land, but with islands large and small,

tall and flat, where once battles were fought and the flags of different European nations hoisted in quick succession. And even where there is no land close by, there will almost certainly be other ships, and an abundance of sea birds will usually be with you. If you are unlucky, you could sail into a violent storm, but you will seldom be even chilly. Cruise prices are naturally higher in the American and British winter, lower when it gets steaming hot in summer.

Two ports often separated by a visit elsewhere, although they are close to each other in the Windward Islands, are those on which Cunard operate luxury hotels – Barbados and St Lucia. Since both have good air services, there are packages including cruising and time at one of the hotels. In each case a visit to the hotel and its fine beach is featured on the extensive shore excursion programme for cruise passengers stopping for the day.

Barbados is often described as the most British of the islands. A busy but not always

thriving mini-kingdom of around a quarter of a million people; like Antigua considerably to the north it has a fascinating though not spectacular interior patchwork of fields, uncultivated hill-tops and busy twisting roads. The vegetation is always welcoming, especially if you have arrived from a northern winter. The coastline is, however, especially worth exploring. Altogether there are 60 miles (96km) of beaches (in an island only 21 by 14 miles (34 by 22km)), while the contrast between the rugged east coast pounded by the Atlantic and the lusher west of the Caribbean Sea is sharp. The harbour capital of Bridgetown is to the west, and a busy as well as picturesque city it is with many things British including old-fashioned tearooms and shops full of the best British goods. Cunard's Paradise Beach, palm-lined, is not too far away to the north.

St Lucia is also too dependent on sugar cane, but otherwise could hardly be more different. It became British in the Napoleonic Wars but retains substantial French influence; it is far more rugged, its hallmark being the volcanic, cone-shaped Pitons; and it is less developed, with barely half the population of Barbados, only one road crossing the lush mountainous interior. It is full of fascinating sights, an active volcano, for example, and reminders of the days when the British and French fought each other. But St Lucia would be the perfect island on which to do nothing but contemplate or play golf, and the ideal spot for that would be Cunard's La Toc Hotel Village, a few miles from the port capital (again on the west) of Castries which still retains something of the primitive excitement of a frontier town. Nothing is primitive at La Toc; here is man-made luxury, a golf course in a fertile valley and a cliffside street of luxury houses and suites on the other side of the main hotel complex around a pool and the beach, in as pleasing a setting as any you will find in the Caribbean. Bagshaws, famous for their printed fabrics as original as any quality item you will find coming from the Caribbean, is only a short walk away.

Prizes are awarded for exercising, walking and even losing weight while cruising

THE GOLDEN DOOR SPA AND CUNARD/NAC

have enjoyed your participation in the
SPA AT SEA PROGRAM

We cordially invite you to join us for our

"SHIP-SHAPE" COCKTAIL PARTY

Friday, May 12th, 1989
at 6.30 pm in the Ballroom

A Toast to Health and Happiness!

SHARON DITCHEOS

MARIA HARRIS

5
SHIPS AND ITINERARIES

AS with everything else, it pays to shop wisely. And shopping wisely on a cruise means planning well ahead and becoming a touch knowledgeable. A cruise is a big investment in expectation, not to mention time and money, and it is somewhat risky to rely on the blandishments of a single advertisement or the advice of your travel agent sandwiching you in between selling package holidays.

Most people begin cruising after the seduction of reading brochures for a season or two. These are in the racks for the picking up at most travel agents. Study them, compare them, pick up the next round, and you begin to get some idea of the options and what might suit you best.

As we have seen, successful cruise lines enjoy a high level of repeat business but find it harder to persuade people to take their first holiday at sea. Many special offers are made of 'taster' trips, often of only a few days, so you can judge from first-hand experience. The *QE2*, for example, regularly features two- and three-day 'party cruises' out of both New York and Southampton. It depends what you want, but be warned that such events are not the favourites of staff or regular passengers. 'Too much fizz and not enough substance', complained one elderly lady finding herself on a party cruise between two longer periods of sailing she wanted to join together.

Until you are sure that cruising is for you, also avoid the bargain 'positioning' cruises such as voyages across the Atlantic on board ships which spend half their year in American and half in European waters. Mind you, if you do get hooked on cruising, you may rapidly join the ranks of those who often complain

TRADE WINDS

These are steady reliable winds that blow regularly from the horse-latitude high pressure areas (sub tropics) towards the doldrum low pressure region (equatorial zone). In general they blow from the north-east in the northern hemisphere and from the south-east in the southern hemisphere. When drawn across the equator the trade winds are deflected by the earth's rotation to become monsoons. In former times these winds were very important for sailing ships, permitting steady speeds of approximately 8 knots for the westbound Atlantic crossing.

about there being too many ports of call in itineraries and relish days at sea. Positioning cruising, usually offering excellent value, is thus well supported, and is ideal for the connoisseur.

To start, it is a good idea to stick to itineraries that would be difficult or impossible by other means. Excellent cruises for first timers are up the Alaskan coast in high summer, to the Baltic capitals and Leningrad, around the Black Sea – again with at least one call in Russia, and through the Panama Canal. On such cruises you have a genuine exploration of new horizons, and will incidentally see many more passengers consulting guide-books than say in the Caribbean where despite the fascination of the contrasts of islands the emphasis is more on sunshine, creature comforts and entertainment. So go to some of the places you have always wanted to visit; then, in the unlikely event of your not enjoying life on board, at least you will have achieved something.

The most desirable itineraries naturally tend to be the most expensive. If other people think it is worth paying the extra for a prime cruise, why not you? Many routes are of course strictly seasonal. Not only is the total Alaskan season short, but voyages in its middle are more

desirable than the rest; in June it is still chilly, and by mid August daylight declines sharply. The Caribbean is obviously more popular out of its steaming summer.

Cruises, like other holidays, are more expensive over Christmas and Easter and in the summer school vacations. If money is a prime consideration, try and pick a time when rates are lower other than for climatic reasons. For example, many people dislike being away from home just before Easter and even more so just before Christmas. The nightly rate might be 20 per cent cheaper on the pre-Christmas as opposed to the Christmas cruise. Then, have you ever wondered why world cruises always take place in the weeks immediately after Christmas? It has much less to do with the weather being perfect than with ordinary demand being at its seasonal ebb. Without the world cruise, there simply might not be sufficient business to keep ships busy. And from this it follows that you can sometimes pick up bargain segments even on the most publicised of world cruises. Then, again, there are political considerations. Whenever a trouble spot erupts, cruises committed to visiting it become unloved and up goes the 'sales' notice.

Only you know when you are free to go, whether for example you might or might not be

Cunard Countess offers informal cruising in the Caribbean

able to kick off immediately before Christmas and do all your shopping on the cruise, whether if most Americans temporarily desert the Mediterranean you want to stay away too. But do not be shunted by a bargain into taking a trip which would not be your second or third, let alone your first choice.

If you are reserving a fly-cruise, make thoroughly sure you understand what is involved – whether for example travel is by day or night. The most exotic itineraries alas often include the most excruciating travel arrangements before and after. For a start, even if you are travelling in the best cabin aboard, the air fare quoted will almost certainly be the cheapest available; often it will be by cheap charter flight with even more dense seating.

For a short flight within Europe that may not matter, but think carefully about what is involved in longer and especially intercontinental journeys. Are you being given a sensible routing or going to be flown zigzag across the States so that when you arrive on the west coast you will be too exhausted to enjoy the first day at sea? Are you going further in one journey, such as to Australia, than you would were you on business?

36

Unfortunately there will usually be a substantial difference between the cheap package the cruise line offers and making your own arrangements, but remember you can always buy just the sea transport and get there and back independently at your own pace. Since most people are in a hurry, having only two weeks for a two-week cruise, the standard package will invariably prevent you really exploring and soaking up the atmosphere of the starting and finishing port. Yet especially in Europe these (such as Venice) may actually be more worthy of leisurely attention than many ports of call during the voyage. As always, be in the driving seat, know what you are doing and avoid being surprised and disappointed at the last moment. Realists, alas, occasionally have to conclude that while a distant cruise would be ideal while actually on the ship, the arrangements before and after are just too much of a strain.

Your choice of ship will be somewhat dictated by where you want to go as well as by your pocket and inclination. There is now an enormous range of cruise ships based on Miami alone. Styles, ambiances vary as sharply as the silhouettes of the ships. And here we have to acknowledge that this is a Cunard book. The cheapest (and it has to be admitted it is often excellent value for money) highly organised partying-all-the-way cruise is not a Cunard speciality. Come to Cunard for style in a great continuing tradition, for solid value, imagination, dignity as well as fun, and of course outstanding itineraries – and for the world's three top-rated ships, with unsurpassed dining. This advice has to be biased, but is based on personal experience and a considerable fund of facts.

The two most important commodities on a cruise are space and service. Space is both the

Above *Evening in the 'inside passage' along the Norwegian coast.* Right Vistafjord *anchored at the head of a Norwegian fjord.*

size of your own cabin and how many other passengers are competing for how large a communal area, indoors and out. Except at ceremonial occasions when everyone tries to be present at once, all Cunard ships are extremely generous in their public areas. You simply never feel crowded outdoors or in most areas inside. If there is a pressure point, it tends to be in the ballroom for evening entertainment. Next, and most important, all but two of the current Cunard ships and one of the *QE2*'s four restaurants can seat everyone at once. Even on famous transatlantic liners of the past – such as the *France*, now a Caribbean cruise ship the *Norway* – and even in first class, two sittings for meals were normal, as they are on most of today's cruise liners including nearly all of the recently built ones with spectacular designs.

The advantage of single-seating is enormous. For a start, you are free to come to your seat at your convenience over a long time-span. This is often more important in practice than it might seem in theory: you may wish to come back late from touring a port, or go to the movie or do something else after dinner. Not having to hurry is vital enough. When people are free to come as they wish, they tend to stagger their arrivals, and that makes for more gracious service. Your waiter has time to hear how the day has gone, and discuss the menu in depth. But if you are on second-sitting at say 8.15 and the waiters have already served one full house and now everybody pours in together, it inevitably feels like a production machine. In fairness, those in double-sitting restaurants, Cunard and other, do not seem to complain, and in the *QE2*'s Mauretania Restaurant (formerly Tables of the World) there is anyway some flexibility of space; but to experience shipboard food and service at its best, as provided in different styles by the Grill Rooms on the *QE2* and the single, large restaurants of *Sagafjord* and *Vistafjord*, single-seating is undoubtedly essential.

So is adequate room between tables. A good way of assessing the quality of cruise liners is to note how many tables for two are provided in the dining room. Most brochures have ship plans that tell you, though you may need to use a magnifying glass. Some people, of course, prefer eating at large tables, enjoying conversation and the chance to make new friends. But if, after a busy working period, you are looking forward to the cruise as a means of getting to know your spouse again, it is greatly disappointing not being able to enjoy personal tête-à-tête dining as in a quality restaurant on shore. The food will almost certainly compete handsomely against land, space being the vital consideration.

So compare tonnages and deck plans with the number of passengers carried. Consider how much time you will be spending in your own cabin, how much at table, in the lounge, bars or on deck. Especially do not think that because you have a glamorous-looking cabin there will be automatic spaciousness elsewhere.

While public areas are universally generous on Cunard, cabins are extremely varied, from the most luxurious suites afloat at the top of the *QE2* and on the two *Sea Goddess*es, to the small and simple cabins on *Cunard Princess* and *Countess* and the lower priced of the *QE2*. You pay for what you get. But what is it you want? Again, how long will you spend in your cabin?

It pays to examine the plans showing the different grades of cabins in some detail. Those of quite different size and character are often graded together, for example size being offset by a less desirable position. In other words, the least desirable cabin in any particular grade might actually be the largest. Desirability includes deck (the higher the better) and position (the closer to midships the better), and sometimes also outlook (some cabins especially in the bow might have a restricted view or a view over the area where crew work and sunbathe). And all that is without mentioning the obvious of whether there is one or more porthole or a larger window, and whether you have permanent or convertible beds, a bath, and so on.

Preference is very personal. If forced to give advice, the author would not mind saving money by going a couple of decks down provided the cabin was not too far back. Midships is ideal, but forward better than rear where the 'kick' in rough sea and vibration from the propeller will be most felt. He would place heavy emphasis on at least a peep out to sea, believing that even a single small porthole achieves seven-tenths of the advantage of the largest picture windows afloat. Unless there are frequent days at sea, when you may wish to use the cabin as your drawing room, size is usually not of the utmost importance, but two lower beds permanently in position will inevitably give greater comfort than another arrangement. Private shower and toilet are now universal, but tub-baths are still rare on cruise ships as a whole because of the expense of providing the extra space and especially the extra water. All Cunard ships have some tub-baths, and how important that is to you will depend on personal choice. However, if you want to eat in one of the grill rooms on the *QE2*, you will have to pick a first-class room that automatically comes with tub-bath and many other facilities including, these days, your own television and video.

Service is the other vital element. The ratio of crew to passengers is the clue, but knowing the nationality mix of crew also helps. The availability and scale of room service is another important measure. Nobody ever went hungry on any Cunarder, but there is inevitably a wide gulf between the 24-hours-a-day room service of the top accommodation and the mini-continental breakfast menu of *Princess* and *Countess*. A large proportion of the world's luxury breakfasts served afloat are on Cunard ships. A quick run round the deck in the personal robe provided and then back to the dining room for a ceremonial champagne and smoked salmon breakfast with your spouse is

a highlight on many people's cruise. Such individuality demands people. A high guest/staff ratio was ever the hallmark of the luxury hotel, but few hotels now achieve the level of service provided for the top half of Cunard passengers.

One man's meat is another's poison. We all have experiences of recommending friends to something we have especially appreciated ourselves only to hear them debunk it. So personal recommendation is not universally reliable. Yet when you have familiarised yourself with what is available from the brochures it is most helpful to meet a few people who have actually done what you have in mind. The better travel agents not merely ask their customers how things worked out but may be prepared to introduce you to those who have been before. Getting onto the mailing lists of one or two cruise lines will not merely bring you the brochures (and possible special offers from time to time) but sooner or later invitations to forums where you will be able to meet staff and others interested in cruising, some with practical experience. Such forums are regularly held by Cunard in major cities during the winter months. Travel agents specialising in cruising also sometimes hold their own events at which the latest documentary films on cruise ships and slides are shown; some agents also have sophisticated mailing programmes. Finally, some cruise lines have formal 'supporters clubs' such as the Cunard Club in Britain. Membership costs only a few

The classic lines of Vistafjord, *cruising Europe in summer and the Caribbean in winter*

pounds a year; in exchange you receive a chatty monthly newsletter usually offering some last-minute bargain. While the best rooms on the most popular cruises invariably sell many months ahead, sudden changes in fashion and demand plus the difficulty of selling space on the less popular 'positioning' cruises mean that there will always be some bargains, for once a ship sails with berths unoccupied revenue is lost for ever. Often the pattern of bargains is repeated, and by studying the offers you may be able to do yourself a favour.

As to whether you should make your

reservation direct with the cruise line or through a travel agent is a personal matter and must depend on whether you have a good agent. Many agents well deserve their commission, but while a cruise may be one of your life's highlights, it may just seem routine business to the agent. Lack of knowledge or just plain prejudice can be dangerous. Disgruntled passengers on ships are more likely to be upset by a shortcoming in their travel agent than the actual cruise operator. 'He told me that since our cabin faced forward we would have a view like the captain's, but with all the equipment out there I can hardly see the sea at all', complained one passenger from Mid-Western America. An agent specialising in sea transportation would have known better. You are more likely to find flowers welcoming you to your cabin if you reserve through an agent, and of course there will be someone to argue on your behalf if things go wrong.

To sum up: decide what you really want and at least for your first cruise don't compromise. Become your own expert as you would if you were spending that amount of money on perhaps remodelling the kitchen or even buying a small car.

One final thought: do not dismiss an itinerary out of hand because you have already been to several of the ports. The joy of cruising includes equally a chance to see more new places and countries than would otherwise be possible and the opportunity to look up old favourites. Even if you spent a solid month at a resort and did all the things there are to do, arriving by sea for another day at a different time of year opens up an entirely new dimension. 'This is my twenty-first visit to San Juan [capital of Puerto Rico] and it's sad I won't live long enough for another twenty-one', said the Manhattan lady setting off for a round of nostalgic calls. We all envied her rich perspective of the city.

Even in Spitzbergen, in July it is warm enough for light clothing

Above *It is hard to be tense in the Caribbean of white beaches and palm trees*

Below *Malta's sandy-gold buildings always demand your camera's attention*

6

BALTIC

ALL around there is a spectacle of lights as dusk falls over Stockholm's very Scandinavian skyline. Passengers who earlier walked round the deck with its grandstand view of the cleanly designed buildings dispersed over many islands, linked by a grand miscellany of bridges, now linger for a quite different impression of Sweden's capital. With its sparkling waterways and spacious parks, the city is pretty enough by day, but magical after dark.

That loving couple we have been watching on their post-dinner stroll are on their first cruise. We heard something of their doubts about coming when they joined the ship at Hamburg. No doubts now. 'What a week', he declares, and they check off some of their memories – of the departure down the busy river from Hamburg; going through the Kiel Canal by moonlight; their first ever visit to a place behind the Iron Curtain, Gdynia in Poland; the marvellous but tiring two days in Leningrad; the shorter stop in Helsinki, relaxing once they were back in the west; and now this the first of two days in Stockholm. They have been on a tour of the sights today, but tomorrow plan to be on their own and take lunch in the old city over there, and then after departure at the end of the afternoon to make sure they enjoy the sail down through the thousand islands between city and sea.

Like so many newcomers to cruising, they have already started talking about when they might take another trip. And like most passengers, newcomers and regular cruisers, they have used up all the film they brought for the two weeks in the first of them. And still another day here and three more ports including two further Scandinavian capitals.

The Baltic is an excellent choice for a first cruise, an absolute must for regulars. In just two weeks you will see sights, hear tales, experience ambiances, make better sense of the history, geography and culture of an important portion of the world, than most people get to do in a lifetime. Of course you would have liked more than two days in Leningrad, hope to come back for a whole week in Stockholm one year, and so on. But life is short, the world large, and unless you favour Scandinavia to the exclusion of most other regions the fact of the matter is that unless you take a cruise you will reach forty, fifty, sixty without having sampled each of the countries and their capitals, leave alone experiencing Poland and Baltic Russia.

On this cruise more than perhaps any other, people come with a mission to learn and experience, to taste the different ways of life and political systems. Lectures on the ports are attended by nearly everyone, and a lot of reading goes on – sometimes aloud even on the tour buses! And naturally there is a great deal of discussion, especially about things in Poland and Russia. It is not a particularly restful cruise, the two (usually) days at sea being more than normally welcome especially by those who take their studying of new countries and cultures seriously.

As to the weather, it is inescapably northern European, ie varied, but most passengers return with at least a vestige of suntan and the Baltic itself often provides ideal cruising conditions, the days at sea being very much open-air occasions. You are surprisingly far north at Leningrad and of course go on the cruise when daylight stretches two-thirds round the clock.

Itineraries naturally differ, but often you start (after a few hours sailing down the Elbe, first through the high-class suburbs of Hamburg and then into open country) by turning right into the Kiel Canal, taking a short cut to the Baltic. Many passengers' only real disappointment in the whole cruise is that they do not see much of this grand canal as it winds across the northern neck of West Germany. Most of the transit is by night, though if you are up late and early you will catch the start and finish, and many a passenger has made first use of the personal robe provided in the cabins to sneak a view from deck during the night.

The map of the route displayed in a couple of public areas is particularly well studied on this cruise, but you will do even better to make sure you bring an appropriate map or maps with you. Even when you are not actually in sight of land (which you often are) it is good to note what country lies just beyond the horizon. As you sail east from the canal, you

---

THE BALTIC

The present area of the Baltic is about 184,000sq miles (422,000km^2). Communication to the North Sea and thus to the Atlantic is by three shallow channels off the Danish archipelago: the Great Belt, the Little Belt and the Oere Sound. The greatest depth, approximately 50 nautical miles (92km) south of Stockholm, is 240 fathoms (440m); but the average depth is only about 30 fathoms (55m). This fact, and the low salinity due to the great amount of river water the Baltic receives, encourages freezing in winter.

travel between the Danish island on which Copenhagen is situated and East Germany.

The three neighbouring cities of Gdynia (the port where you land), Sopot (Victorian-style resort, now for the masses) and Gdansk (Hanseatic city wonderfully restored after the war whose mood is reflected by the ubiquitous floral displays, also birthplace of Solidarity) make an excellent introduction to Poland. You will hear much history, ancient and recent, have plenty of opportunity to spend your American dollars or use your credit cards (local jewellery and handicrafts are well worth-while looking at) and probably be taken to Oliwa for a recital on the famous organ. This is a surprisingly relaxed, fun day, the highlight probably being walking round on your own through the centre of Gdansk with its gates and town hall, squares and narrow streets by the river, all looking truly ancient though again rebuilt from rubble after World War II.

The cultural shock is perhaps greater between here and Leningrad than between the West and Baltic Poland. Tension rises as you approach Leningrad, across the route of frequent hovercraft services, past a submarine depot and other naval areas, even alongside blocks of flats, until you tie up with a bird's eye view of part of the city of massive buildings and wide streets of sparse traffic. Most passengers will be coming to Russia for the first time, not sure quite what to expect or how best to plan their precious hours. Certainly you still need a visa to explore (or even to go to the terminal to buy a postcard) on your own, and without one you perforce have to take one of the organised tours or stay on board.[1]

As the cruise director will emphasise, you cannot do everything, and to take up every possible tour will be tiring. Above all you have to decide whether you want an impression of Leningrad and how these Russians live, or whether your preference is to concentrate on as many of the famous buildings as possible (of course still seeing something of the city on the way from the ship). There is certainly no

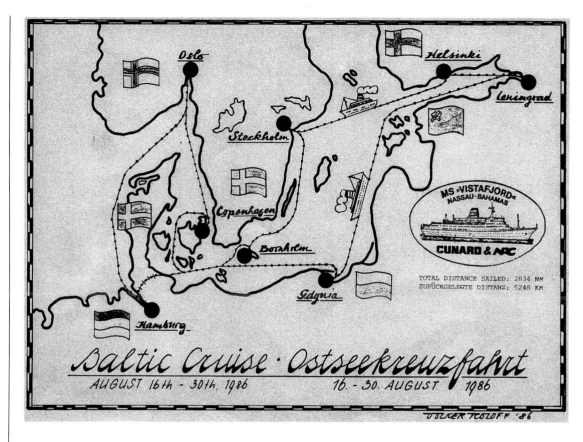

Your friendly restaurant section manager might draw you an itinerary

shortage of top-class attractions, led by the Hermitage, the Russian museum of museums housed in the Winter Palace, home of the last six czars and itself a major architectural attraction. But be prepared for crowds that dwarf those of most commuter rush hours being marshalled for their turn to enter. Inside, the crush is eternal as guides harangue their jostling groups in different languages, the Russians themselves always predominating.

And you will not exactly enjoy liberal space at Catherine's Palace at Pushkin, built by the same architect determined to give Russia its own style of grand royal palaces. Again you will be awe inspired, but enjoy the bonus of a 20 mile (32km) drive out of Leningrad through the countryside and later a walk through the grand park surrounding the palace. The Petrodvorets, another monument of Russian architecture and landscaping, is rather further from the city, on the Gulf of Finland. And so the list goes on.

Most people start with a general tour of Leningrad. Everyone comments on the scale of everything, and the relative lack of colour and brightness after Poland, though steadily clothing is more Western – especially for younger people. Passengers paying their first visit to Russia find that every detail counts: the nearly empty streets with the broken-down bus, the petrol station where one motorist is saving fuel by pushing his car along the queue to the pump where he has to pay in advance,

[1] Things are likely to change rapidly in Russia during the next few years. This was as in 1989.

Left *A visit to the old city of Gdansk (a few miles from the port of Gdynia) inevitably means a discussion about the changing face of Eastern Europe*

Below *But the grand buildings of Leningrad are unaffected by politics*

Above *The Baltic like all oceans offers great diversity of light including splendid sunsets*

Right *For many people the first glimpse of Russia is of the Leningrad shipyards through their portholes during the early morning approach*

the lack of display in shop windows, the arches leading into courtyards surrounded by apartments, the queues for vegetables at street stalls and for almost everything else too.

Leningrad was built to give Russia a window on the West, and one still feels very much as though, coming across the Baltic, one is peering through that window into an unfamiliar world. You may be tired and even tense, but you will not be disappointed. One detail is that you will wish to make minimum use of the toilets (and take paper from the ship).

The Russians who looked blandly at the ship while we were in port (when we waved at the children from the observation deck the only reaction was that the adults made sure the children did not respond), now enthusiastically send us on our way. Everyone waves as the Red Flag is amplified. Children on bicycles race us past the blocks of flats alongside the first part of our route. We talk more openly. How, the Americans ask and ask again, can Russia possibly become efficient unless there is the profit motive? When we were taken on an expedition to a special visitors' shopping centre, the Americans were scandalised that the assistants continued their discussion rather than start taking dollars. And the tour office arranges a refund for a small group who waited as instructed for their guide to take them round Pushkin only she never came back.

Tension relaxes. In truth there is nothing so remarkable about a visit to Russia these days; it is just that few of us have yet been, few have bothered to obtain an individual visa, and the concept of being unable to leave the ship even to walk a few steps down the quay is alien.

And so to the first of the Scandinavian capitals, Helsinki, neat, dignified, somewhat in limbo between East and West. For most people it is a bonus rather than a top priority to be here, and after two days in Russia there is a natural desire to do your own thing. And Helsinki is compact, most places of interest within easy walking distance.

Then Stockholm, probably for another overnight stay. Most people are more than pleasantly surprised here, not realising how utterly varied the city is or even that it is built on so many islands and has a fascinating waterway system. This is undoubtedly the place that the greatest number of passengers determine they will revisit one day. They should of course remember that the weather is not always as welcoming as in the short cruising season and that, as in the rest of Scandinavia, many drinks on shore cost far more than on board. Shopping is excellent, glass at the top of the list, though collect some Christmas decorations from one of the little shops in the charming streets of the old city at whose end you will catch a glimpse of your ship.

The next port is usually the joker in the pack, the place that nobody would especially join a cruise for, but which turns out to be most enjoyable if only because there are no great expectations. Sometimes it is the island of Bornholm, a charming piece of Denmark so far to the east of the rest of the country that it is ever repeated that any further world war would first be known about here. But the island is too relaxing to be worrying about wars and we only briefly note its invasion in World War II. It is a holiday island, utterly well ordered in the Danish style, separate cycle tracks and sidewalks even where there is little traffic, glitteringly clean fishing villages and tourist marinas – and a mini shopping paradise.

So to Copenhagen, certainly one of those places everyone does want to know and so arrives at with great expectations. Visitors are seldom disappointed. The city is lighthearted, even joyous, a visual feast in its totality and well ordered in its details. Wonderful indeed, ever colourful even in the uniforms of its workers. Though its historic buildings are particularly magnificent it is also a city to celebrate as a whole, and certainly one you can explore comfortably alone on foot. Tivoli, the fantasy amusement park right in the city centre, is certainly not to be missed, by day or night. But an equally well-ordered countryside dotted with historic villages and castles beckons beyond the city borders. One of the best Cunard tours the writer has patronised was called the Danish Countryside and in five hours by bus and motor launch down a millstream and lake gave a splendid sample of different types of countryside and country activities, including a walk round a museum of old houses and farms collected from different parts of Denmark.

Do not think you have finished with Denmark when you rejoin the ship. The departure is spectacular, but more is to come. As you sail north you pass through the narrow channel (castles either side glaring at each other) between Denmark and Sweden. The intercom is always used sparingly on Cunard ships but this is one of those occasions when you are all too pleased to have your attention alerted and learn the details of geography, war and peace.

Oslo is another of those cities you only really fully appreciate when arriving by sea. Since it is at the head of a 60 mile (96km) fjord it means a really early start. Headlands, inlets, islands, villages and ultimately dockyards and the city itself, are all at their best in the crisp morning sun. When you tie up, the capital of Norway lies right in front of you within easy walking distance. If you are on a full day's shopping expedition, you can easily use the ship as your café for lunch; there is no more animated setting in which to eat in the whole of beautiful Scandinavia than at the heart of Oslo under the castle's battlements. But there are many top-class specific attractions, especially museums, both within and near the city, competing for attention.

7
PORTS OF CALL

SOME passengers select their cruises almost entirely for the choice of ports; others regard stops and shore excursions as an irritating interruption to enjoyable life at sea. One thing is for certain: the enjoyment of your cruise will depend much on your decision as to how to spend time in port, even if you sometimes opt to remain on board.

If there is one general piece of advice worth giving after watching thousands of cruisegoers agonise over their decisions, it is to listen to your feelings. The fact that you have an opportunity to tire yourself out visiting more ancient sites than you can possibly enjoy does not mean you have to seize it. Get your priorities right. If relaxation is top priority, relax. If you hate organised parties and are allergic to bus travel, why travel in an organised party by bus?

It is of course not quite as simple as that. There are places we will all make a sacrifice to see, and sometimes it is hard to tell if it will be possible to make your own way there other than by the official tour. But the generalisation is worth repeating, for overall a cruise cannot give you what you most want from it if you continually do things you dislike.

In particular there is a temptation to get over enthusiastic when the list of official tours arrives, usually at home well before sailing. Yes, it might be interesting to go here and there, but that does not mean you necessarily have to do it by organised party. Many people who can afford cruising would not normally travel by bus and are irritated by the inevitably slow pace of a party of forty or more. Moreover you do not necessarily save money by taking the official tour. Read the tour guide carefully,

noting when mention is made of much walking or the need to wear special clothing. Sometimes it becomes obvious that the tour will get to places that might not be generally available to the public. In some cities the safety of being with an organised party might make a difference. In some places you may not even be allowed off the ship unless you have an individual visa if you do not take the organised tour.

But frequently you will not have have adequate information to make sensible decisions in time. In many ports, for example, the ship might berth close to the city or to taxis, or inconveniently away. Even the captain will probably not know until an hour or so before arrival. A few points are, however, worth making.

Generally people are more pleased when they do their own thing than when they stick with the tour. Often doing your own thing enables you to start later and get back sooner, so avoiding the crowd. Often, too, it will be no more expensive to take a taxi than two seats on the bus, and perhaps cheaper if you find a friendly couple with whom to share. But language *is* frequently a problem where not even pidgin English is spoken, especially if you want to go off the usual beaten tourist track. Having a map showing where you want to go, plus a postcard of the ship to help get you back, is sound advice.

Remember that the ship's tour office is normally flat out just handling the sales (and cancellations) of tickets for the organised tours. The staff will try to answer your individual questions but will not make car rental or other arrangements. Moreover, while their advice will be well intended, they themselves will not have been everywhere and anyway conditions change rapidly. Then, again, at some ports the local tourist organisation will provide useful guide-books in several languages; at others there will not even be a simple map on board to help you, and as you walk down the gangway you may be pointed in exactly the wrong direction for the train station.

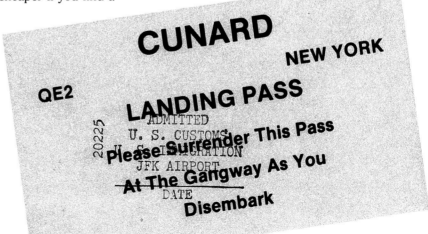

Above *Vancouver's modern liner terminal is close to down town.* Above right *A chance to sample a local drink before rejoining QE2 in evening sunlight at Cadiz.* Right *And always a chance for last minute shopping before rejoining the ship at a Turkish port*

Left *The* Cunard Countess *at Guadeloupe*

So be self sufficient! That means early planning and making sure that you have a map of each port. If you want a self-drive car, not only can you make sure by reserving in advance, but it will probably be cheaper. There is naturally a run on self-drive and chauffeur-driven cars especially at small ports when a large ship visits.

You also need to be opportunistic. There are top-grade tourist places where nearly everyone feels obliged to do the conventional round of the sites. But more frequently it is a matter of personal taste, and even then of fine-tuning when you see what the weather and the traffic are like, how fresh or tired you are, whether you are in the mood to shop or have spent too much money at previous ports, whether per-haps there is some local celebration taking place. Never be afraid of changing your mind. What memories one has of a happy afternoon including a leisurely teatime in an old-fashioned café after abandoning an expensive but totally boring tour of a civic building. It was when the guide told us to stand on the stairs in a certain way – the better to believe her judgement that they were particularly *comfortable* stairs – that we knew we had had enough and, like a couple of school kids, escaped into the world and into our great personal enjoyment.

Another aspect is that it is sometimes pleasant to get away from fellow passengers. Seldom does one feel that the ship is over-crowded; the opportunities for doing your own thing at sea are endless. However, following forty other passengers in and out of the bus and around the tourist traps is another matter.

Most people will go on some organised tours, of course. They are an insurance policy to ensure you see the really key places especially in locations where there may be some doubt about the safety or comfort of travelling alone. Do not overdo it. Use taxis, regular buses, trains or just your feet to discover magical corners that nobody else from the ship will see, sip a drink with the locals in a sidewalk café, enjoy what lesser, uncrowded galleries and churches have to offer, experience being part of the scene rather than just observing it through the lens. The best memories are born of sharing experiences, enjoying contacts, earning yourself a welcome from the café or even from the mountains next time you call. 'Each time I've repeated something familiar and done something fresh', said a passenger who had been many times before as the ship passed the castle into the magnificent harbour. 'Mind you, I've written it all down or I would have forgotten.' She added that when she had first come as a young woman she assumed it would be her one and only visit. Cruising is ever habit forming, and the sooner you record *your* days ashore the more rewarding they too will be.

Of course all this only touches on the issues that will face you. Do you make that very long trip to some magical place inland? (Probably yes if you have dreamed about it, but you organise quieter days before and after.) Do you take your new shipboard friends to share a taxi? (Again probably yes, but for many people cruises offer a rare opportunity to spend real time with your spouse and that may need protecting at all costs.) Do you visit a famous or favourite restaurant? (Depends on your budget. It has to be a particularly superb restaurant to throw away dinner in one of the *QE2*'s grill rooms.) Do you plan to come back to the ship for lunch? (You do not need to decide in advance.) Do you do shopping in town or at the quayside? (Always more colourful in town but also irresistible when real

---

FLAGS

When entering a port, the following flags are raised:

Aft: National flag

Mast: Flag of the country being visited

Mast: Yellow (letter 'Q', until the health authorities have cleared the ship).

You may also see a yellow and red flag (summoning a pilot) and a white and red flag indicating that there is a pilot on board. The company flag (Cunard Lion), Chaîne des Rotisseurs (the restaurant group to which some restaurants afloat belong) or the flag of the charterer of the ship are also occasionally displayed.

displays are created alongside the ship.) How much local currency should you take? (Not too much since big purchases can usually be by credit card or in pounds or dollars, though taxis may need local money.) Should you look up friends in port? (An ocean liner makes a grand way to arrive; never miss the chance.)

Some people like going back to the same place on vacation two or three weeks, years and even decades on end, and certainly they gain a depth of knowledge that more casual visitors cannot share. But properly, though not over-planned, days in port can unlock a rich heritage of experiences, both general and in your individual or specialist mould. Start mixing return visits along with new ports and you truly appreciate the privilege that cruising bestows. Not only will you have visited more places than nearly all who do not cruise, but you will have seen some of them in different moods, even under different political systems.

Days in port are for living and for remembering for ever, even if occasionally you will return early to the ship to pick up the routine of life on board and revel in the comfort of familiarity after the adventure, and to no longer have to wonder if the food is safe.

Arrival in New York has always been a real event and one wonders how many lives were changed by this particular one

---

R.M.S. " QUEEN ELIZABETH "   From Southampton, May 25, 1950   **THE CUNARD STEAM-SHIP COMPANY LIMITED**

THE ATTENTION OF PASSENGERS IS CALLED TO THE FOLLOWING

ARRIVAL.—Weather and other circumstances permitting, the ship is expected to arrive at Pier 90, North River, New York, at approximately 5.00 a.m. on Tuesday, May 30, 1950.

IMMIGRATION.—It is expected that Immigration Officials will board the vessel at approximately 6.30 a.m. and be ready to examine passports and other Immigration Documents and stamp Landing Cards, as below.

U.S. Citizens.—Examination will start at approximately 7.00 a.m. in " A " Deck Smoke Room and passengers are requested to assemble in the Winter Garden on the Main Deck, from whence they will be escorted to the Smoke Room when the Inspectors are ready.

Non-U.S. Citizens.—Passengers are requested to assemble as under :
(1)   Parents accompanied by children under the age of ten years in the Cinema, "B" Deck. **Regardless of visa.**
(2)   Passengers holding Re-Entry Permits, Transit and Visitors' visaes in the **Winter Garden.**
(3)   Passengers holding Quota and non-Quota visaes in the **Smoke Room,** "A" Deck, after the examination of U.S. citizens has been completed.
   Passengers will be conducted from the above points to the Immigration Inspection when the officials are ready.
   Passengers are reminded that baggage may not be taken to the various assembly rooms.
   Your kind co-operation will expedite this important and necessary formality to the advantage of all.

BREAKFAST will be served at 6.30 and 7.30 a.m.

U.S. CUSTOMS DECLARATIONS.—Declarations duly completed should be handed to the Bedroom Steward or to the Purser's Office as soon as possible.

REVISED U.S. CUSTOMS REGULATIONS.—Recent legislation by U.S. Authorities has introduced a more liberal allowance which provides for a Customs exemption of $200.00 to residents with merchandise purchased abroad not oftener than once a month, and an allowance of $500 when at least six months has elapsed since the last prior importation and the returning resident has been out of the United States for a minimum of twelve continuous days.
   When all your baggage is under the initial letter, you

T.C.

should then present your baggage declaration stub to the desk of the Deputy Collector of Customs, who will assign an inspector to examine the baggage.

   Passengers are reminded that it is unsafe to leave their baggage unattended on the pier after it has been examined by the U.S. Customs and their "Examined" stamps affixed thereto.

CHECKING BAGGAGE ON ARRIVAL IN NEW YORK.—Passengers may arrange with the Ship's Baggage Master for the transfer of baggage from the Company's pier to any point in Greater New York, Jersey City and Hoboken, including railroad terminals, hotels, residences, express companies or warehouses.
   Representatives of the HENDRICKSON TRANSFER COMPANY, a reliable organisation, will be found on the UPPER LEVEL of the Company's Piers.

BAGGAGE IN BOND.—Passengers desirous of using this facility should make their arrangements with the U.S. Customs Authorities on the pier.

BAGGAGE.—Passengers are requested to have all cabin baggage packed and ready for removal from their cabins by 6.00 p.m., Monday, May 29, 1950.

BANK.—For the convenience of passengers the Midland Bank will be open from 10.00 a.m. to 12.30 p.m. and from 2.30 p.m. to 5.00 p.m. on Monday, May 29, and will not re-open after this hour as they are not allowed to function in U.S.A. or territorial waters.

MAIL.—It is expected that a small amount of mail will be received on board at Quarantine and this may be claimed at the Purser's Office, "R" Deck. Passengers are requested to enquire at the Mail Desk on the pier for any mail which may have arrived after the ship has arrived alongside the dock.

HEAD TAX.—Passengers visiting the United States for less than 60 days are exempt from the Head Tax of $8.00 per person, provided they inform the U.S. Immigration Inspector of such intention at the passport examination on arrival.
   Passengers who deposited Head Tax when booking passage and who are exempt therefrom on any ground, should obtain U.S. Form 755 from the Immigration Inspector and present such to the Purser before leaving the steamer or at any of the Company's offices in order to obtain refund.

Approaching Malta

The Russian Riviera, Yalta

Liquid refreshment for passengers returning to Vistafjord *by tender from Geirangerfjord*

Opposite *Three pictures conveying a touch of the excitement of a transit through the Panama Canal. Directly opposite is shown the approach to the locks on the Pacific side; the top right-hand picture shows a Cunarder catching up a container ship on the parallel lock; and, top left, in the central reaches beyond the tropical area*

8
PANAMA CANAL

JUST to sail along the canal would be one of life's memorable experiences, but the true appreciation of Panama has to be taken in the context of an ocean-to-ocean voyage, a day of bustling activity yet much tranquillity between sea-going cruising.

By the time you wake up, the ship will probably already have slowed. The sea that was empty last night may now be full of vessels, some waiting their turn to precede or follow you through the great waterway that remains one of man's major achievements against natural features and adversity. This is not the place to recite again just how many men lost their lives over how many years moving mountains of earth and rock, the problems with disease and landslips, but the story of the building of the canal (the dream of centuries but only opened in 1914) never fails to impress. A guide will probably come on board and tell you about it; if a film or video is shown on the subject, make it a priority to watch. What concerns us here is that it is one of the great pieces of cruising on inland water (and on fresh water high above sea level) that you can enjoy in the luxury of an ocean-going liner. The sheer romance perhaps hits you most when you do something mundane like taking clothes off on one ocean that you put on on another. The experience of the Panama Canal is many faceted and though it lasts the best part of the day is never too long.

The canal toll exceeds what many Americans earn in a year, and most ships that use it are therefore really going places. The exception are the occasional cruises just to Gatun Lake, the 168sq mile (435km^2) artificial lake or reservoir near the Atlantic end whose slight drop in level as the result of ecological changes, possibly caused by the burning of the world's rain forests, has already alarmed the experts and might be a warning of real difficulties for the canal in the years ahead. Gatun Lake cruises have their adherents, but then some people are happy enough to go to a restaurant only for a starter.

The full flavour of the Panama Canal, as already mentioned, only comes if you start on the Atlantic and finish on the Pacific, or vice versa. World cruises usually patronise the canal as do voyages around South America. Otherwise it will be a cruise to or from Fort Lauderdale and somewhere on America's west coast, to Mexico or perhaps Los Angeles; and unless you take the same journey in reverse that will mean flying one way. Few cruises call at the ports at either end of the canal, Panamanian cities (who earn greater profit from catering for the more earthy demands of sailors) not being rated highly by tourists. More cruise ships opt for the undeveloped San Blas Islands. These give a taste of a different Panama where Cuna Indians on picture-postcard beaches with bamboo huts under the palms overlooking crystal-clear sea, practise their own form of community life, women always in the lead including selling their colourful *molas* or blouses. The San Blas Islands are undoubtedly different from any of the Caribbean islands that provide the other stopping places on the Atlantic leg of trans-Panama cruises (see Chapters 3 and 8). Yet you will enjoy more of mainland Panama from the ship's deck than you see of the interior of most countries you visit.

The first excitement is naturally watching the ship fit tightly into the first lock-chamber and be harnessed to the electric locomotives or 'mules' that ride with you as they pull you up through the locks and keep you steady. The railway with steep gradients at the lock rises is the only thing that has changed since the canal was opened; at first animals did the guiding. You go up three locks, the surprise being that another ship, perhaps a large container one, is paralleling you going up the other of the twin sets. Everything is beautifully ordered with split-second timing, the two ships ahead still visible when you get into your first lock-chamber, the following pair seen down there below the stern as you prepare to leave the final chamber. Forty or fifty ships a day come this way, strictly timetabled, the ladders of locks being wholly devoted to climbing or

---

NAUTICAL MEASUREMENTS

A nautical mile is 6,080ft or 1.8532km (1.852km for international nautical mile); a land mile is 5,280ft (1.6093km). A knot is a nautical mile in a time/distance relationship: ft (km) per hour. The term dates from former times when the speed of a ship was calculated by means of a log tied to the end of a line knotted at measured intervals. This was thrown over the side, the number of knots passing through the hand in a known number of seconds as it fell gave the speed of the ship in knots. More nautical measures: 6ft = 1 fathom = 1.8532m; 100 fathoms = a cable length = 185.32m (185.88m international measure).

descending ships at different periods to allow maximum capacity. But it of course takes time for the fresh water from Gatun Lake to gush down to the next level after the paddles on the gigantic gates are opened – and most people take far more photographs than intended.

So into Gatun Lake with its islands which used to be tops of peaks, including the nature reserve of Barror Colorado Island to which many animals retreated as the water level rose in 1914. All around is lush, verdant jungle, many tall trees topped with exotic climbers. Where else do you sail peacefully past such a spectacle?

Then into the Gaillard Cut, the deepest excavation of the canal across the continental divide; 60,000,000 tons of explosive were used to make it possible for ships to take this short cut. Though it is narrow, with sheer cliffs towering overhead, ships pass each other with no more fuss than buses on a road. Ships of all shapes and sizes, nearly all cargo, such a great everyday traffic that it is stunning to realise that but for the canal they would all have to go around the tip of South America and that that was indeed the route from the east to the west seaboard of the United States until 1914. There are 8 miles (12km) of the Gaillard Cut, and awe inspiring they are. But you are closer to unspoilt nature after descending the Pedro Miguel Lock and again have jungle around you. After the wide expanse of Gatun Lake and the narrow Gaillard Cut, Miraflores Lake is a more natural waterway. Note the bridges of the Panama Railway (once the world's most profitable) over its inlets and tributary rivers. All around on a generous but not overwhelming scale there is green beauty, peacefulness. This is where many passengers satisfy their emotion by a toast in champagne, but it is a place for quiet, personal rather than an organised, noisy celebration.

And so down through the two Miraflores Locks into the Pacific, under the 5,000ft (1,524m) long Puente de las Americas straddling high above the final sea-level section of canal, and onwards past Balboa and Panama City.

Most of the canal is 85ft (26m) above sea level, and your climb and descent will use more than 50,000,000gal (227,000,000 litres) of precious water. You descend an average of 7in (18cm) less than you rise, since the Pacific is higher than the Atlantic, though your actual sea levels will of course depend on the different states of the tide at either end. It will not, however, be details like that you will remember, but the total experience of crossing the isthmus, the glimpses of cities and ports with their furious activity, the utter peace even when passing a ship going the other way in the more open parts of the canal, a serene clear waterway through the jungle.

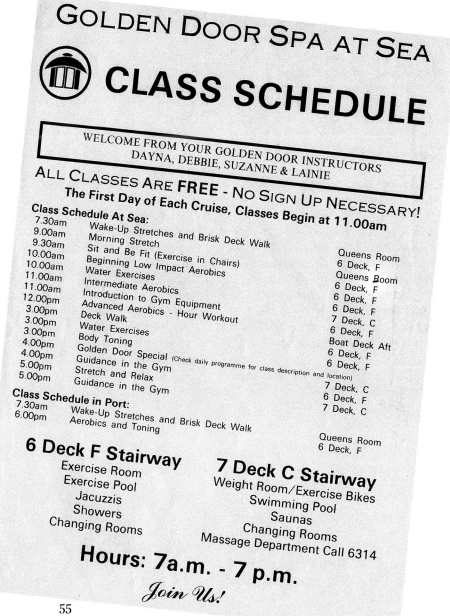

9
SOUTH AMERICA

FOR most of the small party who assembled on the dock overlooking a hillside of both well-built houses and a shanty town, it was their first ever footsteps in South America. We were the people who had put down our names under a handwritten letter on the ship's notice board: 'I am arranging a small party to visit Colonia Tovar which is a German-speaking village in the mountains beyond Caracas. We found the trip very enjoyable the last time we came to La Guaira. It will take about six hours including lunch.'

It was a Sunday morning, and as happens in much of the world things were slow to get started. Eventually two vehicles to accommodate the fifteen or so of us were ready; we took our seats, and off we went. To begin with everything was new: the American-style car plates and road signs, the boldly engineered modern highway (nearly empty now but which we were told already clogged up at commuter rush time) and the check points where everyone had to slow down and be seen by the police.

We climbed. First up the highway to Venezuela's rapidly expanding capital, then well above the city which we could look down upon from a layby higher up the mountains. Now the road was narrow and twisty and took us through villages of long, untidy main streets. Then our first glimpse of Colonia Tovar still higher, and the final climb to this little well-kept piece of Germany where we found ourselves just another set of tourists amid the hundreds of Venezuelans visiting it for a fun-Sunday lunchtime. Everything glittered in the clear sunshine, quite different from the haze hanging over Caracas. Decorations strung across the street fluttered in the breeze, souvenirs sold rapidly in the busy gift shops, even the orderliness of the German cemetery caught the imagination. One of the joys of cruising is that all of a sudden you find yourself sharing a tourist treasure with the locals who, though of course not having so far to come, are nevertheless on an expedition to see it. The visitors photographed especially the costumes worn by the Colonia locals, and little girls were discreetly changed into a gay new outfit to celebrate the mood.

When our waiter heard where we were going, he had said, 'Wonderful! Pigs' knuckles and Sauerkraut!' The country house restaurant was almost more German than Germany, but pigs' knuckles were not obligatory! Strange to be speaking Spanish while ordering German dishes, though a few of our party tried out their German successfully and some of us as usual resorted to English/American. Our organiser had by now become a popular man, for until we saw his letter none of us had even heard of Colonia let alone had a desire to visit it in preference to the capital, yet now we were universally agreed it was a super way to spend our Sunday ashore, and were generous in our tips as he collected payment for the bill.

After lunch there was more time to walk around and visit the shops, the only disappointment being that the florist did not take credit cards nor even US dollars. Then came the winding descent, and another pause to take in the enormity of Caracas, city of contrasts with mansions and makeshift corrugated-iron homesteads in layers up the sprawling hillside. And so back to La Guaira, being visited by two of Cunard's largest ships together, giving the staff a day of toing and froing, renewing old acquaintances and making new ones.

The *QE2* was the first to leave, and a handsome sight she made – disappearing, it seemed, through the rigging of a large sail-training vessel. We followed in *Sagafjord* an hour later as the sun sank behind the hills and cast long shadows over the port and town which we would always remember as our first South American landfall.

Cruises to and round South America have a special appeal to those who want to go somewhere different, and see for themselves what this vast sub-continent that accounts for 12 per cent of the world's landmass and for some of its greatest mountains and river systems is really like, without having to spend a lifetime making separate visits to various countries and often widely separated destinations within them. At one extreme many Caribbean cruises include one or two ports, often indeed La Guaira, letting passengers experience perpetual spring in Caracas, the capital in a hurry to get bigger and yet more impressive; sometimes Cartagena in Colombia with its splendid walled old city, a place to explore on foot. At the other extreme are the occasional cruises right round South America. People who have patronised them swear by them as a kind of purposeful mini world cruise, offering a spectacular variety of sight and experience that even today is still for a very select minority.

One of the highlights of Round South America itineraries is the passing through the Panama Canal and, taking you back to the ocean you set out on, the voyage through the Straits of Magellan, 330 miles (563km) long, between Patagonia and the Tierra del Fuego archipelago. Here indeed is romance: an inhospitable landscape of towering cliffs, snow-covered peaks and, closer by, ice-floes and numerous near-barren islands where the residents are penguins. You will of course come in their summer and, to emphasise just how far south you are, at the longest day you will enjoy sunshine (or at least the possibility of it) for nearly twenty out of the twenty-four hours. But sun or cloud, and to some extent even in mist, there is great clarity of vision in the pollution-free environment. And there is much to enjoy from a host of other points of view. The area abounds in natural history and, especially when you have Argentina on one side and Chile on the other, you will learn much about the passions of South American history and indeed about the discovery and exploitation of the V-shaped seaway between the world's two greatest oceans. You will see Punta Arenas, the only large town in these parts where, before the opening of the Panama Canal, ships carrying much of the Americas' trade used to stop to coal and generally revictual. Few preferred the more exposed route farther south via Cape Horn, and the price for transferring between oceans by the Straits is that you yourself will not experience that possibly even more romantic yet undoubtedly more fearsome route. Incidentally, across the Strait from Punta Arenas is a town on Tierra del Fuego whose population of about 4,000 is almost all Yugoslavian, descendants of those who left before World War I to avoid being caught up in Austro-Hungarian military service. Germans, Yugoslavians and many more ethnic settlements dot South America, a whole new world waiting for most of us still to explore.

Between the Caribbean cruises that just add a South American destination for variety and

Above QE2 *seen leaving La Guaira (the port for Caracas, Venezuela) through the masts of a sail-training ship.* Right *Sunday in Colonia*

Many of South America's most famous sights can be viewed on shore excursions. This is Machu Picchu in Peru (Imagebank)

often nicknamed the 'Paris of South America', here is a city owing no allegiance elsewhere, a city you need to experience even to begin to understand it and its nation.

The grandness of South American cities is matched by that of the natural scenery and phenomena such as giant waterfalls even away from the Andes. And nobody explores in the footsteps of the Incas who does not think how wonderful it would have been had Roman and Greek treasures not been discovered (and pillaged) until 1911, when the ancient fortress city of Machu Picchu was first seen by modern eyes. A visit to Callao, 8 miles (13km) from Peru's vibrant capital of Lima, may make it possible to catch one of the world's most memorable trains and then bus to Machu Picchu, the archaeological site that, according to many enthusiasts of bygone civilisations, beats anything European. Once there used to be a ship round South America weekly; now you have to take your chance and plan how to use precious time carefully. Just occasionally Callao is at the beginning and end of a sector, enabling those joining the ship to visit Machu Picchu the previous day and then leave the day after. That is certainly not an opportunity to be missed, though if you are only off the ship for a day trip you have the alternative of Pachácmac, 20 miles (32km) south of Lima where the holy city once occupied 4 square miles (10km^2) high above the pinky-grey desert, the Andes one side, the Pacific the other.

There are, of course, things that cruising on a large ship does not make possible. Ecuador you may sample at the port of Guayaquil, where about half the country's total population lives and works, but you cannot even taste the mainland's diversity let alone enjoy the Galapagos Islands and their unique wildlife. The Galapagos are the prerogative of much smaller craft with strictly limited numbers of passengers. Thousands of miles away, and in another ocean, the Falkland Islands are now being placed firmly on the tourist map, again largely for their natural history. But politics

those great all-round South America itineraries, there are opportunities to taste something worthwhile of the sub-continent, most often Brazil. Once more, this is not meant to be a guide-book, but to help readers select and make the most of their travel experience. Even a single visit to South America starts unravelling the deep mysteries – especially that ever-present mingling of past and present, rich and poor – of the sub-continent so different from the rest of the western hemisphere. But such is the variety that however many ports you visit you will never exhaust the treasure.

Some especially enjoy the sheer splendour of many of the cities, notably the capitals. Many people say that a visit to Buenos Aires is worthwhile just to see the great banks and railway stations; others that what really struck them was the scale of the famous tree-lined avenues, the animation of the people. Though

prevent the logical routing via Buenos Aires, and that discourages the inclusion of Port Stanley, the Falklands' capital, in itineraries.[1]

You can sail up the mighty Amazon to Manaus, but that is a cruise which disappoints some. Though you are on the river for a solid 1,000 miles (1,600km), at Manaus it is still so wide that people complain they do not get a feeling of intimacy with the banks and the jungle, and that Manaus (though not without points of interest such as the magnificent opera house built out of the wealth of rubber before the Malay peninsula took over much of that trade) hardly has the feel of a city in the middle of the world's greatest rain forest. To get the best out of the Amazon, again you need to take to a smaller – much smaller – craft, and to do so for more than half a day's ride. People going up to Manaus are often especially disappointed after the promising start at Belém, gateway to the river and its riches, a city of wide boule-vards and grand buildings in the middle of the forest. It is sometimes described as being at the Amazon's mouth, though in fact the Atlantic is nearly 100 miles (160km) away – a small distance when the river is twice that number of miles wide and stretches inland for well over 3,000 miles (4,800km), Manaus not being any-thing like halfway to the limit of navigation. So broad is the river below Manaus that indeed often you cannot even see the banks. True river enthusiasts recommend flying to Manaus and making that the starting point for a voyage on a smaller ship to Iquitos; not of course that you do not catch some of the feel for the world's largest river and its traffic from the luxury of Cunard.

What seldom disappoint are the Brazilian coastal calls, including Belém, sometimes the first American port after South Africa on a world cruise. Rio de Janeiro would make any top ten. You will never forget its setting, whether seen from the ship as you approach or from a

[1] This was as in 1989. Tensions have eased considerably since.

BAROMETER

Next to the mariner's compass and chart, the barometer is one of the most important aids to navigation ever devised. Invented by Torricelli at Florence, Italy, in 1643, it is an instrument for recording changes in the weather by measuring weight, or pressure, of the atmosphere. A rising barometer signals the approach of fair weather and a falling one signifies the reverse, while a sudden drop warns the seafarer to be on the watch for severe storms. The ship's barometer, which is kept in the chart room, traces a barometric chart and records the atmosphere throughout the voyage.

---

vantage point during a tour. As the guide-book puts it:

> The first view simply takes your breath away. The blue sweep of the bay dappled with islands and surrounded by green hills; blind-ing white beaches fringed with palms; tower-ing Sugar Loaf Mountain standing like a giant rock sentinel at the entrance to the harbour. You were prepared for the wonders of Rio – the gaiety, the carnival atmosphere, the dazzling women – but not for the sheer beauty of the sight.

The *Berlitz* guides which are bound into your cruise programme are always eloquent where eloquence is called for, and obligingly tell you about the history, the principal things to see, the shopping and what to eat (lest Cunard should leave you feeling hungry), but are somewhat variable in the quantity and quality of other information, only sometimes providing a basic map. So whether you are visiting one or many South American ports, take care to go properly prepared and, incidentally, remember that the sub-continent straddles the equator and that on a cruise round it you will experience big climatic variations.

São Paulo, Brazil? Sounds a great place in which to spend a gentle day. But *Berlitz*, while describing it as New York gone mad, gives no map of the bubbling metropolis of over 10 million people and you could as easily be miserable as exhilarated. Recognise that most South American city calls are potentially dis-orientating and exhausting and then you will get the most out of them. Enjoy their self-

centred lifestyles mixing ultra-sophistication and exaggerated architecture with ample evidence that the frontier was pushed back only yesteryear, the very modern being cheek by jowl with ancient buildings and monuments. The arrogant drivers who make Italians seem tame stuff at the wheel, the astronomical inflation rates that we more normal people cannot quite comprehend how anyone copes with, the ability indeed to progress rapidly without ever quite conquering – they are all part of the unique South American and especially Brazilian character. Not surprisingly, more people opt for the organised tours here than in most places, yet you only experience the city's full flavour when mingled with the crowd.

Brazil is the world's fifth largest country, and what happens in it is of great importance to us all. Its wealth is such that on most cruises, say in Europe, you will probably find a handful of Brazilian passengers. The diversity of its ports, mainland and island, will hopefully be steadily better exploited by cruise ships. *Berlitz* tells us, for example, that Salvador is without equal:

> Colonial mansions and Baroque churches decorated with ornate gold leaf coexist with holiday hotels, shanty-town huts and elegant restaurants. And surrounding the peninsula on which the city stands is mile upon mile of hot empty beach with room for just about everybody in Brazil.

Recife, the 'Venice of Brazil', Fortaleza, key to the nation's sunshine coast – the list goes on, and one suspects they are all places which are going to become much more part of our world.

10

MEDITERRANEAN AND ADRIATIC

IT was the last arrival but the least forgettable. Even many of those who had not worn them before put on the robes thoughtfully provided in the cabins and wandered on deck soon after six. The first reaction was disappointment: visibility was restricted by a heavy mist clinging to the Adriatic Sea. But as we passed through the entrance into Venice's lagoon, we rapidly appreciated that the mist, now rolling in banks a few feet above water level, added a serene if not mystical touch.

The water was still, almost glazed, and you

Land is in sight more often than you expect. Yugoslavia's Adriatic coast never disappoints

could hear *Vistafjord*'s bow gently cutting through it, and the faint noise of her engines aft. Everything else was silent except for the very occasional passing of a fishing vessel whose crew – seen only momentarily through the now effervescent mist – quietly raised their hands.

Then, as if by magic, first the blurred outline of Venice's waterfront and then individual buildings came into vision, often to be lost again, reappear more vaguely then in greater clarity, until those who knew Venice could pinpoint their exact bearing and tell the story of that church and point to the entrance of the Grand Canal.

By now the engines had slowed, and muffled sounds could be heard from land. Just everyone was on deck, proud to be at this geographical spot at this moment in time. And there, look, stands the familiar silhouette of St Mark's – and exactly over it a pale, orangy ball of sun peering through the top of the mist just as the bell sounds seven. One is compelled into the present tense, so great is the joy, so at peace together are all the passengers who within hours are to be dispersed across much of the globe.

As the sun gains strength, steadily all Venice comes into sharp focus. However well you think you know Venice, you have not fully experienced it until arriving by sea, and ideally at different times in different weathers and lights. But now we are on the route crisscrossed by the ferries and gondolas many passengers have taken on previous visits, and can go down to the dining room for breakfast without too much sacrifice.

After the leisurely meal with the usual last-morning fond farewells and tipping ritual, it is not long before the tender ferries us to the waterfront just off St Mark's Square. We are to meet there in two and a half hours for the water-taxi that will take us via an interesting selection of canals to the airport. Meantime there is the choice of an organised walk with a tour guide, or of disappearing into the crowd on our own. Venice is a marvellous city at which to begin or end a cruise. Nobody can possibly tire of it, most of it is so conveniently explorable on foot, and every moment brings some new juxtaposition of vista and light, a work of art that veritably envelopes the soul. Canaletto, for instance, realised that the ever-

changing light on the canals gave Venice an ethereal quality.

Some passengers wisely sacrifice the seat bought them on a charter flight as part of the cruise package and make their own arrangements to celebrate Venice a couple of days longer, and to celebrate to the hilt there is often the possibility of starting or ending your cruise with a trip on the *Orient Express*.

This particular cruise, titled Around Italy, had begun ten days earlier in Genoa and included a selection of Italian, Greek and Yugoslavian ports plus Malta. Genoa, Italy's largest port and another city everyone is glad to have a chance to explore before or after a cruise, Venice itself, maybe Piraeus (port of Athens) or elegant Barcelona or Malaga, queen of the Costa del Sol, occasionally Southampton or even New York, are starting or finishing points for the Mediterranean's endless variety. Nowhere else in the world is there a greater diversity of route, and even if some of the ports are fairly frequent common denominators, the total choice and order are seldom the same. The range is moreover increased by the fact that two or more short cruises can often be conveniently and economically strung together. From time to time, though mostly regularly, all four of Cunard's styles of cruising can be enjoyed here, from the yacht-like splendour of *Sea Goddess*, unobtrusively slipping into ports not open to larger ships to take her natural place beside some of the world's most exclusive privately owned vessels, to the bargain style of *Cunard Princess* making it possible for entire families to experience the most important sites in the history of man. At the time of writing, *Princess* has been stationed for year-round cruising mainly out of Venice and Malaga, incidentally with the option of a train journey from London to Malaga or back.

Unlike the Caribbean, where most people

By sea and tram it took barely half-an-hour between leaving Vistafjord *and taking this photograph of her off the coast of Capri*

cruise for the overall experience, the exact ports often matter enormously here in the Mediterranean, for millions of discerning people want to see some of the great cultural and historic cities and individual ruins much more than others. So Mediterranean itineraries are examined in far more detail than most and, like other cruise lines, Cunard pays more attention to passengers' ratings of the ports here. The Mediterranean is both large and studded with top attractions. It indeed offers almost limitless variation, for the essence of the story of the world's greatest civilisations and of western religions unfolds if not on the actual waterfront then certainly within easy reach of convenient ports. Even inland cities like Florence are regularly included in the day-tour itineraries.

The Mediterranean nations, from southern Spain and all but far northern Italy through Greece to Israel and Egypt, can be largely explored by cruise. Many who reckon to know the region intimately have made *all* their visits by ship. Thoroughly to get to know anywhere you need longer than a few days, yet if you have visited say Venice, Rome or Athens five or six times by ship, beginning or ending a couple of cruises there, you will not be doing badly compared to the tourist who has made a single trip even if that stretched a week or longer. Certainly few people have the time and resources to spend that long in each of the Mediterranean's top dozen destinations.

The ports you are most likely to repeat are the very ones that you could happily spend a whole year in if human life were infinite. And how often one hears of a friend spending a holiday of a lifetime somewhere special only to be disappointed that it was the wrong time of year, the weather caused some special upset (for instance in hot, dry weather the smell in Venice was obnoxious) or that the visit to the gallery that was to be the apex of the visit could not take place because of a strike or maintenance work. 'This time', say cruisegoers setting off to make another attempt.

If you have never yet visited the Mediterranean, all this talk of repeat visits may seem beside the point. It is not. For if you take one cruise, you will almost certainly want to come back some later year, and so set a pattern of exploration. One thing is absolutely certain: your first cruise will unlock more of the treasures of this unique region than any comparable time spent on a land tour, and in greater style and with more relaxation. Of course you do not have to commit yourself to never making a land tour any more than it would make sense to say that cruising was not for those who had already explored by train, coach or car. It is just that cruising is a highly appropriate, practical means of getting round, and wherever you go you will be using that great common factor that knit the region together throughout historic times – the sea.

A few other facts about Mediterranean cruises. Spring and autumn are the best seasons, high summer being unbearably hot especially among the Greek ruins. Remember that shops close for long afternoon siestas, and even in spring and autumn the morning and evening will often be more enjoyable out and about. Sensible planning should begin with early starts. You are almost certain to attempt too much; so do not resent the quieter day at sea or on an island for relaxation that Cunard might skilfully weave into the itinerary. Driving conditions in places like Rome and Athens are among the least appealing in the world to those coming from more traffic-law-abiding cultures. And while in the course of ten or fourteen days you would be exceedingly unlucky not to have much sunshine, the Mediterranean is by no means immune from storms, as indeed the Bible makes clear.

Neither, unfortunately, is the region free from political upheavals. Ports come and go in itineraries according to the latest pressures. It is years since Beirut, once a tourist mecca, was a regular port of call, and also since Libya welcomed Americans. Israel and Egypt suddenly get wiped off future itineraries when

tensions are high, though already planned visits have continued – often with bargains for those prepared to take the place of cancelled passengers. If there is going to be a hijacking or a shoot-out at an international airport, it will most likely be in the greater Mediterranean, against which the vast majority of cruises make you no more aware of the political divisions than the brief reports of the latest happenings in the shipboard paper.

What you certainly will enjoy is a great diversity of cultures. This chapter began with Venice. Often the ports immediately before or after are in Yugoslavia, but along the sun-blessed picturesque coastline of island paradises, yachtsmen's harbours and ancient cities and villages. Eager guides, restaurateurs and other traders delight equally in serving you and in taking your pounds and dollars. Hardly the average westerner's idea of life in the communist world, Dubrovnik is the port most frequently visited, and it is easy to see why. The walled city with its jewellers and other shops well worth studying, its grand cliffs and even its cafés and tourist hotels, make it one of the most welcoming resort towns anywhere, intimate yet dramatically varied. Ancient Split is another common calling place: a large port with a huge market where you can bargain to your heart's content, an interesting old town with outdoor cafés and a steep hinterland which taxis will be only too pleased to whisk you around, stopping for photographs of the port including your ship. Split is always colourful, yet it is some of the smaller places (one or two of them, such as Korcula, just occasionally on *Vistafjord*'s itinerary) and the narrow channels between mainland and islands, or between islands, that make this so fascinating a coast.

If one had to select just one piece of coastline where you need to take to a smaller cruise ship to enjoy the best, it would be this Dalmatian seaboard rivalling Norway's in its complex indentations but blessed with a perfect climate including a daily average of twelve hours of sunshine in summer. If you can afford it, one of the *Sea Goddess*es sometimes comes this way, popping into discreet village harbours and through channels where other Cunard vessels could not possibly go, and making occasional impromptu stops in particularly delectable spots for sea bathing. If that is out of your league, then here as nowhere else the advice has to be to one day take a smaller non-Cunard ship, possibly out of Venice.

Another route that ships as large as *Vistafjord* cannot take is through the Corinth Canal, though many cruise liners do make their passage through the 4 mile (6km) long deep ditch, more intriguing than inviting, by night. So before or after a visit to Athens (the port of Piraeus is half an hour from the city, and the peacefulness of the ship even if tied up for an overnight stay will be especially welcome after a busy, noisy and dusty round of Athens's sites, unbeatable though they are), it has to be the long way round the whole of the Peloponnesus peninsula to get to Itea for Delphi. Never regret this time spent going round the Greek coastline or threading between the islands. Whenever there is light – even from the moon – to see it, there is an ever-changing panorama of landscapes in which so much of the history of civilisation has been enacted. This is no place for detailed history, but here is the kind of thing you will read from the guide-books you will hopefully take with you and which will make Mediterranean cruising so much more vital than just snapping pretty views:

The Peloponnesus forms the southern extremity of the Balkan peninsula and takes its name from the ancient island of Pelopos. In the Middle Ages it was known as the Morea, due to the fact that the mulberry flourished. It is a highland region with more than half of its area above 1,500ft. Its imposing ruins illustrate more fully and comprehensively four thousand years of history than anywhere else in Europe.

Mycenaen, Greek, Roman, Byzantine, Frankish, Venetian and Turkish remains reveal the province's complex evolution. In 1821 it was the Germanos, the Bishop of Patras, who raised the standard of revolt against the Turks, and the Peloponnesus formed the core of the early nineteenth-century kingdom. Nauplion, in the Argolis district, was the first capital of independent Greece. Otho, first king of Greece, disembarked at Nauplion in 1833, remaining until the government was removed to Athens in 1834.

If Athens overwhelms, even disgusts with its pollution, (though it never disappoints), Delphi instantly enters the very soul with its combination of dramatic setting on the beautiful slope of Mount Parnassus and its rich historical and mystical associations. For many Delphi is the ruins above all other ruins, and extensive they are too, visual evidence of the sheer wealth the seat of Apollo and the Oracle was based on.

Though Itea on the long Gulf of Corinth is delightfully situated, it has little in itself; for centuries, however, it served as port for the pilgrimage up the mountains. Just think of all those who have set out on this road before you. Since it would be too risky to rely on taxis being available, make sure to reserve the official tour, though in truth this is only a bus ride, ever climbing up the green hillside. 'Flat, comfortable shoes recommended', says Cunard's *Berlitz* description of the expedition, adding: 'To maintain the best possible standard the guides and some transportation have been transferred from Athens.' Since it is too much to ever expect to have Delphi to yourself in popular hours (and its sheer scale in rich layers up the hillside devours crowds), the extra Cunard touch is more welcome than intrusive. Whatever your emotional capacity, it will be pressed to the absolute limit; if the whole of the rest of the cruise had been spent stationary in the Mediterranean, most

passengers would think just this visit made it all worthwhile.

Rome is another magnificent calling place where most people will devote much of their time to exploring the great remains of the classical world. Naples, whose great bay it seems a privilege to enter, makes possible visits to Pompeii and, closer to the teeming city with the world's second densest population, possibly the even more dramatic excavations of Herculaneum where within easy compass you can relive the life of an upper-crust resort of two thousand years ago now complete with facilities like wine shop and laundrette.

Volcanoes, active and passive, apart from all the disasters they caused in bygone times,

Above *Special trains are often run for Cunard passengers such as this one in connection with a QE2 visit to Corsica*

Left *Your ship usually docks within easy walking distance of St Mark's Square, Venice*

Below left *The walled city of Dubrovnik and its spectacular cliffs yards away are also a pedestrian's delight*

Throughout the Mediterranean one of the main attractions is of course ancient ruins. Who could possibly forget a visit to Delphi?

Below *An Italian welcome: cruises often start from Genoa*

occur surprisingly frequently. You may be lucky enough to pass the island of Stromboli whose volcanic top is throwing red cinders into the sea; many cruise ships contrive to show this natural firework display in late evening. If you stop at Messina, guarding the strait between Sicily and mainland Italy, or at Catania to the south – there is a spectacular coast road between them – you are bound to come under the influence of Mount Etna. Hope for clear skies so you can snap its smoking top even if you do not take the journey by road, cable car and foot to Europe's largest active volcano. Those who do, descend with a sense of thrill and achievement; but then again those who explore one of Sicily's unspoilt villages, shopping and sipping wine with the natives, hardly feel that their time has been wasted either.

It is the magic not only of Sicily but of dozens of varied smaller Mediterranean islands of many nationalities that each in its own way sharpens your senses and makes you appreciate the very act of living. Even on the larger islands such as French Corsica and very Italian Sardinia, which however hard you try you can only sample during a day's call, you still imbibe the highly individual flavour and leave believing, most decidedly, that it was worth going. For many who cruise later in life there is the very welcome experience of paying brief return calls to earlier holiday sites such as Mallorca or Minorca, Malta or one of the enchanting Greek islands, and seeking out familiar haunts that make a unique link between past and present life. Certainly it is hard not to feel superior passing the ugly rows of cheap hotels providing mass-produced holidays which, at this very moment, many people from your own home town will be in the middle of. But even on a day's visit, there is no need to linger in the hotel belt and it is usually perfectly possible to get to enjoy whatever part of the island attracts you most.

The best island days are often those on which you take impromptu decisions, like abandoning the official tour of Greek's greenest island of Corfu and (since there may be nothing else) renting a jeep for a drive to the idyllic beaches of the north coast. For the even more adventurous, light motor cycles can be rented cheaply. Mediterranean island days are mainly for kicking off and, as already mentioned, for taking a break in an otherwise hectic schedule of traditional ruins of the ancient world. Yet two things should be borne in mind. A few islands have top-class attractions themselves, so reserving the official tour to ensure you have a good English guide might be desirable, while at many smaller places car rental facilities are limited. Also remember that, especially in Greece, it is much cheaper to rent a car in advance than locally. So some homework is desirable, though hopefully leaving ample opportunity for last-moment changes of mind like forgetting about yet another night of luxury dining on board to experience the simpler but tasty fare of a taverna.

One thing is certain: no Mediterranean island, and certainly not one that Cunard calls upon, will fail to charm, even if it also teases. And even if you stayed on deck during time in port, or simply migrated to the nearest beach, you would still have picked up much of the flavour. For a substantial part of the fun is threading through and making the act of calling at the islands, especially the Greek ones, often in the company of simple ferries taking the place of the buses of most of the world. You quickly get into the rhythm of taking in every new angle as the ship makes its gentle turns and realise that, even if all the mainland were taboo, the richness of the islands would still make the Mediterranean a great cruising ground. And while you arrive at yet another relaxed island paradise in state, you may recall that on an earlier trip you or friends found the ferries just a little too simple and subject to the motion of the swell.

But if the islands are for kicking off, most passengers on most cruises will be ready tomorrow or the day after for another serious round of visiting somewhere wherein our own or a previous civilisation was fashioned. No ports are approached with more serious intent than Haifa and Alexandria. For many people only cruising provides a practical means of getting to Jerusalem and Bethlehem, Cairo, the pyramids and the Sphinx. Nowhere else in the world are the worrying details of security and comfort more readily delegated to Cunard. But be prepared for gruelling days. Though you may feel like kissing the clean walls of your ship when you return from the bedlam and by western standards squalor of Egypt, she is hardly anchored close by the main attractions. Everywhere the traffic on the roads and the traffic of sightseers at the attractions will slow you down and make it tiring.

Geographically it makes sense to take these two key historical ports one immediately after the other, but to lessen the pressure on passengers sometimes an intermediate diversion is taken, to say Limassol in Cyprus, for a gentler time ashore. In any event, and even if the ship spends a night in Haifa and/or Alexandria, your precious time in Israel and Egypt needs careful planning. For many it will not be a choice of whether to take one of the ship's own tours or not (as in China, you would need to be very confident to prefer to make your own arrangements), but which and how many tours one is to take, possibly with options as ambitious as a one-and-a-half-day tour to Luxor including charter aircraft.

At the eastern end of the Mediterranean, Israel and Egypt today are nearly always destinations in their own right, and if you sail on the Suez Canal it will far more likely be by a short-crossing ferry rather than a cruise liner taking the traditional route from the Orient. Though passenger liners do occasionally still pass through the canal, even most round-the-world cruises now take a different route. Yet for many years after the war this continued to be the way that nearly everyone came and went – for Australia as well as India. That had the oddity that years ago you would frequently meet people who had not merely passed through the Mediterranean but achieved some of its splendid sights (Alexandria was a regular call, and some more adventurous passengers would catch the next ship a week later) well before cruising was accessible to other than the ultra-wealthy.

Malta was another common calling place for ships bound to and from the Suez Canal, and memories of those days mingle into the unique historical maritime blend that makes up the Malta character. If there had to be but one port that summed up the Mediterranean, it would have to be Malta, a mingling of cultures twixt Europe and Africa, Gibraltar and Suez, where even today it somehow seems more natural to enter Valetta's marvellous harbour, surrounded by stone buildings of various ages that glow golden in the sunshine, than land at the airport. Arrival and departure are always exhilarating, and even when at anchor you soak in the historical richness of the surrounding panorama.

Like so many Mediterranean ports, Valetta offers a great variety of options, beginning with the decision whether to take a bus or taxi from the ship's side or exit the other side, down the steps to the launch providing a frequent courtesy service across the harbour. Valetta itself is full of interest. The citadel and former capital of Mdina (walk rather than take the horse-drawn bus around it and enjoy a leisurely fill of the view across the Maltese mini-kingdom) is only 6 miles (9km) away, and if you go by taxi you will probably also be shown a picturesque harbour with brightly painted fishing vessels. Indeed, your only problem might be getting the taxi driver to adopt anything like a straight line: 'It's my duty to show you everything', is a somewhat intimidating approach.

But there are so many different faces of the Mediterranean that not even Malta, in fact nowhere, sums it up. Could there be a greater contrast, for example, than that between the Spanish and French, and then further along the French and the Italian ports close to each other but on either side of the border. Americans, used to experiencing the whole spectrum of life, geography and climate in their single United States, are perpetually fascinated by the unity yet the political, linguistic, architectural and other diversity. After a day in Barcelona and before one in Livorno (for Pisa and Florence) they wake to find the ship anchored off Villefranche in the French Riviera, take perhaps their first exciting step in the Riviera and very shortly find themselves in the independent state of Monaco (different nations down opposite sides of the same street) and then puzzlingly learn that business is only kept going by a large daily intake of Italian workers.

Whether or not the Riviera is your choice for a full holiday, the day the ship spends anchored off Villefranche is an excellent example of what cruising makes possible. It was our first visit to that famous part of the world. Even from the ship's deck before breakfast, the setting was seducing, and the tender-ride lives on as one of the most sparkling in the memory. We felt lazy and spent the morning exploring small Villefranche itself, taking a narrow street to see the railway station, returning to the square by the church watching the locals turn out in force for the passage of a colourful procession led by a band. It was Sunday and all around us families were ceremoniously getting together for a long lunch. Our leisurely lunch was to be on board with no definite plans for the afternoon until, back at the small harbour about to take our return tender, we spotted the notice of Riviera Motors. A one-man business, we discovered here a charming chauffeur with perfect English driving a beautiful car. Often he is reserved for cruise ship calls well in advance; today nobody had claimed him. So we decided on a quick buffet lunch and arranged to be back in an hour or so, and in the afternoon lived to the full.

Within a few hours we had taken in a distant view of Nice, patronised the various corniches (the roads at different levels along the Riviera coast), walked through a hill-top walled village where all France seemed to be unwinding, toured Monte Carlo with a lap round the race track (usually a normal road) and through the complicated one-way tunnel system, sauntered round its harbour, stopped at a cliff-top hotel for quality afternoon tea with piano music, and drove down the peninsula close to Villefranche admiring its grand houses and hearing of its famous residents including Somerset Maugham. And repeatedly, from different heights and angles and with extremely diverse foregrounds we saw our ship, adding the final touch to a delightful scene.

Like many passengers, we had never even heard of Villefranche until studying the itinerary. Like most, we would happily go back – to nearly every one of our Mediterranean ports as enthusiastically as we would love to fill the numerous gaps that remain. The scale as well as the variety is endless, in fact greater even than in the Caribbean. You will not enjoy so much lazy time here, but will undoubtedly return with unbeatable memories and photographic record. And while it may not be as exotic as the South Seas or the Orient, the Mediterranean is ever about the shaping of our own culture and life.

THE MEDITERRANEAN

The Mediterranean covers almost 1 million square miles (2.6 million km^2) and is thus four times larger than the North Sea. It is the remains of the original, earth-spanning Thetys sea, the mother of all oceans. Through continental drift, the Mediterranean achieved its present shape. The deepest part is north-west of Crete, at 16,500ft (5,000m). In the depths of the Thetys sea all mountain chains were formed, from the Alps to the Himalayas and the Andes. This is why fossil fish, shells etc are found on mountain peaks.

11
DINING

DINING is one of the highlights of cruising. Whichever ship or restaurant they use, and whatever their personal taste, nearly everyone comes home singing the praises of the food: the choice, the quality, the quantity. And most people inevitably put on a little weight.

Whether you want to experiment or just indulge in more of your favourite dishes, set out to make the most of meals at sea. It sounds a little trite, but work with the system (each restaurant has its own), with your waiter or waiters and your section and wine waiters. For if you are at odds with them, ever complaining or just plain bored, they will be unable to give you the satisfaction that the vast majority of them dearly want to convey. Yes, they really do care, and while they may totally misunderstand what you want to begin with, almost always they will steadily get into your ways and provide appealing personal touches.

The desirability of single-seating in the dining room, and of choosing the right kind of table for your personal preference, has already been touched upon. Again, do remember to check up on your table as soon as you board the cruise and find the table assignment waiting for you in your cabin. The head waiter will do his best to make changes, but flexibility decreases rapidly as things settle down, especially on a popular cruise.

If you have requested a special diet, make sure the information has reached your waiter. But many requests can be accommodated on

Above In Alaska a boat is lowered to collect ice for evening drinks. *Left* On every Cunard ship dining is a great occasion – none more so than in the QE2's Queen's Grill

a day-by-day basis and there is no question, for example, of having to eat solidly vegetarian or not.

While working with the system and your waiters, never be intimidated. There is something especially sad about someone eating a dish he wishes he had not ordered or which disappoints for some reason. If you have especially enjoyed something served sparingly, do not be afraid to ask for more. If the waiter indicates he will select your salad or buffet, tell him straight that you would prefer to make your own choice. Do not let the wine waiter force you into finishing a bottle; part-used bottles are routinely set aside for the next lunch or dinner.

Breakfast is the most flexible meal, taken in the dining room, café or your cabin. Lunch can be a formal dining-room affair or taken more casually in café or on deck. If in the dining room, you will have a chance to study the dinner menu and make special requests and order wine. If it is a fine red, it will be breathing on the table well before you come for dinner, an improvement over most restaurants where the bottle is often opened too late.

Special dishes are a subject on which some regular cruisegoers wax eloquent. Caviar or smoked salmon to start, and on some ships such a special order will be of higher quality or more generous than standard portions doled out when they are on the menu for all. Caviar Belini in one of the grill rooms on the *QE2* takes some beating; but then so does a specially ordered soup such as lobster bisque, infinitely better prepared individually than on the grand scale. The chef may refuse to make it with less than thirty-six hours' notice so as to allow it to marinate properly. Your section waiter will flame it with brandy at table.

Flambé dishes are a QE2 *speciality; indeed many of the dishes presented to passengers are works of art it seems a shame to destroy*

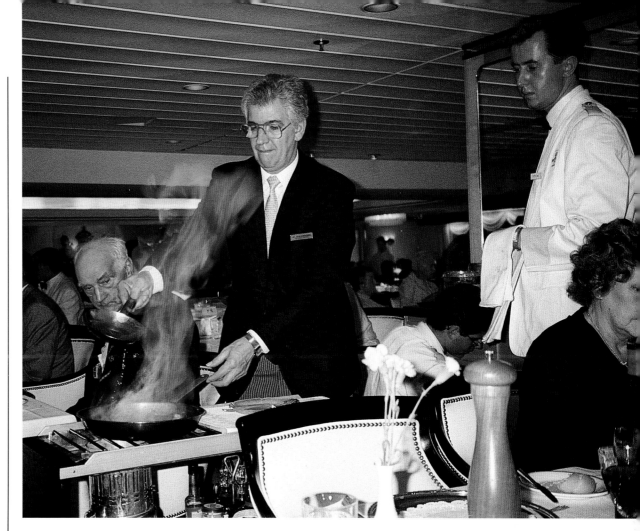

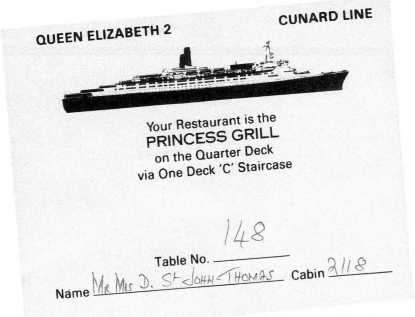

QUEEN ELIZABETH 2   **CUNARD LINE**

Your Restaurant is the
PRINCESS GRILL
on the Quarter Deck
via One Deck 'C' Staircase

148

Table No. _____

Name *Mr Mrs D. St John-Thomas*   Cabin *2118*

Duck à l'orange, beef Wellington, rack of lamb, Dover sole, cheese soufflé, golden buck rarebit – the special orders come, neatly marshalled to their correct table with minimal delay and, in the case of soufflés, with split-second timing. Many diners in the Queen's Grill request four or five special courses a night, having whole turkeys cooked for a single portion, pairs of pheasants and other game birds for a couple. Everything is to the highest standard. Naturally, you will not get this standard in lower-grade accommodation – but

then, on the *Sea Goddess*es every dish is a special one, cooked individually.

There are of course some gastronomic drawbacks about being at sea: you cannot pick fresh strawberries or even lettuce in the mid-Atlantic! Experienced ocean travellers take their fill of fresh produce when they can at the voyage's start. Freezing is now a fine art but, for example, some fish (especially Dover sole) freeze better than others. Fine red wines are never at their best after a couple of days of force 10.

You will also come across the occasional language or cultural problem. Chicory in Britain is endive in most of the rest of the

world, for example. British endive is something quite different, a kind of lettuce. Getting it right can be important, especially because after several days at sea chicory is often in better condition than lettuce. Ensuring that you get the water you require (bottled water is consumed on the grand scale since the ship's own supply is not the best for drinking), and that tea and coffee are to your personal taste are also extremely important. If your waiter does not know how to make tea, request boiling water and make your own.

On most ships there are a series of special dinners, each it seems with greater aplomb. Whatever it is, the ingredients are the best, chosen, stored and prepared with a passionate attention to detail as any tour of the kitchens and store rooms reveals. Indeed, when did you hear of someone saying he or she would not go cruising again because the food was not good enough? That people cannot resist it and so put on unwanted weight, yes, that is occasionally cited as a reason to stay firmly on land. On ships with the health spa 'The Golden Door at Sea', the suggested lighter range of dishes is often eagerly accepted.

The extensive menus are minor works of art, usually incorporating a touch of Cunard history, and not surprisingly are taken as souvenirs by many passengers. But it is the memory of the meals themselves that lives on. Most cruisegoers have had their repertoire of favourite dishes steadily extended and use the dining rooms afloat as the standard by which they judge restaurants on land. But even that misses a vital point. Once you have paid your cruise fare, all food is included. Quite apart from whether you can afford luxurious dishes, you avoid the problem of even seeing what it costs, wondering if it is sensible value. But even those who take the best cabins on the *QE2* would very probably balk at the cost in a famous city restaurant of a Queen's Grill meal of five courses, starting with a generous helping of caviar and including three dishes liberally flamed with spirits at the table.

CAVIAR

Caviar, the roe (egg) of various species of Acipenser (sturgeon), comes in several qualities and has been known as an article of food since the sixteenth century. The word is common to most European languages and is supposedly of Turkish or Tartar origin, but the Turkish word *khavyar* probably derives from the Italian *caviala*; the word does not appear in Russian. The best caviar, which can be made only in winter and which it is difficult to preserve, is loosely granulated and almost liquid. It is prepared by beating the eggs and straining them through a sieve to clear them of their membranes, fibres and fatty matter; it is then flavoured with salt. The beluga sturgeon, the major source of commercial caviar, is a freshwater fish that lives in the Caspian and Black Sea and swims upriver to spawn. Some belugas have reached a length of more than 20ft (6m) and weighed as much as 300lb (136kg). Sturgeon have long lives, some living for well over a hundred years.

QUEENS GRILL
CAPTAIN'S GALA DINNER

15TH OCTOBER 1989

CHEF'S SUGGESTION
Russian Malossol Caviar
Mock Turtle Soup
Cold Lobster QE2
Lime Sherbert
Prime Rib of Beef, French Green
  Beans, Baked Potato with Sour Cream
Caesar Salad
Fresh Strawberries with Vanilla Ice Cream

VEGETARIAN SELECTION
Watercress and Orange Salad with Pine Nuts
Eggplants Parmigiana Served with
  Whole Wheat Noodles
Flamed Peaches with Vanilla Ice Cream

THE GOLDEN DOOR SUGGESTS
(No Salt Added, Low Cholesterol)
Honeydew Melon
Broiled Breast of Chicken, Steamed Vegetables
Caesar Salad

A Selection of Freshly Baked Breads
and Fresh Fruit from the Salver
A Platter of International Cheeses served with Crackers
Figs, Dates and Butter Cookies
Petit Fours

#94 Chablis 1986   *#52 Château Beau-Site 1982*
(Domaine Long Depacquit)   *Cru Bourgeois Exceptionnel*
                                    (St. Estéph)

#109 Piesporter Göldtropfchen
Spätlese Mosel
(Langguth) 1986

Executive Chef - Bernhard Stumpfel
Chef de Cuisine- Jonathan Wicks

MENU

SPECIAL TONIGHT
Fresh Garlic Bread

HORS D'OEUVRE
Russian Malossol Caviar Served with Chopped Onion,
  Egg and Sour Cream
Smoked Scottish Salmon with Horseradish Cream
Fruit Cocktail with Blueberries and Maraschino Liqueur

SOUPS
Mock Turtle Soup with Cheese Sticks
Cream of Fresh Mushroom Soup
Chilled Vichyssoise

CRUSTACEANS
COLD FRESH SPLIT MAIN LOBSTER QUEEN ELIZABETH 2
Served with Sauce Cardinal and Condiments
OR The Traditional **LOBSTER THERMIDOR** Fresh Lobsters in Fine Wine
  Sauce, Sherry, Mornay Glace, Saffron Rice

SORBET
Lime Sorbet

MAIN DISHES
ROAST AMERICAN PRIME RIB SERVED AU JUS, with French Green
  Beans and Baked Potato with Sour Cream and Chives

VEAL MEDALLIONS SAUTEED IN BUTTER, Served on Bell Pepper Strips
with Mushrooms and Gorgonzola Cream Accompanied with Macaire
Potatoes

BREAST OF CHICKEN STUFFED WITH MANGO, Breaded with Almond
and Coconut Crumbs and Served on a Bed of Zucchini and Carrots

VEGETABLES
French Green Beans
Zucchini with Tomatoes and Herbs
Sautéed Green Peas

POTATOES
Baked   French Fried   Macaire

SALADS
Caesar Salad a La Mode du Chef Prepared by Your Chef in the Dining Room
OR Mixed Salad, Dressing of Your Choice

DESSERTS
Hazelnut Soufflé with Strawberry Cream
Apple Pie with Cinammon Cream
Fresh Strawberries with Vanilla Ice Cream and
  Whipped Cream
Lime Sorbet
Tiramisu (Italian Cheesecake)

DIABETIC DESSERT
Fresh Strawberries, Whipped Cream

ICE CREAM
Vanilla   Chocolate   Banana

DESSERT SAUCES
Mango   Chocolate

CUNARD SERVES ONLY 100% COLOMBIAN COFFEE

Beverages
Celyon and China Tea   Full Roast Coffee   Non-Caffeine Sanka   Instant Coffee
Decaffeinated Coffee   Hot Chocolate   Horlicks   Hag-Coffee
Iced Tea with Lemon   Iced Coffee

Hong Kong seen through the mist of the early morning arrival

A group of Hong Kong people looking at QE2 after her later arrival the same day in February 1990

GODDESS OF THE ORIENT'S SEAS

The exotic waters of eastern seas are the realm in which Sea Goddess II reigns. Gliding between enchanting ports of call, she exudes the style of a bygone age – an age which relished quality and created the style of grand colonial hotels.

With Singapore as base, Sea Goddess II takes her guests on a journey to some of the most alluring ports in the world. Within this fabulous programme, she explores the coast of Malaysia and islands in the Indonesian archipelago, dropping anchor at the exciting cities of Jakarta – on the way to Phuket – and Kuala Lumpur en route to legendary Bali by way of the Straits of Malacca.

In 1990 Sea Goddess II is set to sail into history as mainland China's principal river, the Yangtze and many of her cities welcome her.

There are opportunities with each of these cruise holidays to extend your visit to the Orient with pre- and post-cruise land based options. Depending on your chosen port of embarkation or disembarkation you may stay in the best of hotels in Singapore, Bangkok, Hong Kong, Bali or Phuket. There is even an opportunity for three nights' stay in China's capital Beijing.

ZHANI

SANYA

BANGKOK

KO SAMUI
PHANGNGA
PHUKET

LANGKAWI
PENANG
PULAU PANGKOR   KUALA
                 LUMPUR
MEDAN   KUANTAN
                 TIOMAN
        SIBOLGA MALACCA
NIAS
                 SINGAPORE   KUCHING

                          PULAU PELANGI
KRAKATOA   JAKARTA
                                    SEMARANG
                                    S

NANJING   ZHENJIANG
                SHANGHAI

N   XIAMEN

G KONG

                MANILA

KOTA KINABALU
NEI

A

LOMBOK

12
THE ORIENT

AS the sun rose rapidly over the off island of Nusa Penida, passengers gathered at *Sagafjord's* bow to watch the approach to Bali. Ahead the towering mountain, whose top was blown off in a volcanic eruption well within living memory. There were dolphins prancing and flying fish darting everywhere around – and gaily coloured craft (crosses between canoes and mini catamarans) some of whose occupants were preparing to bombard us with offers of souvenirs as we descended into our tenders for the ride into Padangbay. As we dropped anchor, passengers were saying that the capital, the hotel district, the lake were all two hours away. 'Two hours from the world', commented one. First timers and the lady who had been a regular cruise visitor for fifty years ('my parents started me early') were on the other hand aware of how lucky they were to be aboard this luxury liner at this choice spot.

We landed to the inevitable 'only one dollar' (and harder-to-resist 'buy my cards, ten a dollar, I want ice cream' from a five or six year old girl) to meet a business colleague coincidentally on holiday in Bali and staying the inevitable two hours away. In the morning we made a gentle taxi ride to the village of Amlapura, and went in and out of shops where several generations live and work. Just round the corner from the display area of one, a dozen folk, aged perhaps ten to eighty, were weaving while watching a boxing match from the States. Dollars, 'American Express Cards Welcome', US television (when our business colleague called his wife 'darling' a group of youngsters, who had only heard it on TV, repeatedly mimicked the word), yet so Indonesian, family life still so vital, worship and

dancing united in tribute to the gods that provide plenty. Later we were to see a procession of young ladies return with large bowls of gorgeous fruit from a temple where the gods had first offering before human consumption. And in the evening a grand display of dancing was provided in our ballroom.

Outside the shop where we made our purchases, chickens noisily drew attention to themselves in their round baskets. When one dog disliked an intruder, others immediately joined in a chorus of ritual barking to see him off. Everywhere verdant vegetation and joyous flowers. It had obviously rained during the night and the entrance to the steep village street was still blocked by a puddle. We retraced our way across stepping-stones. Along a white, palm-tree studded beach and there was our ship to be photographed in yet another setting.

In the afternoon we motored up the mountain through a succession of spectacular vistas and past innumerable temples to Lake Batur. The crater of an enormous volcano, this lake now provides irrigation for much of that side of the island. Fascinating it is to watch how the same water is used, and used again, for irrigation and washing as it ever descends towards the sea.

Passengers and staff loaded their shopping, really different at very cheap prices, onto the return tender. Every steward seemed to have his twenty dollar portable chess set carried like a small wooden case. The only discordant note was struck when several passengers criticised a steward for buying a stuffed turtle; holding it proudly almost like a baby with its upturned eyes longingly looking at his, he had not heard

about the endangered species thing and wished he (or it) could melt into air. Mind you, most of us thought we *were* melting – and found the ship's air conditioning especially welcoming. Hours later we still felt the warmth while we saw the dancers off on the last tender as the moon that had accompanied us from Australia lit up the Badung Strait and lightning flickered over the high mountains.

Few days in the Orient fail to be memorable, and one suspects that much of the future of cruising will flourish here. There is everything in its favour: the ability to sample different cultures, to enjoy Cunard's comfort and knowledge in strange and often challenging environments, to avoid those chaotic airports and transfer arrangements and also those colonies of beach hotels more segregated from local life than is the ship. At some of the more obvious destinations, such as Hong Kong and Singapore, the ship gives new perspective as well as staying perhaps two or three days in an enviable location. Some places you would frankly not visit at all without the security of your floating home. This is especially true of some of the rarer ports of call, including several in Indonesia and odd-balls like Bander Seri Begawan (capital of the world's wealthiest nation, oil rich, mini Brunei), an enclave in North Borneo which our cruise visited after Bali.

Nowhere do cruise ships provide welcome access more than in China, where whatever happens politically it will be years before older people will feel comfortable spending vacations on shore. Who does not want to visit Guangzhou (Canton) looking pretty bland on the outside but teeming with historical treasure under the surface, or Shanghai where West penetrated East in bubbling harmony for generations? Which of us does not hope one day to sail up the Yantze River or walk on the Great Wall as well as tour Beijing? Of one thing you can be sure, in our lifetime the proportion of Westerners doing so by ship will be much higher than in most of the world.

You can, however, add endlessly to the list of places you would feel dubious about settling into as a tourist by land, but welcome exploring from the cosseted safety of a Cunarder: Karachi which followed Singapore, Penang and Bombay on the world cruise whose Cairns-Hong Kong segment we had taken, is another excellent example as are various ports in the Philippines. And while at first sight, especially to those of limited means, it may seem crazy to pay for a cabin periodically to leave it on expensive extended tours, you quickly realise how much more acceptable those nights away from the ship taking in Kathmandu and Nepal are to an itinerary totally composed of air and road journeys. Only the privileged few will ever be able to afford the best of both worlds, ship plus extended expeditions, but do not underrate the privilege.

The rest of us can of course extend our cruises by taking land packages before and after, Hong Kong and Singapore being frequent joining and leaving ports. Other possibilities (especially by *Sea Goddess*) include Pattaya (the port for Bangkok), that exotic but all too rapidly developing island of Phuket in southern Thailand, Osaka in Japan, Bombay, occasionally even Bali.

Whether you are in search of warmth, civilisations predating our own, value for money and gifts that are truly different, never-to-be-forgotten street scenes, mountain paradises and verdant rain forests with intriguing natural history, possibly the most interesting buildings on earth, museums of endless fascination, even harbours whose very ships are shaped unlike ours, and that endless fascination of the ploy between traditional religion

and contemporary commerce, entertainment and family life – the East has it in infinite abundance. It is so vast, perhaps so challenging, as to deter the faint-hearted and those who only seek sun and fun and whose needs are met closer to home. Yet make a start, and quickly patterns emerge encouraging you to build your own experience and vision of the Orient. Above all, do not fret if your second or third cruise repeats the same ports, or indeed your first one takes in (as is very likely) places, such as Hong Kong, you have already visited. For the Orient is distinctly not just a map of ports to be ticked off as done, but a vast library of experience to savour, real understanding necessitating a mixture of repetition as well as new discovery, reading as well as seeing, listening, smelling, just being as well as shopping. Even at the same time of year in identical weather, no two arrivals at, say, Colombo, will ever be the same and each trek by road or rail up to Sri Lanka's ancient capital of Kandy will open up quite different visions and thoughts as well as enhance the familiar.

If you have never visited the East at all, then Hong Kong, Bangkok, Singapore and the Malaysian resort island of Penang make excellent starting points. The last two are especially comfortable, unlike, say, Jakarta (the Indonesian capital) or even Bombay which inevitably overpower – though as maritime key to the magic of India, Bombay will sooner or later be irresistible to the devoted traveller. But then perhaps Singapore and Penang are too comfortable! Though the sea approach through the crowded shipping lanes to Singapore is always impressive, and there is certainly much of beauty in and around Penang, in both commercial modernity seems to have become too great a goal. Such generalisations are dangerous – certainly forgotten over afternoon tea at Raffles – even when basically true. So the best beginners' choices are Bangkok and Hong Kong, both with excellent international air services.

Even Bangkok, astride what must be the

busiest river on earth, is hardly for the faint-hearted. 'After ten minutes I realised there was no way I was going to cross the road', said one passenger. But it is utterly unique, full of overall flavour and innumerable individual attractions of the highest calibre – and also has many a perfect haven, including several of the world's top hotels. It does not matter that the ship will be joined a short distance away at the resort of Pattaya, but fully to experience Bangkok you really need to have your base in its heart. Cruisegoers who sleep on the ship at the resort inevitably lose a touch of 'hands on' experience.

Also utterly unplastic, inimitable and never-to-be-tired-of is Hong Kong, the world's best bazaar, where even if you took a score of world cruises each at rest here for three full days you would still only touch the surface. Who knows quite what 1997, when the British lease runs out, will bring (smaller Portuguese Macao, a full day trip by hydrofoil, goes back to China in 1999), so visit or re-experience it sooner than later. The ship ties up at the ocean terminal on the Kowloon side.

The Star Ferry terminal for Hong Kong and harbour cruises is at the foot of the exit steps, the fabulous shopping of Nathan Road and its side streets just past the Peninsula Hotel. The variety is frankly stupendous, the prices keen, the service efficient and friendly. Hong Kong is totally Oriental yet reassuringly comfortable, genuine in its vastness.

We arrived in the time-honoured way, anchoring out in the harbour in the small hours, alongside other ocean liners and container ships. The harbour boiled with activity, the double-decker ferries, junks, hydrofoils and other craft crossing hither and thither while the ships were called in one at a time. The sun was already high over a still-misty Hong Kong when our turn came to take the complicated, fascinating route to the ocean terminal. There was the bonus of the *QE2* attracting much local interest as she arrived in the afternoon with a Japanese charter.

13
NORWEGIAN FJORDS

THE scene was what travel posters are made of. A hundred or so well-spaced-out passengers were basking in the afternoon sun around the ship's pool taking in the sheer magnificence of the setting: the great mountains rising above the romantic fjord-end, the tourist village nestling under, the waterfall many had passed on their earlier walk during which they had picked the occasional wild raspberry. The play of light between sky and water continually changed as fluffy clouds passed overhead, and there were fascinating patterns of wake and ripples as the tenders gently came and went to *Vistafjord* and a couple of other visiting cruise liners. And then came the car-carrying ferry with its larger wake violently bobbing the cluster of small boats on which a group of boys were spending a lazy, gossipy afternoon of the school holidays. Tractors were at work in the fields at this choice spot for agriculture and horticulture; a gang were lifting potatoes. And having taken in her washing helped by her blonde daughter of about ten, the woman at the nearest house to the ship collected a basket and picked plums. So much to see, yet the only sound was that of our much-loved pianist pouring his heart out with Grieg, appreciated by many including his wife, a bedroom steward off duty in the afternoon.

Today was billed as one of the cruise's highlights, and in every way it was living up to expectations. Geirangerfjord, queen of them all, had impressed with her grandeur and

Left *The Seven Sisters waterfall in Geirangerfjord.*
Right *Viewing the fjord the spacious, leisurely way*

enticed with her subtlety. Every vista at her every twist had made passengers rejoice they were able to take in the ultimate in Norwegian scenic splendour in such style and in such perfect weather – not empty, hazy skies but occasional cloud cutting across the sun, even one or two showers followed by brilliant rainbows. For many the day would be one of the longest ever lived so actively. The keenest of the deck-walkers, absorbing the ever-changing scenery doing their laps, would achieve 14 miles (22km) by bedtime. On deck by 5 or 6, they had discovered that the ship was already well into the complicated network of fjords that penetrate deep into the nation; open sea had indeed been left behind well before dinner the previous evening when we passed Alesund, the city on several islands. In the early morning the scene was compelling to the eye even before most photographers could have begun to cope with the harsh blacks of moun-tains and the banks of mist topped by the red rising sun. At this stage the emphasis had to be on general impression rather than detail. The first pictures taken were of *Vistafjord* overtak-ing a lesser cruise liner approaching Hellesylt where we stopped to tender off those pas-sengers opting for a land tour.

Then it had been back a short distance and right into Geirangerfjord, an utterly remote arm of the sea between sheer walls of curving cliffs, over some of which jump great waterfalls whose very splashes the passengers could feel as the ship passed almost underneath. Of course they had to be named: there were the famous Seven Sisters, and brooding on the other side the Suitor falls. And above, thou-sands of feet up on the plateau, the old farms now being lovingly preserved where once men grew their crops and nurtured their livestock. The animals, like the children, had to be tethered to prevent their falling over the sheer edge into the fjord, whose winter warmth (fjords never freeze) made it possible to farm where only a mile or so away it would have been out of the question.

So this was Geirangerfjord, and everything it was cracked up to be. Over the generations, many of the world's liners have paid their respect to it, few international seaports indeed hosting a more distinguished list of guests than the village at the head that shares the fjord's name. Arrival there has to be an occasion, marked by amplified Grieg echoing in the hills.

Yet while the fjord is generally considered Norway's (and the world's) best, the village is just one of a large collection of enchanting fjord-end settlements cruising takes you to. Each is unique, in its own layout as well as in its setting amid the mountains at the head of different arms of the sea. All share tranquillity, a sense of time having stood still. And when the sun shines in summer, there is real warmth to ripen the fruit in the enclaves of orchards. At each you will naturally see hotels, clean village settlements, coaches linking with water transport, and enjoy the sparkle of clear skies on clean, deep water. To make the best of fjord cruises, combine the excitement of the passage with time to soak in the surroundings when you land off your tender. Your ship which brought you across the open sea before pene-trating the landmass adds a final touch of magic out there dwarfed under the peaks.

Many people say that days such as these are the most restorative they ever spend. There is so much to see and enjoy without the compul-sion of exploring city centres and ancient ruins. And while spectacular coach tours are usually offered, sometimes linking the visits made to separate fjord heads in morning and afternoon, the discerning usually stay at sea level not merely to avoid missing the full pleasure of the transits (quite different experi-ences each way) but so as not to interrupt the sheer serenity and inspiration of staying in touch with salt water.

Moreover, while days up fjords will open up many treasures, you cannot hope to see all Norway from a ship or on coach tours off it. If you are really compelled by the scenery you will surely want to come back another time on

a land tour; so make the most of what the ship uniquely provides meanwhile. Thanks to new roads and terminals, as in so many other parts many ferry crossings are now shorter than formerly, and opportunities for enjoying the full glory of fjords from the water other than by cruise ship have been much reduced, though in places ferries still regularly connect with each other in mid-fjord. Incidentally, if you do travel around Norway by land, you will have great pleasure in noting where your cruise itinerary intersects your ferry crossings. You need to have a large map to realise just how neatly it all fits together, that at times your ship will take you well over 100 miles (160km) inland along the great cuts in the rock made by the glaciers of the Ice Age.

Four main fjord systems are regularly visited by Cunard, though you will not of course see anything like the whole of any system. From north to south, first comes Romsdalsfjord. Your first call is likely to be Molde, city of roses, blessed by the Gulf Stream. Calling point for the daily coastal steamers along the Norwegian coast, it has real character, and one is not surprised when local folk-dancers come on board to entertain. Some passengers will how-ever disembark here for the land tour, naturally enough starting with a ferry crossing, to Andalsnes, reached more gently by the ship for its afternoon stop in idyllic scenery. Andalsnes is larger than most head-of-the-fjord places and actually it is not quite at the head. Regional centre for a large area, it is as cosy as it is busy, the sleeping-cars of Norwegian State Railways labelled for Oslo testifying to its geographical importance.

Then comes Geirangerfjord, a branch off Storjorden. Next Sognefjord, the longest and with the most complex divisions. Such is the scale that the real interest only begins after you have sailed 60 miles (100km) inland, and that is as the crow flies. You would need a week thoroughly to explore all the ramifications, but will not be disappointed when after hours of sailing east you head almost due south to spend half a day each at the head of two deep-cut fjords. The morning call will probably be at Flam, one of those peaceful fruit-growing oases where the sun feels as warm as thousands of miles south. An excursion with a difference is offered here, up the Flam railway, masterpiece of Norwegian engineering, to view a magnificent waterfall. The journey emphasises why near-level ground as at Flam is such a rarity and thus intensively used. One of the most pleasant of all afternoon sails has to be that from Flam making a sharp junction into the other southern arm of canyon-like character with dramatic waterfalls leading to Gudvangen. Those opting to take the land tour between the two will descend by Norway's steepest road – and that is saying something.

Finally there is Hardangerfjord, again over 100 miles (160km) long leading inland from the Bergen district. Much of it is broad, and this far south trees grow at a higher altitude. Islands as well as branch fjords, and rather more towns and villages dotting the shores, add to the interest. Your morning might be at Ulvik, on one of the northern branches, another of those sun-basking holiday and fruit-growing centres, the narrow fjord opening up into a lake at its furthest point – an inviting place if ever there were one, ideal for a dip into Tolkien. And in the afternoon down a south-eastern finger to the pretty village of Eidfjord where there is little of specific interest except the medieval church but a handsome walk around the fjordside begging to be taken, again with wild raspberries for encouragement.

You will not see all of Norway's fjords by Cunard; purists will indeed point out that actually you see only a small proportion, especially of the branch fjords, but there is no doubt that the best are picked and that if you experience even just one day of fjord cruising you will always long to return. It is undoubtedly one of the most special of all cruising experiences.

To get to the fjords, you will of course sail along part of Norway's deeply indented, island-studded west coast and there also enjoy much splendid scenery in sheltered water, with an ever-changing light pattern and strong probability of showers and rainbows. Here you will realise how important a maritime nation Norway is, for you will ever be sailing by, if not calling at, fishing and other ports, and passing (sometimes under bridges linking islands to the mainland) ships of all shapes and sizes going about their regular business, the passenger liner being the summer oddity.

Most fjord cruises spend a day in Norway's second city of Bergen, about which there is one particularly sound piece of advice: take a mac *and* umbrella. It is a delightful city, points of interest ranging from Grieg's home a short but expensive taxi-ride away to the extensive fish market you will be bound to wish you had in your home town, but the sun rarely shines throughout the day. Another likely call is the nation's third city of Trondheim, in a gorgeous setting and with a very personal character deriving much from its rare mixture of facets. It is very much a workaday city yet rich in culture and history, and this somehow has made it all of a piece, and it was indeed carefully planned when rebuilt after fires and neglect. The Gothic cathedral (Norway's single most impressive building with exquisite stained-glass windows) and the colourful warehouses along the waterfront, the great open square and the cafés in the pedestrianised side streets, all fit harmoniously together. History exudes at every corner, and with all the evidence that Trondheim is also capital of a lush agricultural territory you have to be reminded you are only 250 miles (400km) south of the Arctic Circle – presuming, that is, you go in summer. Arrival and departure are particularly interesting; thanks to the Gulf Stream, farming flourishes even on the islands you will pass by and which protect the city.

Norway is the only country to be divided between three chapters in this book, a fitting tribute to the fact that the Norwegians have pioneered in cruising as in most other maritime matters. You cannot be an experienced cruisegoer until you have at least tasted Norway, in its short summer season the provider of the most colourful of all inland cruising as well as of a magnificent coastline and ports of great individuality. Oslo, itself up a fjord, is mentioned in the chapter on the Baltic, while the North Cape is assigned to that on the Arctic.

The question is often raised as to how a fjord cruise compares with an Alaskan one. Apart from the fact that both cruises will take you to sheltered northern waters in days of long sunshine, there is little similarity. The fjords have their unique grandeur and historic associations, while in Alaska among the glaciers and rich natural history one always feels as though one is exploring the last frontier. One thing is certain: you will never be bored in the fjords – no matter how often you explore them. The vista at every turn, the perpetual ploy of light and dark, demands your gentle attention.

FJORD

Three things are needed to create a fjord: a mountain range, a river bed and an Ice Age. These three elements came together in Norway a million years ago. Near the coast the ice-cap was relatively thin. Farther inland its thickness increased, and its weight assumed enormous proportions. Thus, where a river had already dug a valley, it continued to burrow deeper and deeper – sometimes as far beneath the sea level as the harder-rock mountains towered above it. At the coast, however, the pressure of the ice was relatively lighter and this accounts for the shallowness of fjord mouths – the threshold may be only 500ft (150m) below sea level, while in the interior the fjord may be 4,000ft (1,220m) deep. As the ice-cap retreated, saltwater flooded in to fill the enormous basins to sea level – the fjords were formed. Their salinity in combination with the warmer waters of the Gulf Stream is responsible for the fact that they never freeze, except in their remotest branches.

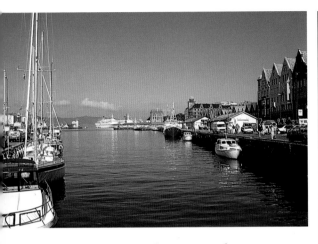

Many lovers of Norway's scenery prefer never to rise more than a few feet above sea level. They are certainly not deprived of variety. *Left Passengers bask in the sun waiting for their return tender to Vistafjord. Above Trondheim. Below Tenders enliven the scene as well as providing frequent service at fjord heads. Above and below right The light changes at every turning in the fjords as well as at their approaches*

14
WORLD CRUISES

WHEN you arrive in Sydney Harbour and tie up near the Opera House and under the shadow of the Harbour Bridge with, it seems, the eyes of half the population of Australia's largest and most cosmopolitan city gazing enviously at you, and know you have two days in which to explore or renew acquaintance with the glorious coastline and beaches, the theatre and elegant shops, you realise that to be taking a world cruise is a very special privilege.

Most people who go on lesser cruises hope that one day they may indulge in the ultimate voyage, three months round the world. Some who have taken one or more world cruises say that they would regard anything less as anti-climax. Those who can afford all 90 or 100 days can occasionally be heard expressing regrets that cheaper, shorter segments are now sold separately. Yes, for all its delights, there is no doubt that there is snobbery in the world-cruise business.

Ships offer their very best for the world cruise, including in this category anything lasting over a month based on a grand, out-of-the-ordinary itinerary, such as a great sweep round the Pacific. Whatever special entertainment pleasures or delights from the kitchen,

you can be sure enthusiasm will have gone into providing the very best. Another advantage is that usually there are fewer passengers, since the cheapest cabins are often not sold at all for long voyages and there are more single occupancies of doubles. It is quality and special attention all the way.

Another enormous difference is the gentler pace. You will literally spend the majority of every week at sea, and in a whole quarter-year may call at no more ports than patronised by a couple of two-week cruises strung together. Sometimes you may spend an entire week crossing an ocean. Your ports will of course include the unusual and sometimes be distributed between all five continents.

Most shorter cruises sell largely because of the popularity of their itineraries. To a large extent the itineraries of world cruises are irrelevant; people come to celebrate an old-fashioned, elegant lifestyle, the big decisions being when to stage your own party, whether to have it in a public room or your own cabin, who to invite, what to wear. 'Reserved for private function' notices go up in bars and lounges as precious necklaces are claimed from the security deposit boxes. There is

nowhere better to show off diamonds and pearls.

On a world cruise, everybody gets to know the captain and has a turn to dine at his table. Irrelevant the ports may be in the sense that they interrupt the social calendar, yet the very best is provided by way of excursions, sometimes including overland journeys involving nights away from the ship. Then there is always the possibility of your ship making a maiden visit; for several ports it is likely to be the only visit made by any Cunard ship in the whole year. Arrivals and departures are thus often great events. And when the world cruise ends you do not usually just get off as though that were that, but invite relatives who are collecting you to come on board and share some of the excitement.

World cruises are necessarily expensive, however good the value; and contrary to popular expectation, they are not always easy to sell. The truth is that they are only run in the first place because there is a lull in ordinary cruising activity in the Northern Hemisphere in the first months of the year. After their popular Christmas and New Year cruises, there is not enough work to keep all ships occupied, which is why Cunard was pleased to have the *QE2* on charter in Japan for several late winters/early springs, disappointing though that was to some world-cruising addicts.

Because of the high prices and the fact that more people seem to be kept busy (such as with voluntary work) even in retirement these days, the number of élite who can reserve the whole 90 or 100 days has declined. More opt for a segment or two. But what splendid holidays they enjoy. Cunard rolls out the red

---

SATELLITE NAVIGATION
Its basis is the US Navy Navigation Satellite System (NNSS), which became operational in January 1964 to serve as a precision-guidance aid for the Polaris submarine fleet. It was made available for commercial use by the release of its operational details in 1967. The NNSS complex consists of a system of radio satellites circling the earth every 107 minutes, in fixed polar orbits at an altitude of 600 nautical miles (1,112km). They intersect at the poles and are spaced to create a kind of orbital 'cage' around the globe, duplicating the familiar pattern of surface meridian lines. Each satellite transmits continuously updated time and position, enabling a ship's equipment to receive and interpret these signals and thereby to plot its location with great precision.

carpet (such as providing charter Concorde flights at amazingly low fares) even if you are only going to be aboard for two or three weeks. On the ship you will still find the very best, none of the key personnel on holiday, for example, and cabins usually given a special freshening up for the year's greatest event. And if you go for one of the more distant and exotic sectors, there will be the opportunity to see more of the starting and ending port than by remaining aboard. There are indeed frequently especially attractive beginning and ending land packages, the only disadvantage being the long air journeys from and to home.

Most regular cruisegoers who aspire to a world cruise or at least a major part of one, take special delight in reading the brochures and seeing the display maps of the routes to be taken. Just where would your journey of a lifetime take you? To Australia, surely, for the sheer romance of sailing to the most distant continent and to enjoy that splendid arrival at Sydney and privileged mooring place in the city centre beside the Opera House. To New Zealand, and hopefully up Milford Sound, one of the world's grandest fjords and certainly one of the least seen by Britons and Americans. Almost certainly the route will take you through the Panama Canal, and probably up the west coast of Mexico and the United States, giving another special arrival through the Golden Gate into the heart of San Francisco near Fisherman's Wharf.

Whichever way you cross the Pacific, there will probably be an island or two for fun days, and to or from the Orient there may be an opportunity at last to get to Bali or see what has changed and what remains enduringly the same in the Seychelles. In Hong Kong and/or Singapore you will delight in using your ship as a centrally placed floating hotel. But for many the highlight of a world cruise will be a visit to China and perhaps a walk along the Great Wall.

Most cruisegoers tick off, at least in their mind, the ports on next winter's round-the-world cruise. There are bound to be many that frequent travellers have visited before as well as out-of-the-way exotic new ports you would not get to in a hundred years except by world cruise. The joy lies in the ability to absorb the contrasts in a leisurely manner, and to regard each visit, however enthralling, simply as a pause on the great voyage.

If you return to New York when it still feels chilly in the spring, you cannot but rejoice that you have cheated by avoiding all the hard weather while you have circumnavigated the world gaining new experience and perspective. Only the scales might warn that now is the time to switch to a more mundane life-style.

Few ports are more accessible than Sydney where world cruises usually stop for several days. Book your opera tickets in advance! (Tony Stone Photolibrary – London)

Above left *Dakar in Senegal.* Below left *Nearly every world cruise will have you bargain-hunting here, the main street of St Thomas in the American Virgin Islands.* Above *And most will also call at San Juan, Puerto Rico where modern development, the charming old town and the castle guarding the harbour entrance are all within easy walking distance of the ship*

Right *You will see many palm-lined beaches like this in Martinique*

15

TO THE ARCTIC

WHILE some passengers were still luxuriating in the sunshine around the pool, steadily more were gathering at the ship's bow peering at the ragged white line that presented itself as an exaggerated horizon. Though the ship slowed, steadily the line grew closer, clearer – ragged indeed, irregular with great bays though basically straight, and actually bobbing about. The *Vistafjord* had once more reached the edge of the Arctic icefield, the North Pole straight ahead as far away as about the distance between New York and Toronto. Cautiously the captain edged the bow into the ice and – crunch, crunch – pushed through.

Now the ship was surrounded by the bobbing ice. Most passengers had perhaps never wondered what the Arctic icefield would be like, or, if they had, they had perhaps imagined it as a continuous cliff. But everyone quickly realised that the edge was merely broken off pieces from the more solid ice toward the Pole, and that this, of course, was just frozen sea. No land; no great icebergs; just frozen sea, but great cakes of ice – sometimes several layers thick – where one had been forced up against another. Imperceptibly, the 24 hour sunshine of a fine Arctic summer's day was slowly pushing the edge of the icefield farther north as the pieces, drifting from the main body of the icefield, melted away. Sobering to think that some months earlier this spot, after months of continuous darkness, would have been well within the icefield, utterly inhospitable. Now, every ice-cake seemed to have its own resident gull, suggesting a bounty of fish.

Cameras clicked, video enthusiasts recorded their commentaries, hot drinks were served to people with sunglasses but nevertheless warmly dressed since you could feel the cold being thrown off by the ice. After everyone had enjoyed a leisurely fill of one of the great sights of cruising in these northern waters, the ship headed back south.

It had indeed seemed as though we had come to the edge of the world, three nights and two days' uninterrupted sailing from our last port, itself in northern Norway. And we were hardly going to arrive back in the heart of civilisation tomorrow. Soon, however, we came across land – Spitzbergen. For hours, before, during and after lunch, we passed white-topped cliffs and mountains without the remotest sign of habitation, though here and there we met small fishing vessels presumably operating from a larger mother-ship out of sight.

Even this afternoon's port of call – subject to the weather and there not being too much ice – was to be to an uninhabited inlet, Magdalena Bay. We were lucky. We sailed into the sheltered bay dominated by several glaciers in still-continuous sunshine, and sat on deck while waiting for the ship's advance party to go ahead and erect a small pier where our tenders would land us. Robinson Crusoe, Cunard Arctic style.

So here we are at the World's Most Northerly Bar they have set up for a couple of hours, and obligingly we pose for the ship's photographer (he never misses an opportunity) to take us drinking mulled wine in this dramatic spot, mountains and glaciers all around, colonised by the ship's crew and passengers for up to three hours most years. The ship itself looks like a toy, dwarfed under one of the glaciers. We walk across the low headland protecting the bay and are rudely made aware we are unwanted intruders: birds whose nests are on the ground between the loose rocks are protective of their young and repeatedly dive-bomb and actually swipe one party of startled Americans.

We all agree that if we saw nothing else in our remaining eight days, the cruise would have been worthwhile. But as we restart our passage south, slightly delayed while the crew collect every last piece of our litter before disassembling the pier, we again keep the spectacular Spitzbergen coastline in view. Then a stunning diversion up Krossfjord and each of the two tributaries into which it divides. Mountains tower over us, and icebergs the size of large houses, but weathered by the sun into fantasy dwellings, slip past on their way to the sea and annihilation.

We become fascinated by Spitzbergen and its history, and hear of the former coalmining at Ny-Ålesund, terminated by a 1962 accident in which twenty-one miners were killed. But coal, we know, is what keeps the capital,

---

ARCTIC CIRCLE

The Arctic Circle comprises the southern limit of the Arctic region and is placed at latitude 66 degrees 33 minutes north. The name 'Arctic' is derived from the Greek word *arktos* meaning 'bear' and is a reference to the constellation Ursa Major, or Great Bear, which appears prominently in the northern sky.

Longyearbyen, alive, and at breakfast next day we drop anchor up the fjord opposite it and see a ship depart with a load of coal. As for Longyearbyen, it immediately takes the prize as the least desirous place we have yet visited, and it is not surprising to learn that the Norwegians spending a year or two here are mainly incited by tax incentives. But then neither are we surprised that a small minority dote on the isolation and rare habitat of the mountainous hinterland.

The sprawling mining town is hardly inviting in sunshine, and the very thought that the sun does not show itself above the horizon for four solid months is unbearable. There is no organised tour, but a free shuttle service up to the sole shop, where everyone tries to buy a memento if only a postcard, and the most ardent of American shoppers find it hard to spend real money. Then to the museum, with a fascinating display of Spitzbergen's natural and man-made history: hardly surprising, we agree, that the hotel once opened to encourage tourism only lasted a couple of seasons, but the wartime carnage is unexpected. Three dozen passengers beaver away writing postcards so that they can be given a Spitzbergen postmark and be flown south to the world long before we return there.

In the afternoon there is one more vision of Spitzbergen: the Russian one. Though the island (about the size of Holland) is Norwegian, under a 1925 treaty other nations are free to share in its natural potential, and Russia maintains a vast mining community (accounting for most of the population). We pass by it slowly and study it through binoculars. It could hardly be more different from the scattered, utterly un-cosy Norwegian town of a thousand souls. Here is a great chunk of urban, industrial Russia, an enormous apartment block and even a massive greenhouse in which they grow fruit and vegetables.

Now a whole twenty-four hours and more of sailing south to view Norway's North Cape from the sea and then to anchor at Skarsvåg for the coaches to take us over the bleak moors of the island of Magerøy back to the Cape where we hope to catch the midnight sun, something you can only do from mid-May until the end of July. The North Cape is surely one of those great promontories that everyone has heard of and everyone longs to have 'done'. Expectations are not quite fulfilled since it has become extraordinarily commercialised, as we fear will be the case by the number of cars and campers we pass on the road and as is confirmed by the enormity of the car park. Forget anything about solitary communion with nature here. There are people everywhere. In fairness, as you would expect from the Norwegians, everything is well laid out, including a long underground walk to a splendid auditorium and viewpoint, though the view from the cliff's edge on top is better. And do not be disappointed if you miss the midnight sun or do not see the sun at all, for fog and cloud are common. You will, however, usually enjoy the great clarity of northern light. As for us, well we half caught the midnight sun. It was a colourful sky, impressive enough as a postcard; and yes it was well worth the trip, which only began after an early dinner served on board. It was half-past one before we climbed up the stairs from our tender, to discover a special middle-of-the-night buffet being served around the pool in bright sunshine. The sun had dipped close to the horizon just before midnight, now it was already high in the sky, and folks back home would take some convincing that these shots were taken at 2am.

In this age of sun worshipping, cruising to the Arctic and through other northern waters may not seem an automatic choice, but there is great enthusiasm among the passengers who go. That northern light again is one of the things that stays in the memory: ever clear, sparkling, with subtle pastel shades often in streaky cloud formations. You never tire of watching it. Continuous daylight has its benefits, too. On this cruise it remained broad daylight for an entire week.

Another northern itinerary that is not particularly easy to sell but has people who go raving with enthusiasm is Greenland, where the 50,000 people mainly living in western coastal communities, unlinked by road, lead fascinating lifestyles at the edge of the world, at the very verge of what is possible. Spend a few days visiting ports here and the rest of the world indeed seems polluted. Everything natural and man-made sparkles. Houses and churches are gaily painted and blend into the unique Greenland scene. Even some kinds of farming flourish, though naturally the emphasis is on fishing. Hundreds of years ago there was a greater civilisation here with many flourishing monasteries. Then climatic changes led to a harder existence. If the 'greenhouse effect' were to increase temperatures a couple of degrees, Greenland is one of the places that would benefit. It incidentally has 1 per cent of Denmark's population but is fifty times the size.

A trip to Greenland or even just Iceland might take in that other surprising outpost of Danish civilisation, the Faeroe Islands, where again everything is well ordered, buildings brightly coloured, and in this case roads dramatically engineered with numerous tunnels. The sea approach to the capital of Tórshavn emphasises the importance of fishing, the drama of the scenery, and the desire of the Faeroe people to make the most of their environment. But do not miss the land tour with its spectacular scenery and focus on history and culture through visits to churches and the more than usually rewarding museum. There is one difference between the Faeroes and most northerly communities; the Lutheran residents do not consume much alcohol, the use of which is strictly regulated, meaning that visitors should bring their own. And surprising though it is, this is undoubtedly one of the ports of call that many passengers would willingly return to for a whole week or two. The population is similar to that of Greenland but in a smaller area, divided between several rugged islands, every community boasting its

Above left *The North Cape is always impressive – whether you see it from the sea or view the coastline from land.* Below left *Spitzbergen basks in bright summer sunshine, enhancing its splendid scenery of fjords and glaciers.* Above *And part of the Spitzbergen experience is the setting up of the Most Northerly Bar in the World at uninhabited Magdalena Bay*

Another glimpse of Spitzbergen's breathtaking scenery. While there is continuous daylight in summer, in winter it remains dark for four months

While visiting Iceland you will pass by the newly-formed volcanic island of Surtsey

The highlight of a cruise to Europe's most northerly waters is approaching the Arctic ice barrier and actually driving into it

as coastal. There are great waterfalls and, of course, the famous volcanic activity and thermal springs which supply Reykjavik with most of its heat.

A single day in Reykjavik is really a tease. There is more than enough in the city to occupy the whole of it, yet not getting into the mountainous hinterland and walking among lava columns and photographing the geysers is a sacrifice. But the point has to be made once more that a tease is better than nothing, and much though we may intend to go everywhere interesting, life is too short. Most cruises calling at Reykjavik also take in the Westerman Islands, and if weather is fine your tender will pop you into Heimaey. These days you have to take the narrow channel almost via the back door since the violent volcanic eruption of 23 January 1973, which led to the rapid evacuation of 5,000 people and the destruction of one of the world's largest fish-processing plants, blocked the main entrance. And you will also pass the new island of Surtsey, which came out of the sea in another volcanic outburst on 15 November 1963, and be told the latest score on the number of species that have now colonised the lava.

The land of the Vikings: sparkling cleanliness, volcanic activity, continuous summer sunshine, skies that ever compel you to stare at them. Passengers come for the sense of adventure and are fascinated by local lifestyles, and of course the utterly unspoilt cliffs and mountains. Cruising to the far north of Europe certainly has much to recommend it. There is naturally much in common with an Alaskan cruise, and if you have enjoyed one you should take the other. There is more sailing across unsheltered water to reach destinations like Iceland and Spitzbergen, and in one other respect Alaska might have the edge: you will see a greater diversity of natural history there. Both offer a sense of exploring the last wilderness; but many fewer reach Greenland or Spitzbergen than go to Alaska, which is thus much more commercialised.

festivals and other cultural events, the Vikings and Norsemen cropping up at every turn.

Iceland shares some of the same characteristics. Certainly you do not go far without hearing about the Vikings, and again the buildings including roofs are brightly coloured, and culture is important. Here they read more than anywhere else in the world, and Reykjavik, the capital, boasts extraordinary good bookshops among many others. The quality of light, the cleanliness, the general far-northern ambiance, are all part of the joy. But unlike the other places so far mentioned in this chapter, Iceland is a major tourist attraction in its own right, thousands arriving during the short summer for touring, camping and walking holidays, patronising the extensive internal air system. Much of the scenery is stunning, inland as well

16

THE ANATOMY OF A CRUISE

ORGANISING a cruise on a ship with a varied itinerary (as opposed to some in the Caribbean which make the same round of a few islands every week) is an extraordinarily complicated and fascinating business. Just how does it all come together?

First there is the basic strategy of what market segment the ship is going for, and how it is to divide its year between which oceans. Past experience (business and weatherwise) will obviously be a strong guide, but there is a continual changing of people's preferences, and competition rises and falls in different parts of the world, not to mention the toll taken by sudden political change or terrorist activity. It has been decided, for example, to lengthen the European season, to cut out calls to Haifa and Alexandria since many Americans are still fearful of travel in that part of the world, but to cash in on the ever-growing popularity of the Black Sea.

The difficulty in all this is that planning has to be done so far ahead – well over a year – that it is hard to react to sudden political or economic change. Though the pattern of advance reservations is studied carefully, generally it is too late to learn from this year's experience for the benefit of exactly the same time next year. Thus a new itinerary that has proved especially popular might not reappear until the year after next. This will apply even more sharply to whether a new port of call in the middle of a cruise has proved popular.

Passengers' long-standing preferences are of course well known, and once more the programme must satisfy the high proportion of repeaters (who will look for something new or at least a variation on a familiar theme) and

GROG

This word is nowadays used for any hot alcoholic drink, but originally it came from the inscription branded on the barrels of rum sent to London, meaning Grand Rum of Grenada. You may very well sample the colourless and very strong Grenadian rum in the form of punch: one part sour (lime juice), two parts sweet (cane or grenadine syrup), three parts strong (rum) and four parts weak (water, fruit juice and crushed ice), plus a few drops of Angostura bitters and some grated nutmeg. You then have the essence of Grenada in your glass.

who are more likely to be attracted by a special offer of two or more cruises together provided there is no duplication, *and* the newcomers who will opt for the more obvious such as the Baltic capitals or Black Sea. Newcomers are still more likely to be earning a living and therefore generally prefer only two weeks from Saturday to Saturday. Another consideration is that while the ship will move around Europe, starting in the Mediterranean when it would be too cold north of the Continent, moving north when the Mediterranean would be too hot, and then returning south again in late summer, the whole thing becomes impossibly complicated unless most cruise segments start and finish at one of a limited number of regular servicing points.

Most passengers on fly-cruises like starting at one point and finishing at another. Here is an obvious advantage over most package holidays using the same airport out and back; and beginning at one port and finishing at another emphasises the sea journey. But starting and ending ports have firstly to be attractive, secondly to have adequate and not too expensive facilities available when needed, and thirdly of course to have an international airport close by. You can see why ports like Venice are obvious favourites.

Once starting and finishing ports have been selected, detailed itineraries can be worked out. Again there has to be a combination of the familiar and change. Passengers' preferences as noted on questionnaires completed at the end of cruises are certainly taken into account, as are reports from the staff, especially the tour manager and cruise director. Any previous delay caused by navigation, customs or immigration, or servicing requirements will be noted, along with the relative costs of pilots, tugs, berthing, refuelling and revictualling. Port charges (and the level of congestion) vary sharply, and are a prime reason for the choice of some Caribbean islands on the itineraries of larger ships in that key cruising area. If they can berth at all, some ships may only be able to do so at the prime, and most expensive, dock. Anchoring offshore and tendering passengers in is unavoidable at some ports, but time-consuming and obviously unpopular with passengers if it happens several days in a row and when there is a long and potentially choppy tender-ride. Another vital consideration is how long to spend in port. There is no point in going to Leningrad for only half a day. Though Leningrad is one of the few ports where ships stay more than a day, ideally the ship travels at night and arrives in port around

breakfast time. Indeed, that is one of the joys of cruising: you have a splendid view of the approach during a pre-breakfast walk, dock while you are eating, and just as you are ready to go ashore hear that formalities have been cleared – and off you can go.

Departure and arrival times are governed not only by the distance between ports but by the speed of travel. Speed costs money. Fuel consumption can indeed double between a comfortable cruising speed and going flat out – which is one reason why the *QE2* is relatively expensive on its fast transatlantic crossings where oil accounts for an appreciable part of your fare. Often the same ships will be in the same ports several days in a row. Note how Cunard normally allows you longer ashore since the cheaper competition takes it slower at sea. But Cunarders are rarely timed to go flat out, so if departure is delayed they can usually catch up (even transatlantic) at a cost to fuel consumption.

While it is the list of attractive ports that sells cruises, especially to new customers, most people travel by ship for a leisurely holiday and become tired of a different port all day, every day. So on longer cruises there will be at least one day at sea to let passengers rest and really enjoy the shipboard facilities, and half-days add variety. Thus while the Danish island of Bornholm must to most newcomers to Baltic cruises seem the least interesting of a showcase of ports, the half-day sometimes spent there is particularly successful and relax-ing. The mere fact that everybody does not have great sightseeing expectations as at Copenhagen, Stockholm and so on makes it different, less tense.

Loading supplies requires detailed planning: leaving even one essential ingredient behind might spoil many people's holiday

Right Lifeboats are regularly checked, and at ports where the ship cannot go alongside they double up as tenders

Once a provisional itinerary has been set, the process of negotiating visits to all the ports is started. Some ports are naturally more businesslike to deal with than others. In some it is first come, first served. If a reservation for a berth has not been made soon enough, the itinerary or dates have to be changed. Even before everything is confirmed, the shipping people will have a good idea of what they want to charge for each grade, taking into account the sales record in previous seasons and (so far as it is known) the pricing policy of competition. The price will usually include airline travel, a decision having been made on whether to fly passengers by scheduled or chartered flight. The level of incentive for passengers taking two or more consecutive cruises is fixed. The brochure is now in proof, colour pictures having been chosen of the main attractions as well as the most up-to-date shots of the ship itself, itineraries laid out, fare-charts completed. Few cruise-line brochures get printed without massive proof corrections. The sales people invariably complain that copies are available too late, though they can start working on provisional summaries of next season's cruises. Changes happen all the time; 'Note itinerary change', says the computer acknowledgement of your reservation.

Computer programmes enable the cruise-lines to gauge the likely final level of response from early reservations. Passengers' reactions often result in further changes, notably to air travel plans. If there are going to be two charter planes back from Venice to London, one will go to Gatwick and, should passengers who would prefer Heathrow (from where they start) be put on that, there will be inevitable criticisms. And since there will be spare space on the second plane, it might also be cheaper to route American passengers home via London. But a large party may suddenly decide they are going to spend an extra night in Venice and make their own air transport arrangements and so upset the applecart again. Getting a charter plane just full is as much an art as a science,

as experience with Cunard's famous *QE2* and Concorde packages shows. Then of course the airline may spring a surprise as when a flight between London and Acapulco was suddenly cancelled some years ago; passengers were offered an extra week aboard *Sagafjord* free if they could leave along with those who were joining the ship at Los Angeles.

As the time approaches for the cruise to take place, a hundred and one other factors come into play. For example, it will steadily become clear who the hundreds of staff will be. Many of the regulars, including the captain and other officers, will have known their rosters months in advance, and the cruise director who successfully conducted the same cruise the last few years is also an early confirmation. The waiters, cooks, room stewards of many nationalities turn over more rapidly, there being a constant process of selection and training. A few newcomers may not make the grade and replacements join the ship for this particular cruise.

Lecturers, clergymen, entertainers all have to be selected and travel arrangements made and accommodation allocated. It is going to be a popular cruise, so only a proportion of the passengers' cabins sometimes available for entertainers will be free, and some crew who on a lightly used cruise might enjoy a crew cabin to themselves will have to share. Some passengers are also going to have to be seated in the corner of the restaurant that at quieter times is set aside for people like the entertainers.

Details of each day's programme steadily take shape. A classical pianist will be with the ship five nights and give recitals on three. Films and their collecting point are chosen. Local dancers are going to come on board at one port and, at two, local chefs will add to the kitchen's repertoire. By now the timings of pilots, tugs, immigration and customs services, refuelling and revictualling have all been agreed. And passengers have been sent details of the shore excursions; literally hundreds of

telexes and faxes have been involved in setting them up.

Three months before sailing and most of the ship has been sold, though not everybody has taken up their option. There is a waiting list of people wanting suites, but one or two of the lower grades are sticking. The decision is taken not to make any special offer for this cruise, but a few passengers find themselves upgraded as the jigsaw of fitting everybody in is carefully completed.

Now the ship is on the final leg of her previous cruise, passengers enjoying a day at sea while the packing up begins. The staff still have some pleasant surprises for these passengers – there will for example be a complimentary ashtray showing that cruise's route and dates; but most management attention is now devoted to the changeover.

The head waiter has received a print-out of the names of joining passengers and their seating preferences and is the epitome of concentration as he makes yet more changes to the seating plan. He is interrupted by a family staying on the ship for the next cruise who make a new request, and a telex comes in from a regular passenger who wants to underline her special request for a quiet table. There are one or two maintenance jobs to be done in port, and some new furniture for the officers' quarters is going to be delivered which means moving out the old. Quite a few staff will be allocated new rooms.

The chef and stores manager and the chief wine steward have their shopping lists ready and hand them in to be telexed. Much of it is routine: thousands of eggs, hundredweights of sugar, yet the chef always likes to give that slightly different touch and has decided to try several new items such as a locally smoked fish. And he makes a note to ensure that this time the endive is better quality than last.

Changeover day has everyone working at full pressure. The waiters may only have a handful of diners at lunch time – passengers staying on for the next cruise who have not fancied another day in a familiar port – but most of them are going to spend long hours moving baggage. Room stewards are hard at it; all the beds have to be remade, drawers checked for cleanliness, bathrooms cleaned and refurnished with towels and soaps, keys placed in position, folders of information and stationery checked, and finally a welcoming note placed beside a small plate of strawberries. The head waiter and his assistant have finalised the dining-room plan and a small envelope containing the table allocation has been delivered to each cabin. Stores come on board for hours in succession; the butcher has reorganised his coldroom slightly differently this time, while the chef has sampled this and that and rejected the first consignment of lettuce. Oil is steadily being pumped on board. And reception desks are being set up to welcome the first of the new passengers.

Embarkation is advertised between 4 and 6, but by 2 o'clock the first of the newcomers have optimistically arrived. They have to be kept waiting a while, for the ship is not yet ready. People may be irritated at being left to kill time, but what would they say if they saw the state their predecessors had left the bathroom in? Embarkation does however start well ahead of schedule. Passengers leave their luggage on the quay, present their tickets and passports, go through security, are photographed at the top of the gangway and welcomed aboard by the social hostess who never forgets a special word to regulars back yet again.

Matching names to people has to be practised as a fine art, and the ship's top staff will have found time during previous days to check the list of joining passengers for familiar names. 'Mr – , we were looking forward to having you in November and I kept your favourite table, but you didn't come; I hope everything was all right', surely makes a passenger feel he is remembered as an individual. Of course, some of it is 'laid on' for effect, but you only have to watch the warmth of greetings

PRINTED ON BOARD

Q U E E N • E L I Z A B E T H • 2

Satellite World News

OCEANSAT

THURSDAY 19TH OCTOBER 1989

Prepared from UPI, USA Today, PA, CItservice and Viewtel by Ocean Satellite Television Ltd. Transmitted at 23.30 GMT, 10-18-1989

Page 1

NEWS AT A GLANCE (UPI)

SAN FRANCISCO - Search crews have brought in heavy equipment and dog teams to help find victims of the Bay Area quake that officials say killed more than 270.

Residents have faced a day of chaos after the quake, the second worst in U.S. history. The 15 seconds of the quake were measured at 6.9 or 7.0 on the Richter scale.

President Bush has granted a Californian request for federal disaster aid. Lloyds of London say the cost of the damage was at least 1 billion dollars.

BERLIN - East German leader Erich Honecker, whose government was weakened by protests and the exodus 60,000 to the West, has resigned citing health reasons.

Officials say the Central Committee of the East German communist party elected Politburo member and hardliner Egon Krenz, 52, to replace Honecker.

KUALA LUMPUR - Commonwealth leaders have demanded more sanctions against South Africa and action to curb environmental degradation and drug trafficking.

BUDAPEST - The Hungarian parliament has approved a constitution based on Western democratic principles to replace a Stalinist constitution adopted in 1949.

The amended constitution declares Hungary is a pluralistic republic and no longer a dictatorship of the proletariat led by a single Communist Party.

BOGOTA - Police say a Medellin journalist was gunned down in front of his home in what appeared to be the latest incident in a war waged by drug lords.

CAPE CANAVERAL, Fla. - The shuttle Atlantis has started a flight to fire the 1.4 billion dollar nuclear-powered Galileo probe on a six-year voyage to Jupiter.

EARTHQUAKE KILLS AT LEAST 270

SAN FRANCISCO (UPI) - Search crews brought in heavy equipment and dog teams Wednesday to help locate more victims in the destruction of the devastating Bay Area earthquake that officials said killed more than 270 people.

The quake was the second worst in U.S. history and Lloyds of London said the cost of the damage was at least 1 billion dollars. State officials asked the federal government for disaster aid.

Shaken residents faced a day of chaos with transportation, communication and power facilities all crippled by the quake, which hit Tuesday at 5:04 p.m. at the height of rush hour.

One of the greatest concerns was Interstate 880, a major double-decked Oakland thoroughfare where the upper tier of the freeway collapsed on the lower level.

Oakland Police Lt. Sydney Rice said four dog teams and heavy equipment were brought in to search for bodies in the pancaked sections of the freeway.

The 15 seconds of rumbling from the quake, which was measured variously at 6.9 or 7.0 on the Richter scale, also crumbled buildings throughout Northern California, started fires and forced the postponement of the third game of the World Series. A major blaze fed by a broken gas line in the Marina district destroyed six buildings.

Officials were faced with the job of inspecting houses and buildings and transportation facilities to see if they were safe.

The Marina district, a neighborhood of mostly low-rise Mediterranean-style buildings on either landfill or sandy soil between the Golden Gate Bridge and Fisherman's Wharf, was hit hard.

San Francisco Fire Chief Frank Jordan toured the area and said a six-block area of multi-family buildings appeared to be severely damaged with sidewalks and streets buckled.

"There may be as many as 30 buildings that have to be torn down", he said. "You look at a building that was three floors and now there's only 1 1/2 floors".

The quake was felt from Reno, Nev., 250 miles to the east, to Los Angeles, 450 miles to the south, and there was massive damage from the posh Marina District of San Francisco to the tiny mountain of Boulder Creek.

More than 30 aftershocks rattled frightened residents, the biggest measuring 4.7.

There were conflicting casualty figures, but Lt. Gov. Leo McCarthy, who was in charge of the state when the quake hit because Gov. George Deukmejian was abroad, said 253 people died on Oakland's Interstate 880, nine were killed in San Francisco, three in San Jose and at least six in Santa Cruz. More than 400 people were injured.

LEADERS DEMAND TOUGHER SANCTIONS

KUALA LUMPUR, Malaysia (UPI) - Commonwealth leaders Wednesday demanded intensified sanctions against South Africa to wipe out apartheid and urgent action to curb environmental degradation and drug trafficking.

"Sanctions must not only continue but

Above left *There are many carefully thought-out touches to help passengers such as this notice put up on departure days at Hamburg train station. Below left Groups of passengers leave the ship on excursions by all manner of transport. Right Members of a QE2 brass band (who like all entertainers are booked many months in advance) blow their hearts out*

Above *The same staff serve bouillon at eleven o'clock sharp – whatever the scenery*

between staff and regulars to realise that many special relationships are based on mutual respect and liking.

Now is the time everybody dreads. Many of the passengers have come thousands of miles for a holiday of a lifetime. They are tired, disorientated, full of expectation of immediate gratification – and get lost, take an instant dislike to their cabin and demand a change, are upset that room service is not operating, discover that even the bars are not open, and for good measure storm into the dining room with a preconceived idea that they have been allocated a poor table. More complaints by far are made during the next few hours than will be heard during the whole of the rest of the two-week cruise. 'My travel agent has let me down.' 'This is a great mistake.' 'No, listen to me, it's this way – oh, where are we now?'

The staff expect it, and smile. Every new-comer seems intent on adding to the mêlée of lost humanity – lost as to their immediate whereabouts and lost as to why they were foolish enough to come aboard in the first place. It has to be said that Americans are the first and loudest to exclaim. But people do steadily find their way around, the bars do open well before sailing time, tea and coffee are available even if you have to help yourself. Once the baggage has been safely delivered people feel more secure, and once it has been unpacked and everything stowed away the cabin does not look so mean after all. And those strawberries were a good idea.

Sailing time. Miracle! The gangways are already down, there have been several announcements about those not sailing tonight having to leave. Over the other side a couple of tugs are beginning to pull. Inches, feet, yards – we edge out from the quay, we're on our way. The ship's whistle gives three emotional blasts and is answered by a tanker, and the Polish musicians strike up bringing tears to most passengers' eyes. A waiter has handed out a small supply of paper streamers; it is beginning to feel as though we are in a movie. Champagne

corks pop in the bars and men furtively carry glasses to their spouses. Only a handful of passengers have friends and relatives to wave them off, but everyone in the small tour-boats raises their hand – with a touch of envy, no doubt. The musicians really do give a rousing performance. Glad you came?

No other holiday starts so emotionally as a cruise, separating you so suddenly from the office cares of only yesterday. Some business-men whose time is precious choose to cruise precisely because the transformation from work to vacation is made so sudden and complete – especially when compared with trips involving long hours of driving.

But the battle is not over yet. Some passengers are at the bureau complaining about their room. Others will not leave their room until their last piece of baggage is delivered, and that might be a little while yet. The head waiter tells those who want to switch tables he will do what he can. The bartenders do a little bit more than possible to serve passengers, but the harder they try the less one disgruntled man is going to be pleased. He clearly needs his own private ship!

Now it is the waiters' turn to come under attack. They do their best to greet their new passengers and to understand special requests, but everybody seems to be coming in and talking together and there is a chorus of impatient pleas for attention. As more passengers begin talking among themselves the mood steadily eases, but take a vote on the quality of dinner and it would not be reassuring. The first night's dinner is always the most difficult. Passengers come to be fed rather than to enjoy gracious dining and many are eating after too long or short an interval from their last meal, and are unfamiliar with the terminology and the presentation. There is a sprinkling of many nations here, among the passengers, staff and the food. The wine helps, though with hardly any advance ordering at lunch and with everyone determined to get started instantly, the Italian and Austrian wine

waiters are hard pressed. There is still time for a greeting to familiar faces, though, and how has life been? 'Yes, we still carry that one, tomorrow perhaps?'

The pace slows perceptibly by the time dessert and coffee are served along with the petit fours and ports. Only the regulars know that over the next two weeks each dinner will seem better than the last. The entertainers have to work harder for their applause the first night, and people slip off to bed early. Tomorrow will see more late risers (and breakfasts in bed) than on any other day.

Steadily, everyone makes the best of the splendid ship and its numerous options, letting Cunard lead them without in any sense losing their individuality. And what a splendid range of surprises the ship has in store: breathtaking approaches to ports, gala dinners and buffets, pretty speeches by the captain, leisure and space, endless smiles and cosseting as smoothly the ship goes, towering above lesser vessels. The staff who were so hard pressed and sometimes abused on the first night now preside benevolently, much as to say 'it is always like this', though they will spring into instantaneous action to smooth any problem or meet a special request that may be required. 'No problem.' 'Of course.'

The best cruise is that which settles down quickly. Cunard are especially good at ensuring this on the short *QE2* cruises, both from New York and Southampton, fitted into the trans-atlantic crossing season. Indeed, they are very good at it on a five-day crossing itself. Pandemonium may reign as nearly 2,000 people come on board for the voyage to Europe or back, but by breakfast next morning everything is in smooth rhythm.

Smoothness does not just happen. It is all carefully planned. The top management team meets daily to consider what might be done better. Every day, every meal, is a new challenge. The art is in making it feel as though it is a natural, God-given way of life. Cunard has it to fine perfection.

17

NATURAL HISTORY

AS touched on elsewhere in these pages, especially in the chapter on Alaska, you can enjoy an amazing amount of wildlife simply by keeping a keen eye out from deck. Dolphins genuinely do come close and cavort leisurely alongside you, and porpoises and whales are not rarities. But it is naturally bird life that is especially fascinating. In his *Oceans of Birds*, also published by David & Charles a few months ahead of this work, Tony Soper vividly describes the joys of bird watching on the seven seas. The following is an extract from part of his introduction.

My seven-year-old son Jack found Cassin's Auklet in the swimming pool one morning before breakfast. We watched albatrosses power-glide down the wake to join us, we sailed through a sea of shearwaters inside the Great Barrier Reef of Australia and rescued some from a sticky end (becoming curry for the Goanese seamen). We gave over our bathroom to a succession of dazed terns and petrels which came to grief on the decks at night and needed peace and quiet. We even learnt to grin and bear it when the loudspeaker system called us to duty with the announcement, so much appreciated by the passengers, 'There is a bird in Tony Soper's cabin'. One of the greatest pleasures of the trip was the discovery that almost everybody on the ship became genuinely interested in the seabirds which passed by and the landbirds which occasionally joined the ship for a rest and some biscuit crumbs.

Wherever we went on board there was someone who was looking at a distant bird or wanted to tell of one he'd seen during the day. There was the old boy who stretched out in his favourite deck-chair round about teatime, on the promenade deck, togged out in his dinner jacket and black tie, and ready to chatter about boobies and storm-petrels. While we stretched out on the games deck, doing our daily dozen, the frigatebirds would soar overhead, doubtless sizing us up as possible breakfasts and thinking better of it. And, best of all, at drinks time in the evening we would lean on a rail with the stalwart band of birdwatchers who girdled the world with us, discussing the day's bird list and admiring the shearwaters as they slanted and turned as we scanned the horizon for whales and the sky for tropicbirds. It was a mind-boggling experience.

In those hundred days we chalked up a list of six hundred and fifty species. But since there are less than three hundred different kinds of seabird in the world and we didn't see anywhere near all of them, our list was bolstered by a lot of birds which we saw at our ports of call. We became experts in planning to get twenty-four hours of birding into an eight-hour stopover.

For the major sections of the classic round-the-world cruise, and the typical North Sea, Mediterranean, Alaskan and South Atlantic voyages, I have tried to indicate the way that the bird panorama unfolds. It is broadly true that you can predict the way in which new species will appear, coast by coast and sea by sea. The pre-ordained sequence of events is one of the great pleasures of the journey – one day out of San Francisco, watch for the Laysan Albatross; approaching Australia offers your best chance of the mighty Wandering Albatross.

Seventy-one per cent of our planet's surface is covered by water, 139 million square miles of it. For every square mile of land there are two and a half of sea. Much of that watery expanse is unknown and unexplored. Yet ocean-going birds have the freedom of those seas and wander them in numbers that stun the imagination. One of the tiny water-walking storm-petrels may be the commonest bird in the world even though penguin cities number their inhabitants in the tens of millions. Albatrosses spend most of their lives soaring the stormy latitudes of the roaring forties, circling the entire Antarctic continent. The sea-

SHARKS

Although this word conjures up the picture of a voracious, man-eating monster, comparatively few of the numerous species are of this nature. The sharks form a large family of hundreds of species divided into dozens of groups. They are found in all waters, cold or warm, and in all shapes and sizes from the eel-like frilled shark occasionally caught west of Iceland to the enormous whale-shark of tropical seas, the largest of all fishes. The latter may exceed 50ft (15m) in length and weigh several tons; it is, however, an inoffensive sluggish creature with feeble teeth, capable of feeding only on small planktonic animals. Most famous are the members of the genus *Carcharadon*, known in South Africa and Australia as white- or blue-pointers, which grow to a length of 40ft (12m). They are man-eaters par excellence and take an annual toll of bathers.

Far left *Sea lions attract passengers' interest on a rock in Alaska.* Left *Whales of various kinds (along with dolphins and porpoises) are frequently seen but not easily photographed. These are killer whales* (Frank Vane Picture Agency). Below left *The Layson albatros* (Tony Soper)

Right *The ultimate natural history experience (which few passengers enjoy) is sighting a polar bear* (The Telegraph Colour Library)

swallows have cracked the problem of winter by criss-crossing the globe and flying through a life of endless summer.

If we choose to follow such birds, we can share something of the romance of their lives. Naval seamen, merchant seamen, weathership crews, cruise ships and their passengers, yachtsmen and all, have a chance of seeing something of these other world travellers. For one of the enjoyable traits of pelagic birds is that they seem to seek out ships and pay them a visit, sometimes brief, sometimes prolonged. Any voyage is enhanced by a small understanding of these travelling companions.

It has to be said that, apart from the birds which actually come aboard and hitch a lift, a lot of them will be rather distant and difficult to identify. Take your eyes off the dipping wings for one moment and they have a disconcerting tendency to disappear behind a wave, for good. So you certainly need to concentrate, to scan the sea from alongside to the far horizon and into the sky. There will be birdless days in the open ocean but plenty of others when, after logging a few dozen excitements, a passing jogger on the prom deck will commiserate with you, saying, 'Not a bird in sight today!', because of course they haven't been looking. Worse still, on days when you're hugging the coast they will say, 'Bad luck, nothing but seagulls today', as if gulls were small change rather than fearsome challenges of identification.

There are no hard-and-fast rules about where to watch from on a ship, since birds can appear at any time almost anywhere. But the afterdeck is as good a place as any, for many birds like to watch a ship's wake for galley waste or for the marine organisms churned up by the propellers. For fishing boobies the foredeck is ideal, for whale-watching you must get yourself as close to the bridge-wings as possible with a forward view. But for every bird seen best from the foreparts of the ship, there's another at the stern, so you must hedge your bets and do some patrolling.

A moderate speed of up to 10 knots is ideal for birding, but it's no good telling that to the master of a cruise liner, or a cross-channel ferry for that matter. On the other hand albatrosses have to make endless sweeps and turns just to reduce speed to keep station at well over 20 knots. And I was overtaken by a couple of razorbills while screaming along in a hydrofoil off the coast of Brittany at 36 knots.

Migrating landbirds sometimes find a great deal of difficulty in landing on a vessel which is steaming fast; they certainly prefer a stationary ship, for example a weathership or an oil platform, especially at night. They are usually exhausted and simply looking for a rest. Seabirds are attracted to ships for different reasons: they provide some shelter in a lee; a roost-place; or most of all because they provide food in the form of the galley waste of which most ships are regrettably prodigal.

The Arctic tern (RSPB)

18

TRANS- AND WEST ATLANTIC

THERE is no experience like arriving in New York after a transatlantic crossing on the *QE2*. For several long (25 hour) days you will have enjoyed the lonely ocean and the great facilities of the last of the world's super-liners. Expectation rises, especially among those doing it for the first time, as the long journey nears its end.

Land! It arrives fitfully. First you may notice an oil-drilling platform off the coast of Newfoundland. Steadily there are more ships, and birds, around. Nantucket lighthouse is the first true American landfall. But the real excitement is held until you are in sheltered water, seeing the United States of America as hundreds of thousands of immigrants from every part of Europe first saw it. The same, yet so different from the days when newcomers to America had first to go into quarantine, when westbound crossings were always fuller than return ones and when emigration traffic from Britain was so great that to ensure it captured its share Cunard found it worthwhile maintaining an office even in a small Cornish mining town down on its luck.

Then the Statue of Liberty. Nothing in the whole wide world causes more universal thrill than passing her aboard the Queen of the oceans. If it is a morning arrival, half the ship will be up, many passengers toasting Liberty with champagne on deck. If it is evening, waiters who have seen her many times before, as well as passengers, interrupt dinner to take their leisurely fill of her floodlit.

On, into the narrows, under the Verrazano-Narrows Bridge which the ship is designed just to clear, and now Manhattan's skyscrapers come into view. If you have never been to the United States (or just not to New York), do treat yourself to this most spectacular arrival. Whether you spot the Empire State building and the United Nations buildings through the thick mist of an early morning thunderstorm or the crisp frost of a pre-Christmas arrival, you will remember it always and have a much clearer perspective of where it fits into the world.

And now you can see individual streets, buildings, even cars. Still plenty of time to go back to your room, since the business of parking the great ship along the pier at right-angles to the street is prolonged, and even then nobody with baggage to be taken off by porter will be allowed ashore until the whole baggage has been cleared.

Now is the disappointment, or at least confusion. Nearly all the piers of the once great passenger port of New York are in ruins, and

WIND SCALE

The most-used scale was introduced in 1806 by the English admiral, Sir F. Beaufort. Wind speed is calculated at a height of 33ft (10m) above sea level; 1 knot = 1.15mph (1.85kmh).

Beaufort Scale of Wind Force

Force No.	Description	Wind Speed knots	Signs on Sea
0	Calm	under 1	Like a mirror
1	Light breeze	1–3	Small wavelets, glassy
2	Light breeze	4–6	Small wavelets, short but more pronounced, do not break
3	Gentle breeze	7–10	Large wavelets beginning to break, foam
4	Moderate breeze	11–16	Small waves becoming longer, white horses
5	Fresh breeze	17–21	Moderate waves more pronounced, some spray
6	Strong breeze	22–27	Large waves (10–13ft; 3–4m), white foam breaking
7	Near gale	28–33	Sea heaps up, white foam breaking
8	Gale	34–40	Moderately high waves of greater length, breaking, foam streams (19–25ft; 5.5–7.5m)
9	Strong gale	41–47	High waves (23–32ft; 7–10m), dense streams of foam, crests topple, spray
10	Storm	48–55	Very high waves (30–42ft; 9–12m) with long overhanging crests, dense streams of foam make sea white with heavy tumbling, visibility affected
11	Violent storm	56–63	Exceptionally high waves (38–53ft; 11.5–16m) long white patches of foam, bad visibility
12	Hurricane	64 and over	Air filled with foam and spray, sea white with driving spray, waves over 46ft (14m)

Space and time are the privileges endowed by an Atlantic crossing. Entertainment and exercise are also important

Right *Arrival in or departure from New York by QE2 is always a great event*

there is unlikely to be another ship beside the QE2. In winter, months may now pass without a single liner calling. And the exit into the city could hardly be less prepossessing. Your porter or longshoreman will compete with others to get a taxi to pull off the potholed street under an ugly viaduct. The contrast with the elegant surroundings of half an hour ago could hardly be greater. And so into the city.

The exit down the Hudson to the sea is just as dramatic. There is, naturally, a commentary from the bridge. The Atlantic ahead, that great ocean of turbulent mood separating the Old World from the New whose passage until the age of the jet was measured in days, in the days of sail in weeks.

However much you may enjoy cruising, no days will have greater magic than those on a transatlantic crossing. The majestic ship cuts through the water hour after hour, day after day, at not much less than 30 knots, a great city on the move, a city of infinite variety and quality where among other things such fine food is served that the caviar consumption is greater beyond comparison than that of any other institution or even worldwide hotel chain. The feeling of wellbeing while being on a real journey and adjusting gently to the time-changes is unique. Service is the very best. In three of the restaurants passengers are positively encouraged to challenge the chefs with original, personal requests. They use spirits more freely in the ubiquitous flaming dishes than almost certainly you will have seen elsewhere.

A few practical points. On its transatlantic crossings, the QE2 is still a two-class ship, though this really only means that the Queen's Lounge is reserved for first class and all can use the two-deck Grand Lounge with its arcades of international shops around the upper deck. Always on the QE2, your cabin choice determines which restaurant you eat in, though actually many passengers decide what restaurant they want first and then pick a cabin in the right category. The top restaurant, the

Queen's Grill, is justly famous and coveted, though the smaller, more intimate Princess Grill has its own keen adherents. The largest of the first-class restaurants, the Columbia Grill, still makes you feel very special. And in the Mauretania Restaurant (formerly Tables of the World) there is an excellent menu and no feeling of being on a conveyor belt.

While a westbound crossing with its 25 hour days is especially relaxing, those who suffer jet lag going to Europe prefer the sailing from New York to Southampton. Some British businessmen who work a few hours each day on the paperwork of their American visit, getting over the time-lag all the while, reckon that taking the ship is no real waste of days. They return to their office in prime condition. Good business facilities are of course provided on board. But gone, alas, are the days when the pair of old Queens provided a departure from New York and Southampton every Thursday, taking in a weekend at sea. Today's economics determine that the QE2 never lingers. She always turns around in the day – a day of total chaos severely taxing the staff between four days of ocean bliss – and has no regular sailing pattern. Even during the summer transatlantic season, European and American cruises are sometimes fitted in between the crossings, and many passengers indeed combine the two. But there are still occasions when you can go straight across the Atlantic and back, and some people enjoy this year by year as a particularly liberating kind of holiday, though it has to be added that the Atlantic is never the warmest part of the globe.

The approach to Southampton is nothing compared with that to New York, though the city and its surroundings have much to offer as described in the chapter on Round Britain. A two-hour visit to a French port (you could always watch the boat train leave for Paris while French cheeses and other provisions were still being taken on board carefully watched and tasted by the chef) was once a regular feature of a transatlantic crossing, but

now only occasional visits are paid to Cherbourg.

Relatively new are the occasional visits to other American ports such as Boston and Philadelphia. These are always special, with a warm welcome given by the city, because of their rarity. They provide a unique opportunity of viewing the sea approaches and harbours from a major ship. As many fewer people normally come and go by sea, there is a growing minority interest in maritime heritage and what a liner can offer, and this is partly also responsible for the popularity of New England and Canadian cruises from New York, normally the province of one of the Fjord ships. The 'fall color' is the natural time for such cruises, calling at a changing range of small and larger New England and Canadian ports, and now sometimes combined with Bermuda.

The highlight of many such cruises is the sailing up the mighty St Lawrence past Quebec City (a stirring sight indeed from the deck of an ocean liner) into the heart of Canada at Montreal. Once Montreal to Europe was a major passenger route quite separate from New York to Europe: the North Atlantic as opposed to just the Atlantic. So little now goes that way that it is good to be able still to enjoy the St Lawrence in real luxury. You are on the river of endless historical association for a whole day. You will be unlikely to see any other passenger vessel larger than a ferry, but pass numerous cargo vessels of different sizes on their way to and from the Great Lakes by the St Lawrence Seaway.

The QE2 and one of the Fjord ships are regular visitors to genteel Bermuda, the nearest island destination from New York and nothing to do with the Caribbean. With a full day at sea there and back and ample time to explore the islands as well as go shopping, it is not hard to see why this has become a popular line in cruising. While bustling Hamilton is a sparkling capital and shopping paradise, do explore both east and west, the latter including charming old St George. And sometimes New York and Bermuda are combined with the colonial south such as Charleston (South Carolina) and Savannah (Georgia), still unseen by the vast majority even of Americans, and to which visits by sea have added spice.

While most of the ships that cruise the Caribbean never go north of Miami or Fort Lauderdale, the possibilities along the whole extensive seaboard right up to the St Lawrence are considerable. But you must plan carefully for the opportunities are by no means regular. You will not, however, see much of the coast from a New York–Fort Lauderdale 'hop', ships going non-stop being on their way to and from greater things. Sometimes the *QE2* goes south after a transatlantic crossing and you may enjoy a couple of extra bargain days on board. There is usually such a sailing just before Christmas, offering passengers from Europe a package including Disney World. World as well as Caribbean cruises from New York make the same journey, passengers steadily getting into the mood as it grows perceptibly warmer hour by hour. You need time, but the sea exit from New York is so immediately stimulating and relaxing that it is a crime to fly.

The South Atlantic to Europe is another different route, usually by Cunard to and from Fort Lauderdale as ships take up their winter or summer positions. Sometimes there is a call at Bermuda or at one of the Caribbean islands. Occasionally, and much to be treasured, is a call at the Azores, one of the world's least-visited treasures, a piece of traditional Portugal floating in mid-Atlantic where there is absolutely nothing else. Your short stop at Horta will give only a flavour of one of the volcanic but beautiful green islands. What a flavour it is! That other Portuguese paradise of Madeira is often the first port of call in the Old World, but sometimes it is Lisbon itself, sometimes one of the north African or even western Mediterranean ports (see next chapter). But on a South Atlantic crossing, generally much warmer and less likely to be rough than a more northerly

Queen Mary *passes* Queen Elizabeth *in mid-Atlantic*

one, the emphasis is strongly on the journey itself with up to a continuous week at sea between the continents. As stated elsewhere, this is not perhaps for newcomers to cruising, but definitely loved by many regulars who complain that the unhurried days with no land distraction pass all too quickly. Naturally the best cabins sell especially well. Those who dislike air travel may take the 'positioning' cruise across the South Atlantic and continue on perhaps to the Mediterranean and Black Sea, returning by sea (perhaps on *QE2*) after five or six weeks of gracious living. All cabins are of course to the same super standard on *Sea Goddess I* and *II* which also cross the south Atlantic but spend summer in Europe; these journeys are exceptionally special occasions with ample time to savour the full *Sea Goddess*

experience at somewhat below the normal daily rate.

There has to be an element of challenge in crossing the Atlantic, especially in a smaller ship. The ocean is ever unpredictable, occasionally viciously violent, seldom plain dull. Sea- and sky-scapes of voyages of years ago still live vividly in the mind. Even in summer you cannot be sure of a smooth crossing, though the vast majority are. In real winter there is a strong probability of some storm, a chance of a day or two of force 10 or even 12. Few who have experienced that would be put off from doing it again. That perhaps is the best recommendation!

*Sunset over Lanzarote, where many UK passengers
return to earlier package holiday haunts*

19
EASTERN ATLANTIC

THE Madeira tasting had been great fun. Now, with two cases tied up with string and marked for the attention of the baggage master, we were being trundled, courtesy of the shop, in a bouncing truck to the *QE2*'s side. Our precious cases disappeared instantly into the ship's bowels between great boxes of provisions for the kitchen; any doubt about whether we would see them again was quickly dispelled by the baggage master telephoning to say he had them safely in his possession. When next seen at Southampton, they had been graciously retied including carrying handles to move them the few yards to the waiting car.

It had been a glorious early winter's day on the semi-tropical island, a demonstration if ever there was one of just how much you can pack into a single day. A leisurely start and walk to one of the great hotels for morning coffee; by rented car across the mountains and through the lush valleys to the high cliffs of the far side, returning by a different route, lunch in true Portuguese style with Madeira wine and fruit; an energetic walking tour of Funchal after the car had been turned in; then shopping ending in the quest for Madeira cake (sign language more than words told the gracious elderly gentleman what was wanted and led to his turning back from his walk home to point to the preferred shop); finally the Madeira tasting as though making the exact right choice were the most important task in the world.

By now it was getting dark, Funchal's Christmas lights adding to the gaiety of the

Santa Cruz in Tenerife, a great port for a lazy day or energetic exploration of the mountainous interior

background though what was happening immediately beside the ship was compelling enough. Hundreds of passengers returning from their exploits of a memorable day were intent on making last-minute purchases: wine, (especially Mateus rosé) by the half-dozen cases at not much more than the price most people are prepared to pay for bottled water; exotic flowers, jewellery, bamboo hampers and great bamboo armchairs. The very idea of carrying all this back home by public transport seemed crazy. Then came the practical, brightly decorated island clothing, Portuguese blue pottery and tiles. 'Always the same', commented an English passenger to a bemused American. Later they met on the promenade deck commanding a magnificent view of the island's Christmas-decorated capital with a firework display adding a further touch of pleasure. The American somehow got talking politics and assumed the Englishman was a capitalist dead against 'Labor'; when the Englishman travelling by the world's greatest ship said he always voted Labour, there was more bemusement but still good companionship.

The green island of Madeira with its hairpin, cliff-hanging roads, changeless institutions like Reed's Hotel once favourite of Churchill, its ancient churches and garden treasures, is always a popular destination on cruises down the Iberian peninsula and to the Atlantic isles. These cruises are noted for their rich variety of nearby destination and such is the choice of ports that seldom are the combinations exactly the same. The cruises are naturally popular with the British who can take their cars almost

to the gangway, but some of the *QE2*'s cruises are also fitted in between Atlantic crossings and thus carry many Americans on longer holidays.

The most common denominator is Lisbon, one of Europe's most relaxed and colourful capitals, full of historic sights, ever a fun place to visit and a wonderful shopping centre. Take a number of these cruises and you may end up in Lisbon each time; you will never regret it, expectation always rising as you sail up the wide Tagus, the Continent's longest suspension bridge ahead, overtaken by the frequent electric trains on the north bank. Plan your day (the first, second or third) carefully, for the options are numerous, including visits to the Portuguese Riviera a few miles away along the Atlantic. Taxis are cheap; ensure you pick one with an English-speaking driver. The only grumble is that the ship docks miles from the animated city centre, and it is not always easy to get a taxi there to bring you back. But someone will always go to great trouble to help you in Portugal.

Praia de Rocha might be another Portuguese destination, gateway for the Algarve; taxis are not plentiful so it is probably a choice between the organised tour and the beach which is why most people go to the Algarve. Other ports are mainly Spanish. Of the Canary Island ones, Santa Cruz in Tenerife is the most popular, giving British passengers a chance to see how the package-holiday brigade spend their time (or maybe renew acquaintance first made on your own package holiday). Relaxing along the water's edge sipping coffee or wine with perhaps a foray into the old town is enough for

most, though the journey over the mountains to the Canadas National Park lying within the perimeter of an enormous volcanic crater, and then on to Puerto de la Cruz on the opposite coast, is ever rewarding. Also in the Canaries, Lanzarote, a much smaller island intensively touristy near the port, intensively cultivated where possible, but in its volcanic centre intensively uncultivable and weird with canyons and still-active thermal activity, has you either loving or hating it. For certain it is different, as again is scallop-shaped Grand Canary, with its own great contrasts of terrain and spectacular views and vegetation.

On the Spanish mainland, to the north, occasional visits are made to Vigo, just beyond the Portuguese border. The fishing town shelters on a great bay forming a fine natural harbour where there has been trading since the beginning of man's history. Taking the taxi a few miles down the coast southward after exploring the town makes an interesting enough day. For many, however, the port offers a unique opportunity to visit Santiago de Compostela, pilgrimage to which once ranked with that to the Holy Land itself. The trip to Spain's holiest city is a lengthy affair generally judged worthwhile.

Another lengthy trip is often offered from Cadiz on Spain's south Atlantic coast to Seville, romantic inland port. Cadiz or Seville, both redolent of history, are archetypal southern Spain, Andalusia, of which they are the main cities, is where the flamenco and bullfights originated and the best sherry is produced.

At another popular port, in truth just in the Mediterranean but more likely to be included in an Eastern Atlantic cruise, you can walk across the border to Spain: Gibraltar, one of the world's most curious enclaves. Get up early to see the Rock as you pass through the Straits of Gibraltar between Europe and Africa. Those who know its turbulent history cannot but be moved, whether it is their first or hundredth sighting. Once, of course, all on their way to India and the Southern Hemisphere via the

THE STRAIT OF GIBRALTAR

This channel of water between Europe and Africa is approximately 22 nautical miles (40km) long and 10 nautical miles (18km) wide. Its depth is between 1,000 and 3,000ft (305 and 915m) and the current flows towards the Mediterranean due to the faster evaporation of water in the latter's hotter climate. In ancient times, the Strait of Gibraltar was thought to be the end of the world and the great rocks on either side were known as the 'Pillars of Hercules'.

Suez Canal scored this sight. Now you can travel the world yet have to make a special point of getting to Gibraltar, with its roads through and up the Rock, its famous monkeys, English-style shopping centre and tearooms, and harbour that has seen more vital days.

For many this will be the first glimpse of Africa, the continent least visited by cruise liners, mainly for political reasons, though some of the more attractive destinations are too far out of the way to be served except on leisurely world cruises. Some ships, especially when moving in or out of the Mediterranean, visit Tangier in Morocco and give their passengers a highly commercialised though colourful view of Africa. As at larger Casablanca, a rarer port of call on the open Atlantic, it offers French-style luxury living in the best of the modern part and a rich panorama of traditional life and trade in the twisting lanes of the souk and casbah. Experience the contrast to the full. But above all somehow try to soak it in during the pauses in the ever-present pressure to buy this or that – a suit or even new dentures made while you wait. Mind you, bargaining here is an art to be practised to the hilt. Knock that teapot down to a quarter of the starting price, have a second thrown in for good measure and you may be inclined to think you have reasonable value – until a fellow passenger reveals she has obtained five for half the price again.

Years ago the wealthy British used to cruise to west Africa for Christmas, and after a gap of at least a decade Dakar in Senegal is occasionally back in the itinerary. Gateway to west Africa it may be, but despite its interesting sea approach the city is dull with undistinguished buildings compared to the Moroccan ports. Shopping is not such fun either, though you will remember the sheer height of the vendors of wooden bowls and other items who set up their stalls beside the ship. The general verdict here is to take one of the tours out of the city, such as to Goree Island which you passed on the way in, or down the coast to a traditional fishing village.

Quite different again are the Cape Verde Islands on the Portuguese edge of civilisation, primitive (including the means of transport offered passengers off the ship), dramatic in their landscape, sorrowful in their memories of once being at a crossroads of trade but largely bypassed since the building of the Suez Canal and now treasured by cruisegoers simply because hardly anyone gets there.

You will have plentiful sunshine on cruises taking in a range of such ports as these, but there is never any guarantee against Atlantic storms. In every way the mood can change more dramatically than on most itineraries.

Lisbon, Portugal (Imagebank)

*Funchal in Madeira is always a favourite port and
one many passengers wish to visit again* (Imagebank)

QE2 *at Funchal photographed by the author as he returned from his Madeira tasting*

Even on a foggy November morning, one's first sight of the Rock of Gibraltar is stirring

The faithful geyser pleases another group of passengers at Lanzarote

An hour's drive from Funchal on the opposite side of Madeira

113

Using a piece of your ship as foreground helps give perspective to your pictures

20

PHOTOGRAPHY

IT may sound a bit obvious, but you will get far more enjoyment from your cruise photography if you have a clear idea of what it is you want to record. We all know there is often an inverse ratio between quantity and quality. While no photographer can ignore the perfect sunset or rainbow, basically you have to choose between producing an overall pictorial record of the places you have visited (taking as it were your own picture-postcard collection), and telling the story of a personal voyage.

For most people, especially those hoping to show off their pictures to friends back home, the story of the personal voyage is more attractive. Friends will see more point in pictures that show what you and yours were doing than a succession of postcards, many of them probably of indifferent quality, that just happen to be about the places you saw. What that says is that you should not endlessly shoot over the vacant sea to distant points, however famous, and that for most of us there is little point in taking yet another bland set of pictures of Roman or Greek ruins. Buy a few professional cards and save yourself the trouble and expense. But you, uniquely, can record your own and family's voyage, with pictures showing the ship and yourselves approaching and actually at the famous places on the itinerary. Alas, you will find that fellow passengers whose inclusion would help give point to a picture are apt to jump out the way in the mistaken belief that all you want is the distant view.

Distance views usually disappoint. You need a reasonable camera even to begin. Foregrounds help enormously, and personalised foregrounds again give purpose. Even if you take a view of the harbour and bay from some vantage point, the inclusion of your ship will make a point. You can indeed have great fun including the ship (not necessarily all of it every time of course) in as many different settings and from as many different angles as possible. You will note how the really keen photographers do not miss the opportunity offered by tender-rides ashore.

Now, a few practical points. Check or change your camera batteries before leaving home and, since even if you can buy it at all, film will generally be more expensive overseas, take plenty with you. Once you get started, you will click the shutter more frequently than on any other kind of holiday. If you are using a new camera, have at least one film developed before you go, and be sure to take the instruction book. A cruise is undoubtedly a good reason to upgrade your camera, but unless you are truly devoted to photography avoid heavy and complicated systems. Even if you can cope with the weight in your baggage, you will not enjoy it on long days ashore, especially on tours of ancient ruins. Handy zoom lenses once despised by those with good cameras have now gained respectability and for cruising are more practical than interchangeable lenses. To tell a personal story, you will almost certainly need some flash pictures – and don't be afraid to give fellow passengers and waiters the fun of pressing your shutter.

But please note that a simple flash cannot light up a distant hill: how painful it is to hear passengers say they will have to use flashlight in order to take a picture of a monument a mile or more across the sea!

In composing your pictures, remember the basic rule to avoid the exact middle. A sea- and skyscape will seldom look good half and half; two-thirds sky, one-third sea, or vice versa, will almost invariably be better. The eye takes in points of interest most easily a third or two-thirds down and across, giving you a choice of four spots for the ship, monument or husband. If you have never done so, give yourself a brief lesson in picture composing by blanking off parts of photographs until you see the best effect. Look how a picture with the horizon in the middle suddenly comes to life if you reduce sky or sea until they are unequal.

Of course, where possible avoid taking pictures into the sun, but if you want to snap a sunset or have to go somewhat into direct sunshine to make your point, manually over-expose to compensate. Be adventurous. Modern cameras cope amazingly with all kinds of situation. Rolling mist, thunder clouds, even rain beating on the deck, can be rewarding. Most amateur photographers are put off too easily; the only really hopeless subjects are those great expanses of bland sea with thin lines of land that the human eye might be able

---

LOOK TO THE HORIZON!

At an elevation of 5ft (1.5m), the horizon is 2½ nautical miles (4.8km) away; at 20ft (6m) it is 5 miles (9km), at 35ft (10.6m) it is 7 miles (13km) and at 100ft (30m) it is 11 miles (20km). On a large ship, the height of the bridge will give the captain a distance, to the horizon, of 10 or more miles.

Tender rides give excellent photographic opportunities if you select your position carefully. Here we are leaving *Vistafjord* at the head of a Norwegian fjord, the tender's wake providing movement

Right *You can see it has been raining, that* Vistafjord *has recently passed under a bridge linking an island with the Norwegian mainland and that a ferry has waited for her passage to make the crossing of the sound. Altogether it makes a more interesting picture than the distant views in bright sunlight so loved by inexperienced photographers. The sun and its reflection add more drama by being roughly a third in from the picture's outer edges; photographs in which the focal point is dead centre are far less effective*

This quayside shot emphasises the sheer bulk of QE2, the name on the lifebelt eliminating any doubt about the ship's identity, and the ship's photographer trying to line up disembarking passengers telling a story

to concentrate upon but the lens cannot. Yet while many people shun close-ups in what they believe might be too difficult light, each day on every ship sees a huge waste of film with those vague attempts to shoot across the ocean to some distant landmark.

Especially if you are in an area like the Caribbean where it is easy to forget what belonged to which port, be sure to note what is on which film. You will probably want to take your film collection back home with you; a great advantage of cruising over travel involving frequent air journeys is that the film will not for ever be X-rayed. When the pictures come and you can relive your cruise, decide how you are going to store them and add details in captions that might later be forgotten. Some people merely enjoy taking pictures and do not care much what happens thereafter; others go in for elaborate storage and retrieval systems. It may be that you will get greater satisfaction from a small prime selection – a mere couple of dozen telling the outline story of the cruise – that will be shown far more often than the whole collection should you keep it all together. You do not of course have to destroy pictures of secondary interest to make a top selection; but you would be well advised to get rid of those that really do not make it at all. Then, how often do we promise ourselves an enlargement of something really special but somehow do not get round to it? A poster-size enlargement of your perfect cruise picture can bring a very personal pleasure.

Photography is sometimes the subject of on-board lectures and demonstrations, and occasionally there are even special photographic cruises with competitions. Remember that should you write up a cruise experience for publication, photographs will be a must. Even today pictures that are to appear in black and white are better taken on black-and-white film, though it is increasingly difficult to come by.

Finally, what about video? Most people will never do anything more suitable for the subject of a personal video film than a cruise. Increasingly you see people walking (occasionally staggering) round the deck with video cameras. Sometimes they drive themselves and their partners crazy with their obsession, being apparently unable to enjoy any experience other than through the video lens. The truth is that making even a quarter-professional video is hard work, and though the result might be very satisfying you do have to decide whether the priority is right for you. To get anything even a quarter decent, you are bound to need editing facilities. Sound taken on deck – 'We are now in the first lock chamber, excuse me' (to the person whose elbow the video operator has bumped), is seldom other than banal without stringent editing. To which it should be added that video cameras are all the time becoming lighter and easier to use. If you are going to make a video film, do not spare the cost of the latest, more compact, equipment. And do give yourself some kind of story line to follow.

The impressive scale of QE2 *is shown off by the minuteness of the small craft in front of her and the low hills beyond* (Ron Baker)

21

THE PACIFIC

EXOTIC images: of coming under the Golden Gate into San Francisco's great bay as the sun melts through the rolling mist enveloping the bridge, and leaving, the sky is lit up red, as the sun sinks into the Pacific; of the myriad green-clad islands popping up through the crystalline sea of the Great Barrier Reef many thousands of miles away; of mini-kingdoms with disappointing capital cities but completely fulfilling their promise of natural beauty with everlasting variations on the theme of volcanic scenery and tropical vegetation; of tranquil lagoons as unspoilt as Captain Cook would have found them, bamboo forests and flower-lined roads along balmy shores that seem so special when folks back home are enduring winter; of ancient customs that impressed Cook and are still vibrant to impress us today, and traditional welcomes ever warm, even at Somerset Maugham's Pago Pago in deluging rain; of the great diversity of Polynesian peoples and cultures, the proud individuality of Tonga, the only island group in the South Seas never to have been colonised; of relics of the vicious battles of World War II and the surprising ancient temples of Bora Bora; and above all of the fraternity of ocean-going passengers savouring the *voyage.*

The Pacific – always the shining sea, as in the song *America* 'from sea to shining sea' – is still relatively undiscovered by cruise enthusiasts and few can claim to have 'done' it all thoroughly. So the sense of exploration is very real. Parts of the great ocean (see also chapters on the Far East, Alaska, Panama Canal, South America and World Cruises) are covered elsewhere. Most readers coming to this chapter will therefore have three types of

OCEAN DEPTHS

The ocean – a general term meaning the great bodies of water on the earth – comprises 142,000,000sq miles (368,000,000km^2). The average depth is 2 miles (3km). The greatest depth so far determined in the Pacific is 32,088ft (9,780m) off the island of Mindanao in the Philippines. The deepest point of the Atlantic was formerly said to be near Puerto Rico, where soundings discovered a depth of 27,366ft (8,340m), a little over 5 miles (8km). However, more recent surveys have indicated that, near the mouth of the River Plate, the depth of the Atlantic is over 8 miles (13km). The deepest point in the Mediterranean is 16,453ft (5,015m), north-west of Crete.

cruise in mind: extensions of other cruises, notably through the Panama Canal, that offer a tease of Pacific warmth perhaps via the Mexican riviera; great Pacific explorations either as part of a world cruise or indeed a circumnavigation of the Pacific as a cruise round half the world in its own right; and shorter variations to groups of islands. For North American passengers, modest island explorations usually mean Hawaii cruises from a West Coast port, but today Cunard also shares in the major business of taking people from Australia and even New Zealand to the rich variety of islands of the South Pacific. Shorter segments with air travel greatly add to the options and, for example, make it possible for those still actively at work to piece together a great Pacific exploration of never much more than two weeks at a time spread over several years.

The Pacific is not for beginners not yet sure of their sea-legs and more interested in seeing things than unwinding on the ocean. Never underrate its sheer size. Vancouver–Fiji (and there is still a lot of ocean south of that) is roughly London–New York and back. Distances are so great that all types of Pacific cruise (even those along the Mexican coast) spend more time at sea than is common elsewhere.

Most of the days at sea will of course be in ideal cruising conditions, days truly to savour, with land however fascinating coming up like an unwarranted intrusion. But like any great ocean and despite its name, the Pacific has its angry periods . . . and at any time of year.

Another feature of Pacific cruises is that seldom will you find the lines of cruise ships that frequent some of the Caribbean and Mediterranean ports. Even when visiting say a popular destination in Hawaii, you will still be among a small minority of those arriving by sea. Excluding Hawaii, there are few islands where you are likely to meet another luxury ship, and at some of the smaller islands yours may well be the largest vessel to call all year – just as important a social as a trading occasion for the local population.

Sensuous landforms, technicolor sunsets, languid ports, and again ever a feeling of space and adventure: 'The rest of the world seemed just a dress rehearsal', said the man from Florida who has been taking several cruises in each of a score of years and now revels in ticking off exotic islands few more ordinary travellers will ever see. Pacific-island hopping is undoubtedly habit forming.

At first nobody is keen to interrupt the melody of perfect days at sea, but after three

Above *Maui's unspoilt coast in the Hawaiian islands*

Left *Fisherman's Wharf, San Francisco, California*
(The Telegraph Colour Library)

Right *Two scenes from New Zealand's North Island: boiling mud and sulphurous fumes in Rotorua's volcanic showpiece, and one of the beaches, never overcrowded, in a suburb of Auckland*

or four of them you face up to the inevitability of land ahead . . . and before you switch off the light you at last read the notes on tomorrow's port and island group whose name you have cherished since childhood wondering if ever you might actually follow in Captain Cook's footsteps. After several lazy morning starts, you have prepared for an early rise by ordering continental breakfast in your cabin.

But excitement overcomes you, and long before breakfast is due you get a tantalising glimpse of heaven through your porthole, pop into your robe and go on deck to see it more clearly. Higher yet higher the mountain peaks appear as the ship sails through a channel between two islands, traditional craft crossing between them. And there it all is: the sea breaking gently over the coral reef; the pure white sand of the untarnished beaches with their palm trees, placed more perfectly than in any man-made arrangement, dancing in the breeze; the fold upon fold of the green mountain-sides topped by humps and pinnacles piercing the clouds; the miniature-sized port to which people are flocking by bicycle, motor and on foot, bent on greeting you, sincerely hoping you appreciate their piece of paradise and of course pay some silly price to take a memento away with you. Then that magic moment of hearing that the ship has been 'cleared' and down the gang plank free to explore yet another famous pin-prick on the map just how you chose.

Eight or nine hours later, feet sore, spirits high, yet more used film and postcards in the bag, you are back to the familiar Cunard cosseting and have a drink still enjoying the changing light playing on sea and land. You now see the opposite island more clearly since during your absence the captain has turned the ship. What a place: the map of the South Seas will never seem the same now you have experienced this. And several more islands on the voyage across the Pacific to come . . . but delightfully spaced with days at sea between, so there is no danger of the memory blurring

them into each other. The sun goes down and the humps and pinnacles seem to lower themselves in the azure sky as you set sail and continue your adventure.

Not that the Pacific is all perfect. The great contrasts of living styles reveal much poverty, poor housing and alcohol problems. And the ocean is not free of tourist traps. Exciting though much of Fiji is, for example, with forests climbing up the sculptured volcanic mountains and a rich natural history in the rain forests and underwater life in the lagoon to explore, the shops of the main streets in the capital of Suva are as undistinguished architecturally as their goods are the mass-produced electronic stuff any duty-free row peddles to bargain hunters (in this case mainly from Australia and New Zealand). Getting out of town is a high priority at many ports, and if you do not take an organised tour, renting a boat or car is highly desirable. Do not, incidentally, dismiss the joys a small boat can unlock especially in sheltered lagoons just because you have arrived by water. Roads and driving standards are what guide-books sometimes euphemistically describe as variable, but you will not have problems finding your way and distances are generally short – though Fiji's airport is a gruelling two-thirds of a day's grind away from the capital by hair-raising roads even if they do go through idyllic scenery. On some roads through the more dramatic coastal scenery of Hawaii, 10 miles (16km) an hour is still an ambitious average. Yet renting a car in Papeete will enable you to take a leisurely circle through much of Tahiti and sample the colourful lifestyle of French Polynesia as well as have your camera working overtime.

Much scenery you can of course enjoy from the ship. Scenic cruising comes especially into its own around Christmas Island, through the Great Barrier Reef, and into the Bay of Islands at the north of the North Island of New Zealand, though if the author had one wish to be granted on a Pacific or world cruise taking in New Zealand it would be to sail into Milford Sound

in the South Island's fjordland. You will not see much of the Mexican coast from the ship, and it has to be said that not everyone is impressed with every port along the Mexican riviera, but something you will not forget (any more than the arrival through the Golden Gate into San Francisco) is the spectacular setting of Acapulco, a truly world-class resort whose grandeur viewed from the sea is breathtaking.

Hawaii is, in every way, something else. The merest fraction of people cruise to it, yet the advantages are enormous. Firstly, you escape being processed through airports where everybody is standardised. Secondly, you have a chance to enjoy rich panoramas of the varied coastal scenery in a way that none staying on land will share. To arrive in 'Heavenly Honda' in Maui by sea is quite out of this world; to experience the setting from the decks of Cunard is a great bonus. Then, thirdly, cruising allows you to sample the splendid variety of Hawaii impossible for those taking a conventional air package of one or two islands. You would have to get in and out of lots of planes and cars to encompass even half of what a few days by ship makes relaxingly enjoyable.

The only disadvantage of an Hawaiian cruise is that though you will of course have several days at sea before and after touching the islands, while there your senses will never be allowed to rest as one panorama is followed by another even more compelling. A sophisticated capital and the famous Waikiki Beach, volcanic mountains and craters accommodating much of the world's pineapple production, rain forests with teeming wildlife and colourful flowers everywhere, the world's highest rainfall only miles away from low-rainfall tourist resorts full of natural and unnatural attractions, and many points of historic interest, Hawaii has just about everything. It is only when they have been there that Europeans can begin to understand how young Americans, when asked where in the world they would most like to be able to go, often reply to Hawaii in their own country!

22

ROUND THE CLOCK ON A CRUISE SHIP

AS the new day begins, a hundred or so passengers have yet to retire to their cabins. They are spread thinly between casino and bars, a small group having an animated conversation in a corner of the ballroom, and a lone man still walking round the deck. Only recently have the last diners left the restaurant's 'midnight' snack, in fact served at eleven.

Regular passengers might recall other midnights when there was much more agog: the birth of Christmas Day when a waiter carrying a cross followed by a clergyman instantly turned a lounge into a chapel, the beginning of the New Year when the Christmas tree that had graced the main entrance to the restaurant was thrown overboard with dozens of New Year's wishes tied to it, the summer evening when hundreds were out watching and photographing the flickering volcano as the ship passed Stromboli, and another summer evening thousands of miles away when it was still broad daylight as an outdoor buffet was prepared for the return of most of the passengers who had gone on a post-dinner excursion to the North Cape to view the Midnight Sun.

Around one in the morning, the last bartender closes up, wandering down to the staff's social centre where a score of waiters and cooks are still unwinding, playing darts or watching a video before turning in for their short night. Soon a mere handful of crew will be on duty. Throughout the night they will of course remain watchful on the bridge. In fact the officer of the watch has just had to telephone one of the forward cabins to ask if its occupants would kindly draw the curtains, since the light is making it hard to see ahead into the night. The engine room remains manned, but since it will be the same speed ahead for the next thirty-six hours, a watching brief rather than hard work is involved. Hard work will, however, be done by the two cleaners on duty all night. They will concentrate on the public rooms where their presence during the day would be unwelcome. Room service is open all night, but the sole person in charge will probably have no call between now and, say, 6 o'clock. The radio room will also remain open but see little activity until the overnight news comes in for the shipboard newspaper. Printing this is one of the first activities of the new day. Baking fresh bread is another. A cruise ship is a town in miniature, small communities of workers repeating familiar routines.

Walk around from 5 o'clock on and you will feel the tempo of activity steadily rise. A few passengers are up, jogging round the deck, amazingly early. By 7.30 there are scores if not hundreds about, one of the staff from the health spa leading the organised morning jog while others bring themselves to life with the first intake of coffee at the café. Now nearly all staff are up, the kitchens are ready for the first orders from the dining room where waiters stand to greet their passengers, while room stewards begin preparing the orders from those having breakfast in their cabin. The café, too, is now offering light breakfasts. Nobody will be in a hurry over the meal for today is a day at sea, a breather for the passengers who have visited a different port on each of the past five days.

The newspaper is pushed under each cabin's door; the captain enquires how the night has gone and looks at the schedule for the day ahead. There are a few messages in from Cunard, one from the agent at tomorrow's port, and a handful of communications from passengers, mainly of a chatty nature though there is one complaint that will have to be investigated with the hotel manager. Stewards start cleaning cabins whose occupants are having breakfast elsewhere and the daily mounds of sheets and towels start finding their way down to the laundry. There are also a couple of hundred bags of individual laundry being passed by the room stewards to the Chinese laundrymen, now hard at work in their very personal environment with its own mini-kitchen.

At 9 o'clock there is the first announcement from the bridge. It will be a fine day. The number of people on deck steadily swells. At first, passengers choose the position for their chairs carefully to get out of the still-cool

---

TIME AT SEA

In the days of wooden ships and iron men, the passage of time aboard a vessel was indicated by the ringing of the ship's bell. The men on watch were relieved every four hours and the bell was rung accordingly. For example at 12.30am one bell was struck, at 1am two bells, and so on until 4am when eight bells rang out. At eight bells the watch changed and the melodious cycle began anew. It is one custom of earlier seafaring days that has survived until the present; think of the noon bell and also the watch cycles of the officers and crew on deck and in the engine room.

breeze, and the pile of blankets diminishes. Soon however it is warm enough to enjoy the sunshine on the main deck around and beyond the pool where the first of many swimmers are already in the water.

By 10 o'clock the ship has settled for that at-sea routine so loved by regulars. Nothing much is happening, but it is happening with great style. Plenty of time to walk around, dip into a good book, talk to fellow passengers, pop into the shop, walk another mile round the deck, remember to change the film in the camera, look to see if the photographs of yesterday's shore highlights are yet on display. A few people are busily writing away in the library. Every machine is occupied again in the computer centre, and every piece of sports equipment is being used by those more actively involved. Soon a small knot of passengers, mainly American, assemble in a lounge to hear today's lecture in the financial series. 'I have to learn how to make enough money to keep on coming', says one obviously millionaire lady from Florida. Rather more go to the travel lecture, with slides, in the theatre. The dining room has finished with breakfast but it is still available in the café for late risers.

The ship's chief officers are in discussion over a few points of detail. A waiter who disgraced himself last night hovers outside the hotel manager's office waiting to be seen and learn his fate. The entertainers are up, the band rehearsing in the ballroom while the pianist plays his heart out on the piano in a bar. The social hostess is trying to organise a group for this evening, and sitting at another table not so far away is Cunard's representative making reservations for forthcoming cruises.

Out on the promenade deck, walkers and runners are not only achieving more laps and miles – what concentration! – but beginning to record them on the pad provided. The winner, who may achieve over 100 miles (160km) on a

There is shopping in great variety on QE2, including a branch of Harrods!

two-week cruise, will be given a prize at a health party for all those who walk, jog, exercise or otherwise use the health spa. The prize? An exercise chart, of course, plus possibly a pair of special shoe-laces.

The walkers are impeded slightly by a pair of deck-chairs placed almost end to end across the promenade, his in the shade, hers in the sun, and by the Filipino maintenance crew's repolishing of a small area of the fine planking. Maintenance work goes on continually, and for the most part is just an enjoyable aspect of shipboard's varied life. The Filipinos will certainly give you an individual greeting, especially early in the morning. Day after day they scrape, clean, varnish, polish and paint. No sooner has the ship tied up in port than they lower a platform from which they precariously paint the superstructure, consuming what must be tons of whitening. Maintenance workers? Yes, it seems, until you anchor well off a port one morning and have to land by tender. It is they who lower the steps and platform that take you to the tender, they who gently help you transfer, and they who lovingly and skilfully navigate around the ship and over to shore.

Breakfast has been washed up in the kitchen, the floors soaked down, and now butchers, pastry cooks, storekeepers, soup makers and many others are beavering away preparing things for lunch, afternoon tea and dinner. Vegetable preparation seems to be by the ton. The soup vat is enormous.

But everything is spotlessly clean. Passengers given the privilege of a tour of the kitchens and storerooms underneath them are invariably impressed by the cleanliness as much as with the complexity and scale of operation. The Chinese cook is also beavering

Below *A passenger sketches an Icelandic island from the comfort of a deck chair*

away at the edge of the laundry. Ships' laundries are traditionally staffed by Chinese who do their own catering. The laundry itself is a tremendous hive of activity with great contrast between the mass-production folding and stacking of sheets and towels and the delicate precision with which passengers' more exotic items of clothing are handled. The piccadillo is sewing away, steadily reducing the pile of sheets which need slight mending. At the printers they are giving the lunch menu a final proof read and making the first of what may be several changes to the dinner menu. The chef insists on his right to change things according to supply and demand, how well the fresh produce is ripening, and so on. The health spa has a keen contingent of body builders, two passengers are having massages, the doctor has nearly completed his surgery and will shortly visit the hospital where there are two passengers, one with stomach trouble, the other with a fractured arm. The beauty salon is flat out, for tonight is a formal night. They could get ahead quicker were it not for the constant stream of callers (in person and by telephone) seeking last-minute appointments.

Bouillon is served at 11: a bit salty for today's taste but still in a great maritime tradition. It is available in the lounge, café and on deck where it is wheeled around as will be afternoon tea at 4. But bouillon is only a minor interruption. The morning continues, most passengers luxuriating in the freedom of not having to do much (in this mood there is more looking than buying in the shop) and staff enjoying the settled time to get things done. In short, everything is shipshape and one realises how hideously busy and unorganised life is on land.

That the morning is coming to an end is signalled first by the noon sounding of the ship's siren and bell and by another announcement of our progress and position from the bridge, and then by a steady drift to the bars. Though some people have already had a couple of hours imbibing their Bloody Marys and other tipples, the noontime cocktail hour

is another great maritime tradition. It is calm today, a shame to be indoors, and no excuse for a 'medical' champagne to quell the suspicion of seasickness.

Lunch on a day at sea is a leisurely affair. Some take it in the café, a quick toasted sandwich minimising the interruption to sunbathing or other non-activity, but in the dining room you get the impression that time is absolutely no object. A little of this, a touch of that, and six or seven courses later all seems even righter with the world. Meantime the wine waiter has taken your order for tonight – the red wine will be open, breathing, before you enter the dining room. And the section waiter has taken details of your special dinner request you thought up last night. Sheer indulgence, of course, for the ordinary menu is varied enough, but why not spoil yourself, for surely you deserve it. Your spouse thinks so, anyway.

Afternoon is siesta time. On a day at sea, many take a short nap in their cabin, while snores can be heard coming from some of the prostrate figures on deck. This is when books seem more for the appearance than the reading. Staff who have to work long hours can also catch a little rest now. Some, again, do so in their cabins, but many more festoon themselves, minimally dressed, over the crew deck, viewed with interest by those whose cabin windows look down on them. But hairdresser, bars, purser's office, shop, keep ticking away. A film is being shown in the theatre, and there is a dancing class in the ballroom. Golf practice in the net, and clay pigeon shooting, are among the sporting activities in steady demand, and even in the afternoon sun as one family finishes a game of shuttlecock another moves in. A lone lady is working on a gigantic puzzle most of whose edging has now been completed. The computer room is as busy as ever. In fact only the computer room, hairdresser and sun deck are anything like fully occupied. You could treble the number of passengers elsewhere, inside and out, and still not have a crush.

Tea-time attracts a small but loyal band of

supporters indoors. The pastries so lovingly made this morning adorn a central table, buffet style, a reminder of grand luncheon buffets laid out once on some cruises – occasions for the eye (and camera) as well as the mouth. But tea is taken round, inside and out.

Four-thirty is bingo time: long lines form to buy the cards. Snobbily, the writer says now is the time to leave – for a couple of miles round the deck while it is warm but not too hot as in mid-afternoon, and then to write a chapter of this book in the cabin. It is all too easy to do nothing on a ship – to do nothing in style. But if you *have* to work, a ship is a great place to do so, with many fewer interruptions than at home or office. And of course room service can provide yet another pot of tea; perfect while the room's other occupant is down at aerobics.

A busy evening tonight. It always is! 'I'm too active to enjoy cruising', says a friend back home. What does she think we do? If only the days were longer. Mind you, you do occasionally enjoy a 25 hour day, and since that is still not long enough it proves the point. The invitation on the dresser reminds that tonight begins with a visit to the captain's quarters for cocktails. The walk there is full of distractions: hearing how the first people we met when we came on board are faring, popping into the shop to see something they have just put out on special offer, and watching others – my, my they *are* dressed up – go by stairs and elevators to the captain's room. All very plush and proper here, a welcoming line of all the chief officers who beam their approval as they shake your hand (the captain compliments three ladies in a row on how particularly attractive their dresses are) and stewards are eager to take your drink order. So you find out what the fellow who has intrigued you for the past few days does for a living and hear the story about the accountant who told his plumber he couldn't charge as much as that per hour to be answered by the plumber that he couldn't either when he was an accountant. The last of the guests having arrived, the social hostess who has announced them all is able to circulate and ooze goodwill; the officers break up their straight line and try small talk. At least it is good to hear the weather will be fine for our port tomorrow.

Downstairs, bars are busy with people drinking, selecting canapés and looking over the dinner menu; waiters are smartening themselves up for the first passengers to arrive for the day's main event and tension has mounted in the kitchen as it does behind scenes at a theatre before curtain up. Outside the deck-chairs have been collected up, blankets stowed away, and decks are being washed down while few passengers are about. Soon passengers will be a rarity anywhere except in the dining room where every seat will be occupied for the short overlap between the arrival of the late diners and the departure of the early ones. It is the chef's special dinner tonight. The food seemed good the first two days, but it seems to become steadily more interesting, exotic, varied. Caviar, lobster, asparagus, Dover sole, beef Wellington – so the menu goes on.

Don't let's hurry, and of course have the bisque as well as the other courses if you would like it. Nothing will surprise the waiters, that is for sure. And the wine waiter who approved of the choice made at lunch pours with a special smile, and asks if we have been to tomorrow's port before. He has some useful advice on how to make the best of our day, never forgetting words of wisdom on the local wine and where to taste it.

While the rest of the ship more or less slumbers, the dining room and kitchens are a frenzy of activity, with queues of waiters carrying stacks of trays going up and down the escalators connecting them. Look round the dining room and you see couples holding hands having an intimate dinner at tables for two, great debates taking place at larger tables, people getting up and going to nearby tables

The daily programme is a mine of information and suggestions for the day's activities

Cruise Director: JOHN WALDRON
Deputy Cruise Director: LINDSAY FROST
VOYAGE 724 No. 2   Sunday, 15th October 1989   Social Director: COLIN PARKER
On Passage To: PALMA
Sunrise: 7.37am   Sunset: 7.00pm
Suggested Dress This Evening: FORMAL

WELCOME
to
Queen Elizabeth 2

Introducing some departments on board...

At 9.15am in the Queens Room
"AN INTRODUCTION TO THE GOLDEN DOOR"

At 11.00am in the Grand Lounge
"STEINERS OF LONDON HAIRDRESSING AND BEAUTY DEMONSTRATION"

At 2.30pm in the Grand Lounge
"QE2 AND CUNARD"

At 2.45pm in the Theatre
"OUR UPCOMING PORT OF CALL PALMA"

to say things to friends they have made, children trying to look adult as they take in new experiences, the head waiter doing his rounds pointing out this and that to new waiters who are not yet fully absorbed into the ship's traditional way of doing things, and serving the special dishes to those who ordered them at lunch. An occasional bedroom steward passes through carrying a tray for someone eating in his or her room. A little later a German waiter who thinks they make the coffee too soon in the dining room slinks off down the corridor with an empty coffee jug and packet of coffee; he has 'a connection', presumably with a room stewardess, and returns beaming five minutes later from some distant pantry where they have brewed up illicitly. Then, while other passengers are told the dark rum truffles have run out for tonight, one who is known to have a special passion for them is provided with a small plateful artfully hidden away by his waiter out of view of others. And 'I've got you two lots of sauce, sir, because I know you like it.' There are hundreds of people in this restaurant, yet the attention is more individual than you mostly ever find on land.

Another great meal. But hurry! Time really has gone on, and the classical concert is about to begin in the lounge. Once ships could fairly be dismissed as a cultural desert: plenty for the body, little for the mind. Not today. Lecture programmes are ever more enterprising, and well-known pianists and other performers add their own dimension to your enjoyment of life at sea. If there is a grumble it is usually about the entertainment in the ballroom, but that is because it is hard to please everybody all the time and a surprising proportion of passengers are anxious not to miss what is on offer. The more discerning pick and choose and spend

much of their evenings in smaller lounges or bars, away from the crowd but often with live music; sometimes with a chance to request what is played. The ship's pianist has been on board for many years, as has his wife, a room stewardess; his memory is excellent and as regulars return he automatically slips into their favourite tune as naturally as he plays the music of the European nation you may be visiting.

About ninety people listen to the Chopin concert and then disperse. Time for a quick tour round the ship, sampling the many different moods and sounds of bars, lounges, ballroom, casino and stairways (let us see how far we have come today). Then out onto the deck, the moon and fairy lights vying to add the romantic touch as three or four couples, young and old, nestle into each other and enjoy the gently swaying motion as they whisper sweet nothings.

Finally to your cabin. It welcomes you as do few bedrooms on land. However you left it before dinner, now everything is in perfect place. The washbasin has been emptied for the second time in the day; the beds are turned down, a piece of chocolate and tomorrow's programme placed on the pillow (as well as a reminder if clocks have to be put forward or back); the curtains are drawn, the bedside lights on; and in the bathroom all evidence of your shower has been removed and there is a new supply of towels and face flannels. Those who enjoy a tub bath lie in it leisurely with the water gently matching the ship's motion. A few pages from the favourite book and then lights out. Most passengers will be soundly asleep before the last few leave the casino or bars, but then retiring and rising times are as varied at sea as anywhere.

The real highlights of cruising are visits to spots like this

23
THE BLACK SEA

ISTANBUL'S mystical skyline, European one side, Asian the other, all looking eastern yet where the western world had its intellectual centre for more than a thousand years, was fleetingly visible through the heavy mist of a heavy thunderstorm. The lightning, though clear, did not even momentarily brighten the sullen sky. Between the rumblings of the thunder echoing across the Bosphorus could be heard the horns of the impatient drivers of cars and trucks overtaking the ship on the parallel road; and then a voice from a mosque calling the devout once more to prayer. And all around were other ships both passenger and cargo, ferries small and large, jockeying for position on one of the world's busiest and narrowest seaways.

For the hundred or two photographers on deck (who had made sure to finish their sumptuous Scandinavian buffet in good time) it was frankly a disappointing passage. Only the skilled with better cameras would be able to show meaningful pictures back home, though those taken of groups of passengers by the ship's photographer were clear enough. But as an experience it was unforgettable, and another reminder perhaps that a cruise is to be savoured from every point of view and not just through the lens. Hardly a soul was not savouring it from the rainswept deck or the shelter of one of the public rooms.

Then out came the sun to add its dimension, rolling the mist into clouds between which the layers of domes with their minarets soaring skyward began to sparkle. Looking backward much of the detail of the three Istanbuls (Asian, and European old and new town, separated by the tributary dead-end sea known as the Golden Horn) could be picked out, sparking plans for how we would spend our time on shore a few days hence. Under the second of the two bridges linking Europe with Asia, passing a procession of cargo and naval ships, dropping the last of several pilots who for centuries have earned handsome livings by splitting the Bosphorus into short 'sections', and so into the Black Sea, Russia ahead.

Black Sea cruises are currently among the most popular, and it is not hard to understand why. Though package holidays in Bulgaria are becoming common, the cruises take you to places you would not otherwise visit, and take you by a route full of excitement. Whatever your ports of call, you have to pass through two narrow straits, the Dardanelles and Bosphorus, between which lies the Sea of Marmara, and so sail for many hours not only within sight of scenic land but past places of great historic fame.

While Istanbul is built on many hills and undoubtedly has one of the world's finest skylines (or rather several of them) seen from salt water, the Dardanelles are gentler, more to be enjoyed from the comfort of a deck-chair than with the alertness that the Bosphorus commands. Yet the war memorials remind that one of the world's bloodiest battles was fought here in 1915 as the Allies unsuccessfully fought to secure an ice-free route to Russia. The whole Gallipoli peninsula, on which tens of thousands died, is indeed a living war memorial, and on any cruise you will discover a small knot of those interested in military history recalling how the Turks were victorious even in retreat and how after the freak blizzard of November 1915 the Allies were forced to withdraw. Some of the shell scars are still visible at Anzac Cove which takes its name from the Australian and New Zealand Army Corps, which suffered especially heavy losses. Any passengers from Australia and New Zealand (where Anzac Day is a public holiday commemorating the nations' loss) will be particularly moved in the inevitable discussion about man's inhumanity to man. The passage through the narrow sea where so many were fruitlessly killed within living memory adds even greater poignancy to the visits to ancient sites (notably Troy) that the cruise also makes possible, while the continual traffic of today's oil tankers through the Dardanelles reminds how Jason and the Argonauts rowed with great difficulty against the treacherous currents as they sought the Golden Fleece.

BLACK SEA

There are many explanations as to how the Black Sea got its name. Some say the Turks feared the open, stormy expanse of water and gave it the epithet *karadeniz* meaning 'black'. Others believe the name was given because of its often very inhospitable, foggy weather. But the nicest story is that though the surface of the Black Sea is of relatively fresh water, the deeper it gets the greater the quantity of hydrogen solids – below 650ft (200m) it is stagnant, not permitting any animal or plant life. In former times the anchors of ships were made of bronze, and if anchors were dropped they turned black by reason of the chemical composition of the water. That is how the Ukrainians explain the name Black Sea.

Most cruises pause at Canakkale, where there is a majestic turn in the narrow sea and you can first spot the funnels of approaching oil tankers over the headland of a peninsula. Canakkale is for Troy, a drive of about half an hour along a modern road through rich horticultural countryside. If you go by taxi, the driver will probably take you up a side road to a hillside in a forest where several of the guns that fired upon the Allied ships are still well preserved – and you are bound to want to stop at a viewpoint to admire the strait with the Gallipoli peninsula and its war memorials opposite, your ship clearly in view.

And Troy is undoubtedly one of those places everyone hopes to visit one day and which the cruise makes easy. Most people are initially surprised to discover that it is in Asia, though everyone knows of how soldiers were taken within the city inside the wooden horse whose intriguing appearance the defenders could not resist – and expect to find the replica outside the crumbling walls today. If some ancient sites disappoint, and more become fuzzy in memory as too many are visited within a short time, Troy is certainly not guilty. You may have only a hazy idea of *Iliad* and the *Odyssey*, and quickly become confused as the guide tells you of the nine different Troys built one over the other from the Bronze Age to the Hellenistic and Roman city (Ilium Novum lasted until AD400 when Istanbul seems to have taken over the trade at the meeting point between Europe and Asia), but its magic is irresistible. Only rediscovered in 1871, and at first excavated primitively in a way that makes modern archaeologists shudder, it of course owes much of its romance to classical associations and its unique position; but is still worth examining in detail and marvelling how a theatre to seat 1,500 people came to be built all those years ago and to reappear for our enjoyment today.

Starting and finishing points and also some intermediate ports for Black Sea cruises vary, and many of them naturally belong to one of the other areas briefly described in these pages, but another common Turkish call is at Kuşadasi for Ephesus where a whole range of archaeological sites are within a short compass. The Arcadian Way, Library of Celsus, Temple of Serapis, Hadrian's Temple next to the Baths of Scolastica, the remains of a Byzantine gate at Selcuk, the Ayasoluk Fortress eight centuries older, the splendour lies in the variety from still majestic buildings to crumbled walls. But Kuşadasi itself has another appeal; it is one of Turkey's great bazaars largely geared to serving the taste of visitors from the West. The choice is great, the prices tempting, but be prepared for the really hard sell. 'May I ask a silly question?' is but one means of getting your attention in the street. Handmade carpets and rugs (from wool to fine cotton so demanding on the eyes of those who work it at home that only an hour's daily labour might be possible) are in great profusion along with leather goods and pottery (especially plates).

Shopping, of course, is also colourful (and with its fragrance as satisfying to the nose as the jewellery and carpets make it to the eye) in Istanbul. A visit to the great covered market is obligatory. Yet here it also tends to be overwhelming, and anyway there are so many attractions and counter attractions in the teeming city. While most places on a Black Sea cruise are adequately enjoyed in a day, Istanbul needs much longer. So if you are unlikely to return, you have to plan carefully. The Blue Mosque is for some people the most exciting religious building they will ever visit; the Seraglio Palace or Topkapi, where the sultans ruled over the Ottoman Empire, is a veritable city within a city with one of the world's greatest collections of treasures in buildings as sumptuous as their setting is breathtaking. And the guide-books will tell you of many more places not to be missed.

Yet ultimately most to be enjoyed is a sample of everyday Istanbul life especially in the old city (though you will be stunned by the best of the new) where you can melt into the crowds. Slow down and join the hordes crossing the bridge over the Golden Horn, watch how local business is transacted and enjoy the combination of street cries, the muezzin calling the faithful to prayer, the ship's whistles and the pigeons. A day in Istanbul may be only a tease, but it will be remembered for ever. Even if the ship does not actually stay overnight, it will be a long day, and much can be enjoyed from deck. If your stop is on the way back from the Black Sea and you are due to arrive at breakfast time, do not be blasé about already having been through the Bosphorus! It looks quite different as the sun rises and is worth forgoing a bit of sleep. And before you leave, the night skylines reveal yet another character.

No matter how exciting the approach and return, the pearls of a cruise to the Black Sea are its own ports well beyond the world with which most of us and our colleagues are familiar. The cruise allows you to personalise another piece of the atlas and put perspective on well-known names and episodes of history. A visit to Russia will of course be the highlight.

Yalta is given one of the highest rankings of any cruise port. Comforting yet challenging, it combines the expected with great surprises. It has a jewel of a setting, and until a road was built from Sebastopol at the beginning of the nineteenth century was only approachable by sea. It was Russia's answer to the French Riviera, and on a cruise calling at both the comparison seemed entirely fair. It has style. The magnificent buildings which once belonged to the aristocracy combine with the splendid hills and cliffs, the fine promenade and lush vegetation of the parks to make it unordinary by any standard. But it is very Russian: you cannot walk far from the pier without passing Lenin's statue and noting how different the shops and their contents (especially the lack of real window display) are from ours. You also quickly note that everything, including the pleasure boats for those staying in the resort, is at full capacity. You may have lunch in the largest hotel you will ever have

Above *The sun rises over the Bosphorus*

Far left *What future is there in the new Russia for buildings such as this one in Odessa. The two nearer pictures show the passage through the Bosphorus, with bridges linking Europe and Asia*

Above right *A whole new world awaits exploration as soon as we dock*

Right *Had a good day in Yalta?*

visited, yet though the construction cranes inevitably dot the hillside Yalta is still relatively small.

Most people will take the organised tour which shows you some of the fine buildings and probably takes you a few miles along the coast to Cape Ai-Todor where a fairy-tale castle is perched on the cliff, the Swallow's Nest, commanding a view of the entire bay. But in spring, just to be able to walk along the promenade crowded with Russians on holiday enjoying the relaxing atmosphere and the fine chestnuts and wisterias was reward enough. As our own day wore on and it became steadily warmer and busier, more and more people enjoying an ice cream, it was hard to remember that this was supposed to be another world. But every few minutes in the afternoon a screeching police car drove through the crowd on the promenade to clear a way for athletes' races.

Today's replica of the Wooden Horse stands outside the remains of Troy

Be sure to watch the fine cliffs toward Sebastopol when sailing-time comes. Sebastopol of Crimean War fame is itself an occasional cruise call. More commonly visited is Odessa, 'Pearl of the Black Sea', another fascinating though quite different place. Once a grand free port with rich cultural life, it still has its opera house of great opulence where maybe a special ballet performance will be given to passengers, nearly all clustered in the boxes wondering who had enjoyed what from those same positions in bygone times. But generally Odessa is more a workaday town than showpiece. Individual showpieces it certainly has, including the 192 Potemkin Steps leading up from the port with its burgeoning ferry traffic to the beginning of the city centre of tree-lined streets. It is a great place for those able to explore individually since everything from port and parks overlooking the fine harbour to museums, shops and outdoor cafés is easily within walking distance.

Odessa is cosmopolitan Russia, and provided you do not display your ship's hat or bag or carry a camera you will be just one of the crowd. Do not be deceived by the guide-book calling it subdued, especially if you set off early while the streets are yet quiet. It is most definitely a second-part-of-the-day city whose old-fashioned charm is put to the test by the crowds who walk and shop and queue for everything, including the trolleybuses and tramcars, in the warmth of the sun. Though the official sights and the guides are interesting enough, inevitably it is always the personal encounter (such as with delightful Russian toddlers) or shopping experience, that will linger in the memory.

You are always advised not to change too much currency and it is unfortunately true that even today there is not a lot you would wish to buy from Russian shops. So there were not quite enough roubles to purchase from a street artist a small painting of a typical Russian forest scene. After sign language showed there was no more money, he agreed to reduce the price but still autographed his creation. The final presentation of a few odd coins and a Russian hug completed the transaction of no great significance except it was between East and West and might be the kind of thing that will one day become universal. Odessa is in a grand bay and it is well worth being up early for the arrival and watching the maritime traffic in the sun of an evening departure.

The other most frequent Black Sea call is Varna on the Bulgarian Riviera. Many people comment that even today there is a greater cultural contrast between Russia and Bulgaria than between Bulgaria and the USA or UK. Certainly if you are on your way back from Yalta or Odessa, Varna will provide you with many details familiar at home. The road system feels western and the road signs are international, for example. Taxis are abundant and most drivers not only speak English but will be pleased to practise and tell you of their ambitions. You will learn that banks offer a higher rate of interest for those lodging foreign currency, that everyone aspires to own his own home and that moonlighting with second jobs is the way to get on. After he has taken you to the Golden Sands, a fine beach but very much an artificial resort catering for the cheaper end of the package-holiday business from western countries, especially Germany, and maybe to a village in the hills where everyone produces wine from their own backyard vines, the taxi-driver will probably leave you outside a shop while he selects a present – to cement your friendship and no doubt encourage a more generous tip. The champagne, alas, did not pop since it lacked a single bubble! But the best of the wine is excellent. The city is small but interesting, and apart from the advertised tourist attractions (nearly all within comfortable walking distance of the ship or at least of the bus that runs from the pier) it is well worth noting how the Bulgarians eat and shop. Flowers are everywhere, dress and costume bright, music almost certainly in the air along with the scent of spicy food.

24

ROUND BRITAIN

BRITAIN is such an obvious destination for tourists by air that many people dismiss the idea of cruising round it as curious. 'Round the British Isles?' they ask, and usually comment that the weather is not the kind normally associated with cruising. Perhaps Round Britain itineraries are not a natural choice for those starting cruising, but they have many attractions and will certainly remain popular. In a few days they show their passengers a range of places that even the keenest car traveller would take years to cover. Out-of-the-way islands are usually included along with mainland ports (some years it is possible to visit both London and Edinburgh) and there is a taste of Ireland. Even familiar places are put in an entirely new perspective approached by sea. The splendour of the coast can be enjoyed in a way not generally possible following the demise of most local steamer services. So the British are among the keenest passengers, enjoying renewed acquaintance with some places and filling in gaps in their knowledge of others.

You will certainly learn a great deal about the country, see parts of the coast that few locals do, and probably be offered some special privilege such as dining in a castle. It will all be relaxed, with no currency or immigration formalities except in Ireland. As to the weather, you chance your luck, inevitably, but in the knowledge that the trip takes place at the warmest time of year with long, light evenings. You might even bask in the sun off the north of Scotland well after dinner.

Southampton will be the usual starting (and or finishing) port. It is from here that a day trip to London is often possible, though the advice

THE GULF STREAM

The Gulf Stream is an ocean current that flows north-eastwards along the east coast of the United States to about latitude 40 degrees north, where its eastward extension becomes part of the North Atlantic Current. Its warm tropical waters originate in the north and south equatorial currents passing through the Gulf of Mexico and along the Antilles, and it influences the climate of the east coast of the States as well as that of the British Isles and the Atlantic coastal areas of Europe, its effect extending as far north as Spitzbergen. The current was discovered in 1513 by Ponce de Leon, and the rate of flow has been calculated at 60 million tons/sec, with a surface speed of more than 2 knots.

to anyone not making a single journey of a lifetime to Europe would be to visit London some other time and enjoy some of the attractions more local to Southampton. These include the New Forest, historic yet prosperous Southampton itself and a whole range of tourist attractions including Britain's largest motor museum. Do not write the day off if you happen to be in Southampton on transit. Hundreds of thousands of British take their own touring holidays in the area especially along the coast to the west, including Bournemouth, while an exploration of the Isle of Wight is also easy.

Visits are sometimes made to one of the Channel Islands, far closer to France than Britain, and the only part of the country invaded by the Germans in World War II. Guernsey and Jersey are full of vitality and individuality, though Jersey in particular has a heavy traffic density. A visit to the unspoilt and smaller island of Sark is especially to be savoured.

The naval port of Plymouth, commercial capital of Britain's South West, offers a variety of well-trodden options with the ship's passengers spreading themselves out over an unusually large geographical area including Dartmoor (England's last wilderness) and Cornwall with its quaint fishing villages and

Arthurian associations. But a ship's visit to the Isles of Scilly, lying off the south-west extremity of the mainland, adds perhaps a third to the local population and makes it desirable to get off the beaten track, perhaps to one of the smaller of the five semi-tropical inhabited islands. The unspoilt Scillies are always a real treat.

Dublin is naturally the most common and popular of Irish ports, a city of gorgeous Georgian architecture and ever-bustling streets. It comes to life and stays alive late; linger as long as possible in one of the classic bars where they put the world to rights each night. Dublin is one of those cities one would surely never tire of spending another day in. Great though the scenery is to the south, it somehow seems a waste not to make the best of the capital itself. To enjoy it to the full you must get away from organised parties and converse with the Irish (who will not be shy).

If there is another Irish port, it will probably be in the south west, such as Glengarriff in Bantry Bay. That will be your opportunity to appreciate something of the unique countryside and very special Irish rural way of life. It will be another place where you cannot hope to inbibe the local atmosphere if you tour en masse, and where just enjoying Ireland is

Above *The tender ride into Stornaway, Shetland.*
Right QE2 *off the Needles, Isle of Wight.* Below right
QE2 *pays a rare visit to Torbay in Devon, attracting
a flotilla of small craft and sightseers to the cliffs*
(Bill Whalley)

Left Sea Goddess I *comes to London. An aerial shot
organised by Cunard*

Leith Docks, Edinburgh (Colin Baxter Photography)

infinitely more important and enjoyable than ticking off the obvious tourist sights.

Douglas, capital of the semi-autonomous Isle of Man, is another likely call and another place where making your own arrangements might be desirable, if only because the island (a mini-kingdom of only 227sq miles (570km^2) but as diverse as you could imagine) is served by a unique range of public transport. There is a horse tram along the promenade, steam railway to Port Erin, ancient tram to Ramsey and mountain rack-railway up Snaefell where you can experience being in the centre of the British Isles by seeing England, Wales, Scotland and Ireland all at once.

Wales is visited rarely and then usually Holyhead on Anglesey, an island connected by bridge to the Welsh mainland. Anglesey, unlike most of Wales, is flat and offers little immediate attraction, so a trip to the mainland taking in Snowdonia, a mountainous National Park, or Caernarvon Castle would be a good way of using your time.

The most likely next stop if the itinerary is clockwise will be in the west of Scotland or on one of the Western Islands. It matters not which, for the whole area is one of the world's most lovely. Here you count yourself lucky not to be in a heat wave, for rain means that when it clears the views will be at their best. Often rainbows add the final dimension to scenes of natural splendour that seem exaggerated when recorded by artists or photographers. Whatever your precise routing, you will cruise within sight of land, and maybe in a channel between dramatic Scottish mountains – the scenery loved and made popular by Queen Victoria and still widely appreciated by the thousands of English who go to the Western Highlands and Islands for their holidays, though new short ferry crossings mean that ever less is readily seen from the water. Skye with its high mountains and colourful clan history is the most visited of the islands and is one of the Inner Hebrides. The Outer Hebrides are composed of a range of sparsely populated, dramatically shaped landmasses well out in the Atlantic but enjoying the Gulf Stream which (out of the wind on the mainland) allows semi-tropical gardens to thrive at an amazing latitude.

Quite unlike the Western Islands are Orkney and Shetland to the north of Scotland, on the way to nowhere and thus only visited for themselves. Yet they are part of the special northern way of life also met in Iceland and the Faeroes. Scandinavian influence lives on in both groups of islands and the Shetland Isles are actually nearer Norway than the British mainland. Both groups have a charming capital on their most inhabited island; both have their populations split between many islands and are renowned for their ancient monuments, productive farms – and fierce winds. There the resemblance stops, the Orkneys lying just off the Scottish mainland, the Shetland Isles much farther to the north and more developed in recent years as the result of the North Sea oil boom. However it is still easy to commune with nature well out of sight of anything man-made and both groups of islands are splendidly approached by sea. You should also enjoy the dramatic cliff scenery of the mainland of the north of Scotland and, as you turn south down the east coast, catch glimpses of North Sea oil platforms.

Edinburgh, whether visited itself or via another port, is again a city you cannot be in too often. While its welcome, like its grandeur, is obvious, it also has subtlety and innumerable details only discovered by those who look. It is especially a walker's city, including the Royal Mile leading down from the Castle.

So in just a few days you will experience something of the extraordinary diversity of culture and dialect, not to mention landscape, that is concentrated within so small a compass as the British Isles. This is a cruise for the active and enquiring, and one for which a little preparatory reading is especially useful. Where better to revise your British history? On-board lectures on the British ports are always especially well attended.

Sea Goddess I manoeuvres beside Tower Bridge, London

25

MEMORIES

STEP up the gangway onto any Cunard ship and immediately you relish participating in a long, rich tradition of fine, safe service at sea. Yesterday's glamour is an ingredient of today's panache. It exudes – from menu covers, pictures on the walls, ship models, conversations about the great days when the fastest you and the mail could cross the Atlantic was by Cunard, when service aboard the luxury cruise ships excelled any holiday available on land. The proud tradition continues with passengers talking about today's ships and itineraries, and about how the careers of the masters and officers have progressed in parallel with their own. They talk about this in almost the same breath as recording the milestones of Cunard's early history.

Anyone interested in the history should read this book's sister volume which officially celebrates the first century and a half of service. *Cunard: 150 Glorious Years* is by John Maxtone-Graham and lovingly records the line's evolution in words and pictures (including many fine colour reproductions of paintings and posters). Here we take a glimpse at some more recent moments in Cunard's colourful story.

Tradition is naturally especially strong on the *QE2*, the last of the superliners, direct descendant of Cunard's very first little sailing steamer (the familiar orange and black funnel already a feature) the Royal Mail Steamship *Britannia*. Even today a handful of the *QE2*'s staff come from the two great Queens that in the short post-World War II heyday of the transatlantic business maintained a weekly service, out of Southampton and New York each Thursday. To travel on one of the Queens, even in the lowest class, was really to be someone in the days well before package holidays. In first class just about every passenger stepped from *Who's Who*; socially and economically Britain and America had moved much closer together, but still five days' steaming time lay between them. It comes as a surprise to younger people to be told that Cunard's greatest year on the North Atlantic was as late as 1957. The first commercial jet went into service across the Atlantic a year later, and within a year of that the jets had captured half the traffic. Soon mere handfuls were patronising the Queens, especially first class in winter. The end was sudden rather than sad, the miracle that after the *Queen Mary* and *Queen Elizabeth* had been withdrawn the new Queen was completed and immediately spent much of her time plying to and from Southampton and New York. The *QE2* was the first ever super ship designed for a combination of 'ferry' work and cruising, and today she regularly sandwiches cruises out of both New York and Southampton between crossings.

The same salient points tend to be recited by all the past captains and officers who so enjoy telling of life on the North Atlantic during the postwar heyday. The majority of passengers were American businessmen and their families, but every voyage included a substantial contingent of politicians and stars; every captain reckoned to receive Christmas cards from some of the world's most famous names. Hardly ever was there a spare bed, especially on westbound voyages on which many of the lower-class cabins were invariably occupied by emigrants. Immediately after the war these included thousands of single ladies, the GI brides going to settle in America, even in the steerage-class restaurant enjoying meals with exotic foods undreamt of in austerity Britain. Conditions were very different from today's. Even captains could not take their wives before 1967 and then only for one trip a year. Unlike the *QE2*, the Queens did not make much of their fresh water and also used far more fuel; having to spend so much time in port taking on these items brought the assumption that it was sensible to mix cargo with passengers.

'If either of the Queens turned round in 24 hours, it was such an achievement that it made newspaper headlines', recalls the former *Queen Mary*'s captain, Treasure Jones, still fondly remembered by many passengers and making the occasional appearance at Cunard events. Along with many other Cunard notables, his early career was with the White Star line, merged with Cunard as a government condition in providing money for the completion of the *Queen Mary*.

Like most later captains, Treasure Jones recalls how painfully slow promotion was during the slump in the 1930s, and he is by no

---

THE TASTE OF LUXURY

Cunard's traditional, spectacular end-of-cruise dessert is Baked Alaska. The recipe originally devised by Oscar, famous chef of the Waldorf Hotel, to celebrate the acquisition of the Alaskan Territory by the United States from Russia in 1867.

means alone in having had his ship sunk by a U-boat during the war. 'At the end of dinner I found this message, just lying around in the chart room though it was urgent warning us of a U-boat. I asked how close we were to the danger point and just as I was being told we were right there, bang and we abandoned ship 300 miles (480km) west of Ireland.' That was a naval ship; throughout its modern history Cunard has seen its top officers go to and from naval service.

Treasure Jones's happiest days were perhaps those immediately after the war before *France* and *United States* were ready for their short transatlantic careers, when Cunard had the ocean virtually to itself. 'You met everyone important from round the world and even the Russian diplomats let their hair down.' And the two Queens were by no means the only Cunard ships on the ocean. While the main sailings to New York had been moved from Liverpool (Cunard's original headquarters) to Southampton in the 1930s, you could still sail from Liverpool to both New York and Canada in ships of substance, and indeed also from Southampton to Canada.

Having been senior first officer on the *Queen Elizabeth*, Treasure Jones was promoted to take charge of the *Media* on the Liverpool–New York run. 'It was mainly cargo but we had 350 passengers, all first class. It was very popular in summer, but a rough ride in winter. Once I was three days late; we had to hove to for 36 hours in 70 to 80ft (20 to 25m) waves. I remember there were only 40 passengers.' And once, when he was commanding the *Saxonia* from Southampton to Montreal he was joined by the *Carinthia* commanded by Jeff Maher on the Liverpool–Montreal run. 'It was April and I had risked taking the shorter route south of Newfoundland to save time. But as we got

The end of an era. Queen Mary's *farewell voyage with* HMS Hermes *manning a flight deck final salute on 31 October 1967* (Treasure Jones)

Queen Mary *first class or, as it was then called, 'cabin class', opulence: the starboard gallery, children's playroom, library and writing room*

Queen Mary *tourist class lounge, cabin class swimming pool and main cabin class shopping centre*

Cunard Cruise

List of Passengers

"*Berengaria*", New Year's Eve Cruise, 1932-33

closer to Newfoundland there was ice everywhere. I got a report from the crow's nest: ice without break. Jeff said "I'll follow you", which put me even more on the spot. We just pushed through the ice very slowly for two hours.'

Treasure Jones took the *Saxonia* to John Brown to be broken up, and before taking command of the *Queen Mary* enjoyed a spell on the *Caronia*, nicknamed the Green Goddess, a much-loved all-cruising ship, mainly for the American clientele:

I enjoyed cruising; you were more your own boss. But when they tried the *Queen Mary* on cruising it was because business had fallen off so badly on the ferry service. Going at 28½ knots across the Atlantic, we consumed 11,000 tons of fuel oil a day, and needed 1,200 passengers to break even. It was terrible when we sailed with half that number, and toward the end it was the first class that was empty. The top people had deserted us.

Even seeing the Queens on the horizon was a moment of emotion for onlookers. Imagine what it must have been like going on board for the officers moving up the promotion ladder. 'When I became chief officer on the *Queen Elizabeth* I looked along the twenty-six lifeboats and at the menus of exotic foods and was overcome,' says Donald Maclean. 'I spent all my money on a new uniform.' He also served on the Canadian ships, 'slow and sitting targets for the U-boats', and was stunned by the *Elizabeth*'s 'amazing 29, sometimes even 30 knots'. Further promotion of course meant taking his first command – back to a slower, much smaller ship, the *Media*, 14,000 tons, 18 knots, carrying mainly the poorer relatives of GI marriages on a Liverpool–Glasgow–New York service. 'No swimming pool, the only entertainment films, but steerage wasn't bad despite very cheap fares. They had the full

A mini Who's Who!

Cunard menu. You could call it a glorified ferry with Cunard trimmings especially in the dining room.'

Then he went as staff captain to the *Queen Mary*: 'My whole social life opened up like a flower. I was in charge of all social arrangements, safety – we refilled the barrels in the lifeboats with fresh water every day.' He recalls many famous passengers such as John Masefield, the poet laureate especially famous for his sea poems, who was horribly seasick four days in a row and missed all his invitations to come to tea with the officers. Then, 'one sunny day I went in command of the *Queen Elizabeth*; I remember my thrill of a lifetime walking up and down my mighty ship.' Finally he commanded the *QE2* for 2½ years. Like all the former chiefs, he daily relives the pleasures of cruising as well as the perils and remembers the friends he made with famous and interesting people.

Another former *QE2* captain, Peter Jackson, has especial fond memories of the all-cruise *Caronia* and its world cruise with a large number of regular passengers treating it as a floating club: he met his wife, a nursing sister in the ship's hospital! He also recalls the slow promotion both in the thirties and after the mid-fifties when Cunard was rapidly selling ships off. 'I had the same job as junior first navigator for twelve years and was held in contempt by those on other lines who had shot ahead.' Like most former captains, he sings Trafalgar House's praise:

> Life on the old Queens was out of this world. It was perfection. The crews knew their jobs and went about doing them with enthusiasm. They were utterly dedicated. Here truly was life. But the slow turn-rounds, the mixture of passengers and cargo, the twenty-seven boilers of the *Queen Mary*, it obviously couldn't last. The company couldn't see beyond the Queens. Then we cut back to three ships, and it has taken Trafalgar House to bring new enthusiasm.

(1939 - 1965)

GALA FAREWELL BALL

Monday, 8th November, 1965

Featuring the artistry of

BOB BURGESS and DOREEN FREEMAN

ROBERT CANNON and VIVIEN MILAN

with

Mike Adams and the Mauretania Orchestras

playing Dance Tunes popular from 1939 to 1965

Auld Lang Syne

Should Auld acquaintance be forgot
And never brought to mind,
Should Auld acquaintance be forgot
And Days of Auld Lang Syne.
For Auld Lang Syne, my dear,
For Auld Lang Syne,
We'll tak' a cup o' kindness yet,
For the days of Auld Lang Syne.

While post-war Britain suffered austerity, Cunard continued to serve the finest meals

Peter Jackson was in command of the *QE2* for seven years including the historic voyage carrying 4,000 highly trained troops to the Falkland Islands – 'a one-way ticket'. It brought back memories of the war years – of 1940, the centenary year that was never celebrated when the new *Queen Elizabeth* was secretly spirited away to New York, and of the famous wartime service across the Atlantic when both Queens went to and fro, carrying troops to Europe, wounded and prisoners of war back to America. At one time there were eight sittings of two meals a day for the Americans on the *Queen Mary*, and such vast numbers of troops that 15,000 were crowded into a space designed for 2,000 passengers. The Queens (the *Elizabeth* was not to make her proper maiden voyage until 1946 when the two-Queen Atlantic service planned in the late 1920s at last began) of course avoided the U-boats. Unlike the smaller ships on the Canadian run,

they could greatly outpace them anyway, and also constantly changed directions and were without lights after dark. So it was again all those years later in 1982 when Peter Jackson dashed by a mysterious zigzag route into the South Atlantic. As the ultimate target, the *QE2* was not allowed closer to the Falklands than South Georgia, 800 miles (1,300km) off, but military experts believe the injection of fighting power and the evacuation of survivors from the several naval ships that were sunk, was a vital turning point in the war. All this and much more Peter Jackson tells in the regular lectures he gives around Britain.

Yet another former *QE2* captain, Doug Ridley, only recently retired, emphasises just how great the revolution has been.

Where it used to take days to turn a ship in port, we now do it in hours. And if you could not clean the steam boilers in port, you had to drop one of them to do it at sea, meaning reduced speed. The reason the *QE2*'s schedules have become more adventurous is

that she's now a diesel ship, and though top speed may not be much different she's able to do it all the time. For example, two days at sea, three nights from Southampton, used to take us no further than Malaga. Now we can get to Palma de Mallorca or Ibiza. So you can do an interesting Mediterranean itinerary in eight days, and go to Norway for six.

Doug Ridley should know, since in 'retirement' he sits beside his fax machine, engaged in planning Cunard's future itineraries. He recalls milestones like the first fly-cruise in 1967, and 'getting tied up with Concorde' in 1973. But there are grim earlier memories of very slow promotion. In 1952 he was number 179 on Cunard's seniority list; in 1964 still only 120. But after the split between the cargo and passenger fleets, he was in the 'lucky' third staying with passengers. Having eaten a very lonely Christmas dinner 'all by myself looking up at the minstrels' gallery' aboard *Aquitania* in 1949 while they were deciding her fate, and taking her to the breakers in January 1950, it then fell to him to go to the Clyde yard for the *QE2* when she was brand new in 1968.

But excitement quickly turned to disappointment. Firstly the world's last superliner's turbines failed on trial; it was almost as though Britain itself was on trial as the world watched whether the problem would be solved. It was, of course. But after a few busy voyages the *QE2* herself was poorly patronised, often with only 200 passengers first class, on the transatlantic crossings that occupied two-thirds of her year. It was only new management and the ascendancy of the marketing men that saved the day – the marketing people who now fill seven ships instead of the three the fleet had been reduced to. As one of them said:

'Yes, we all get very nostalgic about the more leisurely days when there was time to make friends with the world's most famous people, but the ultimate satisfaction has to be giving people what they want at prices they can afford, and that means full ships.'

26

QUESTIONS ANSWERED

ANY doubts you may have about cruising are probably countered in the answers to one or more of these oft-asked questions:

I'm a bad sailor. How could cruising possibly be for me?

Most people have felt seasick at some time, if only in their youth. When and why did it affect you? The probability is that it was a long time ago, on a small boat or ship in pretty unpleasant conditions such as in a crowded public place smelling of greasy food after you had eaten a pretty greasy meal yourself.

Most cruise liners and ferries are as different from each other as chalk and cheese. Many cruisegoers who have never suffered from any symptom of seasickness on a ship of 20,000 tons or more would still be wary of crossing the English Channel on a small ferry in rough weather. Not only are most cruise liners large and stabilised, but most itineraries are in calm summer seas.

However, it would be wrong to deny that rough weather can occur at almost any time throughout the world, and that some people on cruises are inconvenienced, sometimes seriously. What needs to be emphasised is that many fewer people are actually affected by illness than talk about the *fear* of it. And if one asks most of those who were temporarily laid low whether they would now wish to go on another cruise, the answer is an almost universal affirmative. One reason: 'It's quite different when you can lie down in your own private luxury and ask for things to be brought to you.'

Injections are available at the doctor's surgery on board for those who want to avoid seasickness. They work efficiently but may make you feel sleepy. There are other remedies, some of them new, and talking to your doctor at home would be useful.

There are so many places to visit that surely you cannot get to know anywhere properly?

Of course one or two days in a city or district will not tell you all there is to learn about it. Nobody, for example, would suggest you could exhaust New York if your ship were in port there for ten hours. But with sensible use of your time and perhaps taking advantage of the tours laid on for passengers, you get to experience each city and community far more than you might expect. Remember that you do not have to clear customs or immigration, but as soon as the formalities have been completed for the ship as a whole (probably while you are still having breakfast) you are free to walk off and do what you want. Places of interest usually begin close to the dock; certainly you do not have the equivalent of a taxi journey in from the airport, meaning you save time in both directions. Indeed often the ship is so central to the area you want to explore that it is as quick to return for lunch as to eat out.

Cruises are arranged to give you the maximum of prime time at the most attractive destinations. Ask those who have spent a day and a half in Leningrad if it were not too short to be useful, and you would receive very emphatic replies about all that had been achieved. But of course if you wanted to explore everything in Leningrad and nothing else on a holiday, you would not pick a cruise. And sometimes people who have worked hard at exploring a different place every day for a week feel they need a break, and welcome a day at sea or, if the ship is in port, take only a stroll away from it. Even then there is usually much to be seen and learnt from taking an intelligent interest from the deck.

One other point: while you will have ample time for a thorough sampling of each port and its lifestyle, there is a danger of one or two of them blurring in the memory months after the cruise. Remember to keep a record of where photographs were taken and perhaps write yourself a few notes. The last few pages of this book are for your personalised cruise log: complete each page as soon as you return home.

CORAL

The scientific term for coral is madreporaria, and there are approximately 2,500 species. Most of them are true stony corals, divided into various groups such as the colonial corals, to which most species belong, and the solitary corals. The colonial reef-building corals are found mainly in warm seas like the South Pacific and the Indian Ocean. They are protected by a substantial, limy skeleton secreted by the epidermis, so that the skeleton almost completely surrounds the polyp. Reef-building corals live only to a depth of about 90ft (27m), the reef-colony in good conditions growing some 1in (25mm) a year. Solitary corals, however, can live in depths up to 26,000ft (8,000m) and some are found in cold waters as well.

Isn't all that food just too much?

In these exact words, but also in a thousand-and-one variations, this question obviously seems to worry many people. In truth, some people give up cruising simply because they eat too much. But why?

You cannot get the best from a cruise unless you have the attitude of mind that you will be selective and not do (and eat) everything simply because it is there. Compare the dining room on board with some of your favourite restaurants on shore and the big difference is that you can have as much as you like on the ship without further charge, while on land you have to pay separately for each course you order. But does that mean you have to eat nine courses?

Most people will undoubtedly eat well and leave the ship having gained some weight, but there is moderation in everything. These days many who occupy the more luxurious cabins on, say the *QE2*, are by nature light eaters. Nobody will force you to have more than you want. Diets and eating habits vary so sharply that frankly no request will surprise the seasoned waiter. Nowhere in the world are you actually freer to do exactly what you want (or your doctor ordered) with less fuss.

And the facilities for exercising and keeping a check on your physical condition are also better than even the most luxurious hotels provide.

Does it matter that I don't have formal clothes?

Today, not in the least. Once formal attire was universal at least among first-class passengers on appropriate nights, and any man in a lounge suit would have looked out of place, though even then there were some who were brave enough to do just what *suited* them best. Today everything is very much a matter of individuality, save that on many ships you cannot go into public rooms in a bathing costume and men are expected to wear a tie (on some ships on formal nights also a jacket).

Will I meet interesting people?

Of course it depends on who you think are interesting, and where you are cruising. As mentioned earlier, there is a higher intellectual element on cruises exploring seas such as the Mediterranean and Baltic than on those to the Caribbean. Pick your cruising ground and your ship carefully. If you want one long organised party, there are ships that will happily provide it, though they are not run by Cunard. If (and as a reader of this book that seems more likely) you want to meet people you might have something in common with culturally, not only pick the right ships and cruises but attend the right events on them.

It has to be admitted that on most cruises there are plenty of bores: those who have done it all before, who tell you how they are getting more out of the system than you, and who are only interested in the sound of their own voices between eating and drinking. Loud-mouthed though some of them may be, they will never actually be the majority and, if you are looking to make new friends, then certainly other people like you are also doing so.

You meet all sorts. The skill is in being selective, in letting go those who don't seem to share your values and in keeping tabs on anyone who seems genuinely interesting. That last point is more important than it seems since even on a medium-sized ship it might be days before you came face to face with the same couple again. So make a date for a pre-dinner drink.

This much can be said sincerely: regular cruisegoers make nearly all their friends on board, and frequently international friendships develop resulting in visits to each others' homes and even vacation swaps of homes. Your Christmas card list will swell faster than if you spent ten times as long in planes.

I have a medical condition. Is it fair to go on a cruise?

There is hardly anywhere in the world you will be better looked after (a fully equipped hospital only yards away) than on a luxury ship. Of course you do not go on a ship to give birth to a child or with some acute condition likely to require a major operation. But most older people have less than 100 per cent health, and many who would not feel comfortable taking ambitious vacations on land opt for cruising simply because of the level of care on board. And that is the business the cruise lines are in. Many of their best customers are in their eighties or even nineties.

What happens if someone dies at sea?

There are many ways to go. Relatives and friends who have had a dear one die at sea are full of praise for the way the captain managed the situation. Usually there will be the alternatives of burial at sea or of freezing the body for later funeral back home. There is of course always a clergyman on board.

So cruising really is for older people?

Yes, but by no means exclusively. Many more younger people are going on cruises these days, though you will not find them on a three-month world cruise because they have neither the time nor the money. Time and money are what most people have more of in retirement, but younger people will never feel out of place. Family parties with young children are welcome everywhere. All kinds of facilities are provided for kids. It is much safer letting them go off and do their own thing on a ship (organised or not) than at most places on land. There are always special attractions for children so parents usually enjoy rather more peace.

I'm a widow and hate taking vacations by myself. Would I really feel comfortable on a cruise?

Almost certainly more comfortable than anywhere on land. For a start, ships are safe and it is usual for them to carry a good sprinkling of single people of both sexes and all ages. So you will not feel intimidated or a nuisance, or shunted to one side as tends to happen even in the best hotels. There is usually a special get-together of passengers travelling by themselves, but even if you would feel too self-conscious to attend that, you will find it easy to join what is going on and make friends. A cruise ship is *the* place in the world where a lone, attractive woman will be least likely to be sexually or otherwise harassed. But of course romances do often begin on ships . . .

What if I just don't like it?

The advice has already been given to allow yourself a fair trial. Do not be lured into a last-minute bargain of an unpopular sector or (if you want to know what quality cruising is really like) one of those short party cruises when many passengers come just to see what they can get out of it. Take a two-week cruise going to places that you have always wanted to visit.

Experience shows that the vast majority of newcomers quickly come to believe they have made the right decision – and what a pity it is not going to last longer. But only experience can tell you whether, for example, you are going to develop a pathological hatred of the sea!

Isn't tipping a pressure?

If you let it be, and a few passengers do seem obsessed with it. Up-to-date guidance is nearly always given in printed form on board. But there is really no more to it than tipping appropriately in a restaurant, and while many of us dislike the whole business of gratuities we do not hear of people avoiding going to restaurants for this reason. Your tips at the end of your first major cruise will naturally be the largest you will ever have given, but it is only relative and on most holidays on land you will have paid out far larger sums on innumerable extras.

Are things different on a world cruise?

The pace is naturally more leisurely, with successions of days at sea and a predominance of formal evenings. More passengers tend to pursue exercise, competitions and hobbies: there is often, for example, an active craft circle and the creations of its members are displayed in an exhibition of work completed on board. During a three-month cruise the visiting entertainers will change regularly. Fresh produce will be served in abundance for several days after each main port but will become scarcer in the later stages of long voyages. Because of the leisurely atmosphere and the smaller number of passengers, service will be at its best and passengers are addressed by name.

I hate being shut up. Is there really as much room as the brochures suggest?

Cruise ships are mini-towns with their equivalent of parks and other recreational facilities. Space per passenger varies according to the quality (and price) of the product, but for a start forget everything you have ever thought about packed ferry boats and other forms of public transport. Even the lowest-quality cruise ships offer space in a quite different league. It is hard to contemplate anyone being claustrophobic on a quality ship. But storms do sometimes last several consecutive days, especially in the Atlantic, and if you go in say December and snow is swirling outside you will naturally be confined indoors – still with a swimming pool, though a smaller one, and acres of public space.

Is it right that the disabled are welcomed?

These days Cunard and other cruise lines welcome disabled passengers, and you will see them on most voyages. It obviously depends on the degree of disablement, but moving round in a wheel chair is no problem. You will however need to make enquiries early to get the most suitable cabin.

On a limited budget would you advise taking a cheaper, inside cabin on a luxury ship or going by a cheaper ship?

Ask yourself what really matters. To many a porthole giving them their personal glimpse of the sea, and daylight, is top priority; others spend so little time in their cabin that it does not matter. The type of itinerary you take will make some difference. In the Caribbean, for example, you will be ashore most of most days, and many who would require a better cabin for series of days at sea are happy enough in the smaller and much cheaper cabins of *Cunard Countess.*

Do I need a travel agent?

Far more complaints are aired about travel agents than about all the services Cunard provides. That does not mean you do not need an agent, but does suggest you should understand some of the important issues yourself (this book helps!) and be careful in your selection. Many small agents, in Britain and the USA, handle such little cruise business that they cannot hope to be expert. There are specialist agencies, mainly dealing by telephone and mail order, and surprisingly good local ones who have really studied the cruise business. You can of course reserve direct with Cunard, but professionals would say you should have an agent to look after your interests in the same way that it is wise to buy your household insurance through a broker who will fight the insurance company for you should there be a claim. But certainly do not expect the travel agent to know everything, especially about bargains. If you are free to take heavily discounted cruises at short notice, check newspapers' travel pages and get on the right mailing lists. The subject is also touched upon in the chapter on Ships and Itineraries.

SHIP _____   DATES _____   CABIN NUMBER _____

FROM _____   TO _____   TABLE NUMBER _____

PORT

NOTES _____

SHIP _____   DATES _____   CABIN NUMBER _____

FROM _____   TO _____   TABLE NUMBER _____

PORT

NOTES _____

SHIP _____   DATES _____   CABIN NUMBER _____

FROM _____   TO _____   TABLE NUMBER _____

PORT

NOTES _____

SHIP _____   DATES _____   CABIN NUMBER _____

FROM _____   TO _____   TABLE NUMBER _____

PORT

NOTES _____

SHIP _____   DATES _____   CABIN NUMBER _____

FROM _____   TO _____   TABLE NUMBER _____

PORT

NOTES _____

SHIP _____   DATES _____   CABIN NUMBER _____

FROM _____   TO _____   TABLE NUMBER _____

PORT

NOTES _____

SHIP _____   DATES _____   CABIN NUMBER _____

FROM _____   TO _____   TABLE NUMBER _____

PORT

NOTES _____

SHIP _____   DATES _____   CABIN NUMBER _____

FROM _____   TO _____   TABLE NUMBER _____

PORT

NOTES

ACKNOWLEDGEMENTS

THE experience and comments of literally thousands of travellers have helped shape the views expressed in this book; thank you to everyone who has helped. Some may recognise themselves! Many of Cunard's staff, afloat and on shore, have been especially helpful. Eric Flounders, the public relations officer in London, has in particular answered a battery of questions and sharpened my perceptions. Formal thanks are also due to Cunard for providing facilities and allowing me to use a small amount of their copyright material. The natural history chapter comes from Tony Soper's *Oceans of Birds*. I have also quoted briefly from the *Berlitz* series of handbooks provided for cruise passengers, and from a book on Greece by Brian Dicks, now out of print. My wife Georgette and I have enjoyed the research together, and she has also helped in shaping the views and in the selection of facts presented here. Finally, my sub-editor, Norah Luxton, who has spent much of a lifetime working for my company, David & Charles, and who decided to retire just as this manuscript was taking shape, kindly agreed to open up her desk once more to help toward a smooth production for Cunard's 150th birthday celebrations.

D StJ T

INDEX

Page references in *italic* denote illustrations

Paul Hollywood's
PIES &
PUDS

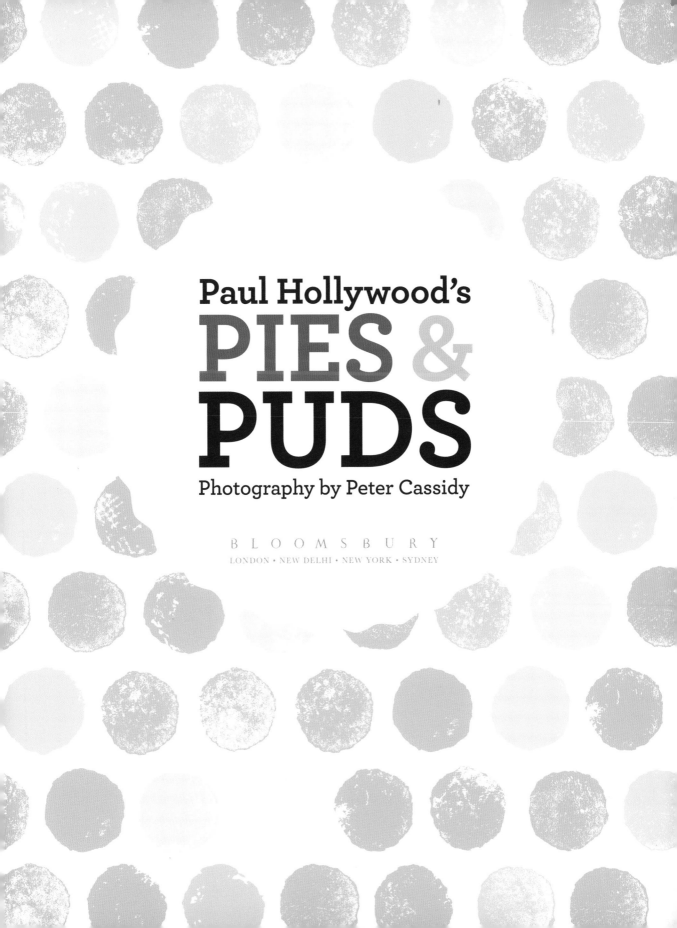

Paul Hollywood's
PIES &
PUDS

Photography by Peter Cassidy

BLOOMSBURY
LONDON · NEW DELHI · NEW YORK · SYDNEY

Note

My baking times in the recipes are for conventional ovens. If you are using
a fan-assisted oven, you will need to lower the oven setting by around 10–15°C.
Ovens vary, so use an oven thermometer to verify the temperature and check
your pie or pudding towards the end of the suggested cooking time.

Introduction

We have a strong culinary tradition in this country, much of it based around the kind of food that fuelled working people: farmers, shepherds, fishermen, labourers, factory workers and so on. Their food may have been frugal and simple but, skilfully made with fresh local ingredients, it could be very good: hearty, delicious and sustaining.

With this book I want to rekindle our affection for that kind of straightforward food, the fare that previous generations thrived on. It's all well and good being able to make a tricky sauce or whip up an elaborate gâteau – those are wonderful culinary skills to have – but there's something about a deep golden home-baked pie or simple steamed pud that warms the cockles of your heart like nothing else. So what you'll find in these pages are simple recipes – unpretentious and comforting – often honed by generations of cooks from particular regions of the country.

I've focused on pies and puddings because I feel these dishes really sum up the strengths of our culinary culture – and because many of my all-time favourite dishes fall into this bracket. Man cannot live by bread alone – not even if the man is me – and a pie can so often give you pretty much an entire meal in a dish.

Not all of these recipes are old-fashioned classics. Some take their inspiration from other cultures – like my spicy chicken and chorizo empanadas and the lovely spinach, feta and pine nut parcels. And some of the sweet options, such as my dark, rich chocolate and prune tart, and irresistible salted caramel and coffee éclairs, are more contemporary. But every recipe is true to the spirit of good, honest, home cooking and at the heart of the book are iconic British dishes such as Yorkshire curd tart, Cumberland rum nicky and my particular take on shepherd's pie.

You'll see that many of the recipes have their roots in the north of England. That's because I'm a northern lad and it's northern cooking that springs to mind when I think of pies and puddings. They remind me of my own youth, growing up in the Wirral. We eat lots of pastry up north and we're very good at making it!

My mum was a great pastry-maker. I remember her one-and-only pie plate, which she would use for all kinds of sweet and savoury pies, every one decorated beautifully with pastry trimmings and baked to a lovely golden brown. As a boy, I would pick sour apples from the tree in our garden, or gather blackberries from round about, and they would all end up in one of Mum's pies. They were the best I've ever eaten: really simple, but so good. She was great at puddings too. The thought of a hot treacle sponge or a bread and butter pudding, waiting for me at dinnertime, got me through many a school day.

Hand-raised pork pies, made with crunchy, hot water crust pastry that broke irresistibly when bitten into, were the stuff of my childhood. And every bakery and chippie where I grew up sold pies and pasties: steak and kidney with a puff pastry top, cheese and potato pie, Cornish pasties with chips – all served drenched with gravy. I was shocked when I moved down south to discover nothing had any sauce!

The dishes in this book do not require great skill or years of baking expertise. Many are the kind of thing our mothers and grandmothers learnt how to cook while they were growing up, and would then be able to turn out for their own families. They may well have made their pastry without even weighing the ingredients, and adapted the filling according to what was cheap and to hand, to create something welcoming and warming out of very little.

Our increasing desire for quick-fix fast food is partly to blame for the waning of this tradition. But I've always believed that time taken cooking a good meal for people you care about is time well spent. There is nothing more therapeutic than putting together a fine suet pudding, nothing more satisfying than the smell of a golden crusted apple pie baking in your oven. And actually, a lot of the time needed to produce a good pie or pudding is not hands-on work time – it's in the chilling of the pastry, the simmering of the stew, or the final baking.

We have also been conditioned to see pastry and sweet puds as unhealthy. But I'd take issue with that. They may not be low in fat, but I would rather eat a fruit-filled pie, topped with pastry made of nothing more than good flour, butter and eggs, than some reduced-calorie, ready-made dessert, full of colouring, corn syrup and preservatives. I'm not suggesting we should all be eating puddings and pasties every night, as people used to do when hard physical labour and huge appetites were the norm, but food like this is a precious part of our culinary heritage and I want to make sure we keep celebrating that.

There are recipes here that will take you all through the year, but you'll find the balance tipped a touch more towards cold weather cooking. For me, pies and puddings are dishes for the autumn and winter, when we all need that little bit of extra central heating. Rain, frost and wind give you the excuse, if you need one, to really ladle on the gravy and be lavish with the custard. Those comforting extras are all part of the experience for me. A pie brimming with savoury juices or a pudding sitting in a moat of hot custard might not be the most glamorous or elegant of dishes, but they are among the most delicious I know. Looks and stylish presentation are not the most important things with these recipes; what matters more is the way they make you feel. This is food that comes from the heart.

Equipment

●●●

It's well worth investing in good-quality baking equipment. You don't need to buy a whole range of cake tins, tart tins and pudding moulds in different sizes – just stock up on a selection of well-made essential items of kit and cooking becomes a breeze, and a pleasure.

Mixers and electric whisks

I'm a great one for doing things by hand but I'd have to say that a mixer or electric whisk can be very useful when making puddings. This is particularly true if you need to beat eggs into a thick moussey state for a light sponge, or if you are whipping egg whites for a meringue. Doing either of these by hand requires a lot of elbow grease! You don't have to splash out too much: you can get a decent hand-held electric whisk for around £20.

Tart tins and baking trays

When baking tarts or double-crust pies (i.e. dishes with a pastry base) you will get a crisper result if you use a metal tin rather than a ceramic dish. To decrease the chance of a soggy bottom even further, it's a good idea to put the tart tin on a preheated baking tray in the oven, which transfers heat directly to the base of the pastry. In all cases, use the best quality metal tins and trays that you can afford: cheap ones are likely to bend and buckle in the oven and can seriously affect your results. The size of tart tins given in the recipes is the diameter or dimensions of the base.

Pie dishes and pudding basins

For pies that have only a pastry top, you can use a ceramic or heatproof glass dish as you don't need to worry about crisping up a pastry base. Choose pie dishes that have a good rim around the edge – at least 2cm wide – so you can anchor the pastry firmly to it.

When steaming puddings, I use ceramic or heatproof glass basins. I also use miniature metal pudding basins and dariole moulds for baking or steaming individual puddings.

Ceramic ramekins and heatproof glass dishes are ideal for baking small custards as they allow the delicate mixture to cook gently.

Cake tins and loaf tins

Again, you need good-quality metal cake tins for the best results. Springform tins are invaluable for turning cakes out easily and stout metal loaf tins are ideal for both cakes and raised pies. I am not a fan of flexible silicone cake moulds: they tend not to hold their shape well, they're not always completely non-stick and they do not conduct heat efficiently.

Rolling pin

I favour a wooden or solid plastic rolling pin. Don't use one with knobs at the end as this shortens the length of the pin, which is unhelpful if you're rolling out a large piece of pastry. I'd go for a not-too-heavy pin which allows you to control the amount of pressure you apply. And of course, make sure your rolling pin is smooth, with no nicks or dents that will transfer to your pastry.

Pie funnel

I often use one of these when I'm making a pie. Placed in the middle of the dish before spooning in the filling and covering with pastry, it supports the pie lid and allows steam to escape, helping to prevent the pastry from becoming soggy.

Knives and cutters

There are a few knives I wouldn't be without: a heavy, sharp cook's knife is ideal for chopping meat and veg for pie fillings; a small, sharp, pointed knife is invaluable for tasks such as trimming the edges off pastry after lining a tin or covering a pie; and a palette knife with a long rounded blade is useful for transferring biscuits and small pies to cooling racks. Sets of plain and fluted cutters are useful for cutting pastry for individual pies and a pastry lattice cutter (available from cookshops) makes light work of creating a lattice pie topping.

Pastry brushes

A pastry brush is a useful tool for glazing pastry and brushing the edges of a pie with water before sealing. I favour the old-fashioned bristle brushes, but modern silicone brushes work well and won't ever shed their bristles.

Baking beans

You can use any type of uncooked, dried beans or rice to line an uncooked pastry case (see page 42), but specially made ceramic beans are nicely heavy and particularly easy to use.

Baking parchment or silicone paper

These are both non-stick, making them ideal for lining tins and baking trays or pastry cases before blind baking. Greaseproof paper is not the same – it does stick, unless you grease it well first.

Cooling rack

This is quite an important piece of equipment because it allows air to circulate underneath a tart, cake or pie as it cools. This not only speeds up the cooling, it also helps to avoid a soggy base.

Ingredients

Many pies and puddings rely on inexpensive, everyday ingredients that you have to hand in your storecupboard or fridge – ready to bring out when the baking urge strikes! My advice is always to buy the best quality you can find.

Flour

It's worth spending a little extra on flour – which is not an expensive item, in any case. In pastries and puddings, it's really the key ingredient so why scrimp on it? There are lots of good-quality flours on the market now, so try out a few different brands to see which you like best.

Most of the flour you'll need for the pastries in this book is plain white flour. This has a protein level between 9 and 11%, which makes it perfect for tender pastry, light sponges and thickened sauces. As with all flours, the quantity of water that plain flour will absorb varies with the brand. So you might find you need to add more or less water to a pastry depending on the brand of flour.

Sometimes I use self-raising flour, which is simply plain flour with raising agents already added. You can convert plain flour to self-raising by stirring in baking powder – allowing about 4 tsp baking powder to 225g flour.

I also use a measure of strong white bread flour in some pastries. Bread flour has a protein level above 12%. This higher level of gluten gives a firmer texture to a dough, which is useful for a robust pastry such as hot water crust, or for pastries that need to hold a high, risen shape such as puff or choux.

Salt

Salt is important in a savoury pastry to stop it tasting dull and bland – a good pinch is all you need for a standard 500g batch. Use a fine-grained table salt that can be easily incorporated into the mix.

Butter

Butter is crucial for flavour in many pastries and puddings, so use the best you can find. I always use an unsalted Normandy butter. As well as a fine flavour, this has a higher melting point than many unsalted butters so it stays firmer for longer as the pastry bakes, and produces a less greasy pastry.

Lard

Lard is rendered down, clarified pork fat. It has a unique, rich flavour and because it is a very pure fat, it forms an impermeable layer in pastry, stopping the pastry from absorbing liquid and thereby keeping it crisp. If you include lard in a shortcrust, you'll get a particularly short, tender and crumbly result, and in a hot water crust pastry, lard gives an incomparable sheen. I like to use a mix of lard and butter – butter for flavour and lard because it lends a unique texture.

Suet

Suet is the fat from around an animal's kidneys. It is very hard and has a high melting point, which gives a unique lightness to pastry. In days gone by, home cooks would buy it from their butcher and chop or grate it by hand. These days, commercially prepared suet is melted down then extruded into little pellets, which are lightly dusted with wheat flour to stop them sticking together. Suet is very easy to use: you can simply stir it straight into your flour, although I often rub it in a little with my fingertips to amalgamate it really well. I usually go for traditional beef suet but, if you prefer, you can use vegetable suet. It will still make good pastry, with a slightly milder flavour and lighter texture.

Sugar

I use lots of different sugars in my baking. Caster sugar is the one I turn to most often: this has fine grains that dissolve easily into a cake mix or a meringue, giving a good, light result. You can use either pure white or golden caster sugar. For sprinkling on the top of sweet pies, I like granulated sugar, which has slightly coarser grains and so gives a lovely crunchy finish.

Soft brown and muscovado sugars are favourite ingredients for puddings and cakes. These contain more of the natural molasses from the sugar cane, which means they have lots of treacly flavour – the darker the sugar, the deeper the flavour.

Icing sugar is very useful for sweetening a pastry dough because it has a similar consistency to the flour and disperses into the mix imperceptibly. You can also use it in a cake or pudding batter if you've run out of caster.

Eggs

These give a rich flavour and colour to pastry, both when used within the mix and when brushed on top as a glaze. The darker and more golden the colour of the yolk, the richer the colour you'll get on your pastry. Of course, eggs are crucial in puddings too: when beaten, they trap air and make for a light mixture, and they are also essential for baked custards, sweet and savoury, where you need the ingredients to set. I use free-range eggs. Generally speaking, the fresher the egg the better – although for meringue, it's helpful to use egg whites that aren't super-fresh, as they are more stable.

Chocolate

I tend to use a good-quality dark chocolate with around 70% cocoa solids for a strong chocolatey flavour that isn't overwhelming. But you can use chocolate with a lower percentage of cocoa if you prefer. Taste the chocolate first: if you enjoy eating it, you'll enjoy what you cook with it.

PASTRY

CLASSIC DOUGHS

TECHNIQUES

PASTRY IS A PRETTY MAGICAL THING. The ingredients couldn't be much more basic or ordinary but, if you bring them together in the right way, the result can absolutely make a dish. We probably all know cooks who have a reputation as fine pastry-makers, and others who say that they're just no good at it. But there's no mystery or secret talent involved. Making excellent pastry is not at all difficult. There are three main things to consider: ingredients, temperature and gluten.

First of all, use good-quality ingredients, and go for brands you know and trust. Don't switch to a new flour, for instance, the first time you make a recipe, because brands can vary, absorbing more or less water. Good-quality pure fats are important too. Cheap butter, for example, usually has an inferior flavour and tends to melt at a lower temperature, making it harder to work with and your pastry more prone to heaviness.

Temperature is crucial with pastry: unless you actually want the fat in the dough to be melted (as in a hot water crust or choux), the cooler your pastry the better. This means the fat is firm enough to work with easily, and stays solid, coating and separating the particles of dough rather than melding with them into a paste. This makes for a light, slightly crumbly pastry rather than a heavy, greasy one. On a hot day, it's even worth chilling your flour for a little while before you begin.

And thirdly, it's important to understand how gluten behaves. Flour contains gluten, a protein which develops into tough, elastic strands when wetted and kneaded. In shortcrust pastries the gluten must be developed only enough to hold the dough together, so a relatively low-gluten flour is used and the dough is handled minimally: too much kneading and rolling will result in a tough, solid pastry. Other pastries have different requirements: puff pastry, for instance, needs a measure of strong flour and a little kneading to give it some structure.

Read my recipes thoroughly and follow them carefully and you will see how the manipulation of a few simple ingredients can lead to an extraordinary range of pastries.

Shortcrust pastry

MAKES ABOUT 450g
●●●●●●●●●●●●●●●●●●●

300g plain flour
Pinch of fine salt
75g cold unsalted butter,
cut into roughly 1cm dice
75g cold lard, cut into
roughly 1cm dice
1 tsp lemon juice (optional)
4–6 tbsp very cold water

The standard proportion for shortcrust pastry is half the weight of fat to flour. Many modern shortcrust recipes use all butter, but I like a bit of lard too. Butter gives a great flavour but the lard creates a particularly short, tender texture. This quantity is sufficient to line and cover a 23cm pie plate.

Put the flour and salt into a large bowl and mix them together. Add the butter and lard dice and toss to coat them in the flour. The fat must be cold when you add it – you want to be able to rub it into the flour without it melting. The fat will then actually coat the grains of flour, helping to keep the pastry nicely crumbly and short.

Now rub the fat into the flour, using your fingertips. Lift your hands above the bowl, rubbing the fat and flour together then letting the crumbs fall back into the bowl. They will trap a little air as they go. Keep going until the mixture looks like fine breadcrumbs. (I prefer to 'rub-in' by hand so I can feel the pastry coming together, but you can use a food processor or a mixer. Process very briefly so you don't overwork the pastry, then tip the pastry 'crumbs' into a bowl, ready to add the water by hand.)

Mix the lemon juice with 4 tbsp water – which, again, should be very cold. The lemon juice isn't essential but it helps to keep the pastry tender because the acid retards the development of the gluten in the flour.

Add the liquid to the rubbed-in mixture and mix in, using one hand; avoid overworking the dough. Add a little more water if necessary, to bring the pastry together.

When the dough just sticks together in clumps, form it into a ball. Knead it very gently on a lightly floured surface to bring it together into a smooth dough. Again, don't overwork it. You can test it by taking a little piece of pastry and rolling it out. If it starts to crack easily, it needs just a touch more kneading to develop the gluten slightly more.

Wrap the pastry in cling film and chill it for about 30 minutes. This firms up the fat and also allows the gluten in the flour to 'relax'. If you leave the pastry in the fridge for much longer than 30 minutes, it may become too firm to roll out easily. Don't worry if this happens, just give it a little time at room temperature to soften slightly.

Adding the diced butter and lard to the flour and salt.

Coating the cubes of butter and lard in the flour.

Starting to rub the fat into the flour, using fingertips and lifting the mixture to aerate it.

Continuing to rub in the fat, breaking it up into smaller pieces.

Step photographs continued overleaf

The latter stage of rubbing-in, when the mixture begins to resemble breadcrumbs.

Adding the liquid to the rubbed-in mixture.

Bringing the pastry together with one hand.

Gathering the cohesive dough into a ball, ready to gently knead.

The smoothly kneaded dough, ready to wrap
and rest in the fridge before rolling out.

Rich shortcrust pastry

MAKES ABOUT 400g
●●●●●●●●●●●●●●●●

275g plain flour
Pinch of fine salt
1 medium egg
1 tsp lemon juice
2–3 tbsp very cold water
135g cold unsalted butter,
cut into roughly 1cm dice

This is made in a very similar way to the plain shortcrust (page 18), but the addition of egg brings both extra colour and flavour to the pastry. This quantity is sufficient to line and cover a 20cm pie dish.

Put the flour and salt into a large bowl and mix them together. Lightly beat the egg with the lemon juice and 2 tbsp water in a measuring jug with a fork; set aside.

Add the diced butter to the flour and toss the cubes to coat them in the flour. Rub the butter into the flour, using the fingertips. Lift your hands above the bowl, rubbing the fat and flour together then letting the crumbs fall back into the bowl. Keep going until the mixture looks like fine breadcrumbs.

Make a well in the centre of the mixture and pour in the egg mix. Incorporate the liquid into the flour and fat mixture, using one hand; avoid overworking the dough. If it is too dry, add a splash more water.

When the dough just sticks together in clumps, form it into a ball. Knead it very lightly on a lightly floured surface to bring it together into a smooth dough. Again, don't overwork it. You can test it by taking a little bit of pastry and rolling it out. If it starts to crack easily, it needs just a touch more kneading to develop the gluten slightly more.

Wrap the pastry in cling film and leave it in the fridge to chill for about 30 minutes.

Variation: Sweet shortcrust

I often use a sweetened version of this rich shortcrust as the base for an open sweet tart. To make enough to line a 23cm tart tin, follow this method but use 200g plain flour combined with 2 tbsp icing sugar, rub in 100g butter and bind with 1 medium egg beaten with 1 tbsp lemon juice and 2 tbsp water.

Adding the egg to the lemon juice and water.

Rubbing the butter cubes into the flour, using the fingertips.

Adding the liquid to the rubbed-in mixture.

Forming the dough into a ball with the hands once it comes together.

Flaky pastry

MAKES ABOUT 450g
●●●●●●●●●●●●●●●●

175g plain flour

Pinch of fine salt

65g cold unsalted butter,
cut into 5mm–1cm dice

65g cold lard, cut into
5mm–1cm dice

1 tsp lemon juice

130ml very cold water

This is a classic pie-topping pastry. Relatively large pieces of fat are trapped in the layers of dough so that when the pastry is baked the fat melts, creating flaky layers, and also releasing steam, which causes the pastry to puff up. This quantity is sufficient to cover 4 individual pies.

Combine the flour and salt in a large bowl. Put the diced butter and lard in a separate bowl, mixing them together loosely.

Take one quarter of the diced mixed fats and rub them into the flour with your fingertips. Combine the lemon juice and water and mix lightly into the flour, using one hand, to form a very soft dough.

Roll out the dough on a well-floured surface to a rectangle, about 10 x 30cm.

Dot the remaining diced fats evenly over the bottom two-thirds of the dough. Now fold the empty top third down and the bottom fat-covered third up over it, as if folding a letter.

Turn the dough 90° and seal the edges by pressing down with your fingers.

Roll out the dough again to a rectangle, about 10 x 30cm. Fold the bottom third up and the top third down over it, envelope-style again. Turn the dough 90° and press the edges down with your fingers. If the pastry is becoming a little soft, wrap it in cling film and chill in the fridge for 20–30 minutes to firm up before continuing.

Repeat the rolling and folding sequence twice more.

Wrap the dough in cling film and leave to chill in the fridge for at least 30 minutes before rolling out and using.

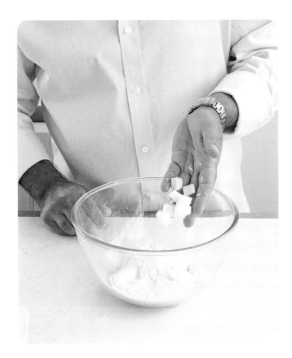

Adding a quarter of the butter and lard to the flour, ready to rub in.

Adding the water and lemon juice to the rubbed-in mixture.

Mixing to a soft dough, using one hand.

Rolling out the dough on a well-floured surface to a rectangle, about 10 x 30cm.

Step photographs continued overleaf

Dotting the remaining fat over the bottom two-thirds of the dough.

Folding the empty top third of the dough down over the middle.

Folding the bottom fat-covered third up over the top.

Turning the dough 90° and pressing the edges together to seal.

Rolling out the dough again to a 10 x 30cm rectangle.

Folding the dough into three again to create more layers and pressing the edges to seal.

Rolling out the layered pastry again after chilling to firm it up.

The finished pastry, ready to wrap and chill before rolling out to use.

Puff pastry

MAKES ABOUT 500g
●●●●●●●●●●●●●●●●●

100g strong white bread flour
100g plain flour
Pinch of fine salt
75–100ml very cold water
165g cold unsalted butter

Puff pastry consists of lots of very thin layers of butter within a dough, created by repeatedly rolling and folding the dough. On baking, the butter melts, making the pastry crisp, and releases steam, puffing the pastry up. The secret to a good puff is to have the dough and butter chilled before you bring them together. If the butter is too soft, it will start to ooze out as you work, and warm dough will become sticky. Chilling the pastry between each 'roll and fold' firms up the butter so you can build up clean, even layers. I use a proportion of high-gluten bread flour to give the pastry the strength it needs to hold its layered structure.

Combine the flours and salt in a bowl. Mix in enough water to form a reasonably tight but still kneadable dough. Turn out onto a lightly floured surface and knead for 5–10 minutes until smooth. Form the dough into a rough rectangle, wrap in cling film and place in the fridge for at least 7 hours.

Using a rolling pin, bash the butter on a floured surface to flatten it to a rectangle, 20cm long and just less than 12cm wide. Wrap in cling film and chill in the fridge.

Roll out the chilled dough to a rectangle, 12 x 30cm. Lay the chilled butter on the dough so it covers the bottom two-thirds. Make sure it's positioned neatly and comes almost to the edges of the dough.

Lift the exposed dough at the top and fold down over half of the butter. Fold the butter-covered bottom half of dough over the top. You will now have a sandwich of two layers of butter and three of dough. Seal the edges by pressing or pinching them together. Place in a plastic food bag and chill in the fridge for an hour.

Remove the dough and turn it 90° so you have a short end towards you, then roll it into a long rectangle. Fold the top quarter down and the bottom quarter up so they meet in the middle. Then fold the dough in half along the centre line and press or pinch the edges together to seal. Return to the bag and chill for an hour.

Remove the dough, turn it 90° so a short end is facing you and roll it into a long rectangle. Fold one-third down, then fold the bottom third up over the top. Press or pinch the edges to seal. Return the pastry to the bag and chill for an hour.

Repeat the last stage of rolling, folding and chilling. The dough is now ready to use.

Kneading the dough to develop the gluten.

Bashing the chilled butter with a rolling pin to flatten it to a rectangle, 11.5 x 20cm.

Lifting the butter sheet from the floured surface during flattening to stop it sticking.

Rolling out the chilled dough to a rectangle, 12 x 30cm.

Step photographs continued overleaf

Laying the chilled butter over the bottom two-thirds of the dough.

Folding the top third of the dough down over half of the butter.

Folding the bottom butter-covered third of the dough up over the top.

Bringing the edges together to create a sandwich of three layers of dough and two of butter.

Starting the final roll and fold sequence: rolling out the chilled dough to a long rectangle.

Folding the top third of the dough down over the middle third.

Folding the bottom third of the dough up and over the top.

Giving the dough a quarter-turn (90°) and pressing the edges together to seal.

Hot water crust pastry

MAKES ABOUT 1kg
●●●●●●●●●●●●●●●

450g plain flour
100g strong white bread flour
75g cold unsalted butter, cut
into roughly 1cm dice
200ml water
½ tsp fine salt
100g lard
Beaten egg yolk, to glaze

I love hot water crust pastry: it's the best thing for a substantial meaty pie, as it keeps the filling moist and tender within its robust, firm crust, which breaks deliciously when you bite into it. The lard gives the pastry a lovely sheen and keeps the pastry impermeable so it can seal in lots of meaty juices without becoming soggy. This quantity is enough for a 20cm raised pie.

Combine the flours in a large bowl. I use a measure of high-gluten bread flour to help give strength to the dough – but not too much or it will become tough.

Add the butter to the flour and rub it in with your fingertips.

Heat the water, salt and lard in a saucepan until just boiling. Immediately pour the liquid onto the flour mixture and briskly mix together with a wooden spoon.

As soon as it's cool enough to handle, gather the warm dough together with one hand, transfer it to a lightly floured surface and quickly knead until smooth.

Your pastry is now ready to use. You need to work fairly quickly with a hot water dough. As the pastry cools, it will become more crumbly and less malleable. Roll it out swiftly (you probably won't need to flour the surface any more as the fat in the dough will stop it sticking) and use it to line your chosen tin, then cover your pie.

I always like to glaze a hot water dough with beaten egg yolk before it goes into the oven, to create a lovely, rich, golden brown sheen.

Rubbing the butter cubes into the flour using the fingertips.

Pouring the boiling water and melted lard mix into the rubbed-in mixture.

Mixing the hot liquid into the flour, using a wooden spoon and working quickly.

Gathering the warm dough to knead until smooth, before quickly rolling out to use.

Suet pastry

MAKES ABOUT 650g
●●●●●●●●●●●●●●●●●

285g self-raising flour

1 tsp baking powder

½ tsp fine salt

¼ tsp pepper

125g shredded suet

About 225ml very cold water

Suet pastry is rich and substantial. Although flexible and soft, it's also robust enough to encase a lot of liquid, so it's great for meaty pies or juicy puddings. You'll get a very different finish depending on whether you steam or bake it: either fluffy and tender or crisp and nutty. In days gone by, cooks would have bought chunks of suet (which is the fat from around an animal's kidneys) and chopped or shredded it by hand. These days, you can buy ready-shredded beef suet (or a vegetarian alternative), which is very easy to use. This quantity is enough to line and cover a 1.2 litre pudding basin.

Mix the self-raising flour, baking powder, salt and pepper together in a large bowl. Add the shredded suet and mix thoroughly.

Add most of the water and mix to a soft, slightly sticky dough with one hand, adding more water as necessary. Gather the dough with your hand and transfer it to a lightly floured surface.

Your pastry is now ready to roll out and use; there is no need to chill it first. Suet pastry is best rolled to a 7–8mm thickness.

Adding the shredded suet to the flour and baking powder mixture.

Adding the water to the flour and suet mix.

Gathering the soft, sticky dough with your hands.

Flattening the dough on a lightly floured surface, ready to roll out.

Choux pastry

MAKES A '4-EGG
QUANTITY'
●●●●●●●●●●●●●

100g unsalted butter,
cut into roughly 1cm dice
Pinch of salt
300ml water
130g strong white bread flour
4 medium eggs, beaten

This is very different to the other pastries: it's a cooked paste, enriched with lots of egg which is beaten in vigorously to create a glossy dough that puffs up quite dramatically in a hot oven. It's crucial to beat the eggs in a little at a time, so the flour can absorb them, and to beat the dough well to make it smooth, thick and glossy. This quantity is enough to make 6 large buns or 16 éclairs.

Put the butter, salt and water into a large saucepan. Heat gently until the butter has melted, then bring to the boil. (Don't let the liquid boil for any length of time, or you will drive off too much moisture.) Immediately remove from the heat and tip the flour into the pan. Beat with a wooden spoon to form a smooth ball of dough that leaves the sides of the pan clean.

Now vigorously beat the egg into the hot dough, a little at a time. This takes some elbow grease! As you add the egg, the dough will become stiff and glossy. Stop adding the egg if the dough starts to become loose – but you should use up all or most of it.

The dough is now ready to be piped or spooned into puffs, buns or éclairs. Work quickly and get it into a hot oven (190–200°C/gas 5–6) as quickly as possible.

When baked, the pastry should be crisp and dry. As soon as you remove it from the oven, transfer to a cooling rack and split open one side of each piece. This allows steam to escape and stops the pastry becoming soggy. Put the choux on a wire rack to cool.

Beating the flour into the boiling water, salt and butter mixture, off the heat.

Continuing to beat the mixture until it is smooth and leaves the sides of the pan clean.

Vigorously beating the egg into the dough, a small amount at a time.

The finished choux pastry – stiff, glossy and ready to pipe or spoon onto a baking tray.

Rolling out pastry

Rolling out pastry well comes down to confidence: the more often you do it, the better you'll get at it. The trick is to work quickly so the pastry stays cool. Use a good rolling pin (see page 10) and aim for an even thickness throughout. If the pastry crumbles or breaks, don't panic, this probably means it wasn't kneaded quite enough to start with. Just bring it together and re-roll. Don't do this more than once or twice though, or your pastry can become overworked and greasy.

Pastry should be rolled out on a lightly floured surface. If you add too much flour, the pastry will absorb it and become drier and you will also get flour transferred to the filling of your pie or tart. Start with just a light sprinkling on your work surface and your rolling pin, and add a little more as needed.

Use a smooth rolling pin that's not too heavy, as this will let you control the amount of pressure you apply. Roll your pastry with light movements. Roll up from the centre, then down from the centre, give the pastry a quarter turn, dust lightly with more flour and repeat until the pastry has reached the right thickness.

Rolling the pastry down from the centre, using an even, light pressure.

Continuing to roll, having given the pastry a quarter-turn, until it is the required size.

Lining a flan tin

There's something particularly satisfying about lining a tin neatly with pastry. It's a straightforward task, as long as the pastry has been kneaded correctly and rolled out well, and it is not too thick. If the pastry seems fragile and breaks easily, it may be too thin, or too warm. Alternatively, it may need to be re-rolled to bring it together a little more.

To line a flan tin or ring, you'll need the pastry rolled out to roughly a 3mm thickness. If it is much thicker than this, it is unlikely to cook through properly, giving you a soggy, starchy result.

If you are lining a loose-bottomed tin, after you've rolled out your pastry place the base of the tin underneath the pastry. Carefully flip the edges of the pastry into the middle and lift the base into the tin. Now unfold the edges of the pastry, allowing the excess to hang over the sides of the tin.

If you're using a tin (or dish) that doesn't have a loose base, the easiest way to transfer the pastry to the tin is to carefully roll it backwards and loosely onto your rolling pin, then lift it over the tin and carefully unroll it so the pastry falls into the tin.

Use your fingertips to carefully press the pastry down into the tin. You want to avoid stretching the pastry as this will cause it to shrink back in the oven, so gently lift and press it down.

Tear off a small piece of the excess pastry, roughly shape it into a ball and use this to press the pastry into the corners of the tin.

If the pastry case is to be baked blind before filling (see page 42), leave the excess pastry hanging over the sides of the tin (it will be trimmed away later, after baking).

If you are not baking the pastry case blind, trim the edges neatly, with a small, sharp knife.

Folding in the edges of the rolled-out pastry on the metal base before placing in the tin.

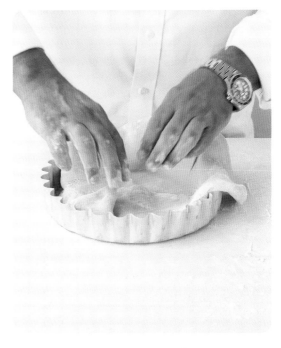

Unfolding the pastry, allowing the excess to drape over the sides of the tin.

Pressing the pastry against the sides of the tin, with the fingertips.

Using a small piece of pastry to press the pastry into the corners of the tin.

Baking blind

To ensure the dough cooks through properly, a pastry case is often pre-baked or 'baked blind' before the filling is added. This is particularly important if the filling (such as a custard) needs to be baked at a lower temperature than the pastry requires, which would leave it undercooked in the finished dish.

Blind baking involves covering the uncooked pastry and weighing it down with baking beans. This ensures the pastry bakes snugly into the shape of the tin and doesn't colour too much.

Line your tart tin with pastry, as described on pages 40–1, leaving the excess pastry hanging over the edge. Keep a little uncooked pastry back in case you need to patch any cracks later. It's a good idea to prick the pastry now with a fine-pronged fork, so that any air trapped underneath it can escape without puffing up the pastry.

Line the pastry with a piece of baking parchment or foil (if you scrunch up the parchment first, then smooth it out, it becomes much more malleable).

Fill the pastry case with ceramic baking beans, or uncooked rice or lentils, pressing them gently right to the edge so they hold the pastry in place.

Bake in a hot oven at 200°C/gas 6 for about 15 minutes, then carefully lift out the parchment and baking beans and return the pastry case to the oven for about 8 minutes or until it looks dry and faintly coloured.

Use a small, sharp knife to trim away the excess pastry from the edge. Use a tiny bit of the reserved raw pastry to patch any cracks or holes if necessary.

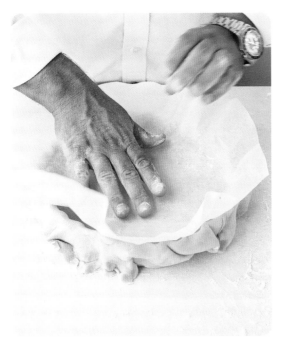

Lining the pastry with a piece of baking parchment.

Filling the parchment-lined pastry case with ceramic baking beans.

The part-baked pastry case with the baking beans and paper removed.

Trimming away the excess pastry from the edge of the pastry case.

SAVOURY

THE THING I LOVE about a savoury pie is the way everything is wrapped up in one neat, tasty package. Anything that goes together well on a plate will go well together en croûte. Take my bacon and egg pie, for instance (page 57) – it offers all the flavours of a good cooked breakfast in a single, tasty parcel. Or the lovely lamb and kidney pud on page 87 – you've got meat and gravy, onions and fresh rosemary, all enclosed in a sustaining suet crust.

Pies have been serving us well for hundreds of years, eaten by people from all reaches of society – from kings and queens who ate elaborate raised pies at their banquets, to working men and women who developed pasties to function as portable meals – the pastry protecting and preserving the filling. Pasties were the original fast food, taken down the mines or into factories to provide a filling and balanced meal. That's how recipes like the fabulous Bedfordshire clanger (page 112) evolved, with the main course and pudding encased in the same pastry package.

Even now, the same principles stand. Pies are still incredibly versatile. You can dish them up as an impressive supper or Sunday lunch, but you can also pop a slice or individual pasty in your lunchbox as delicious fuel to get you through a working day.

You should view every pie you make, I think, as a little work of art. That doesn't mean slaving and worrying over it. I promise you that nothing here is difficult or complicated, I just think it's worth taking real pride in your work. Homemade pastry is a world away from the shop-bought, ready-made stuff, and yours will be even better if you relax and enjoy making it. All of the classic pastries used in this chapter are described in detail and illustrated with step-by-step photographs in the Pastry chapter (pages 14–43), so refer back to these if you need to.

It's incredibly satisfying to bring good pastry and a well-made filling together, then slide them into the oven for that final bake where the magic happens, enabling you to bring out something really inviting. Take your time, savour the process and relish the fact that when you make pastry, you're actively continuing a great British culinary tradition.

Corned beef plate pie

SERVES 4–6
●●●●●●●●●

For the shortcrust pastry
300g plain flour
Pinch of salt
75g cold unsalted butter,
cut into roughly 1cm dice
75g cold lard, cut into roughly
1cm dice
4–6 tbsp very cold water
1 egg, beaten, to glaze

For the filling
1 tbsp vegetable or sunflower
oil
1 medium onion, chopped
1 large carrot, peeled and diced
2 celery sticks, de-stringed
and diced
1 large potato, about 250g,
such as Desiree, peeled and
cut into 1cm dice
340g tin corned beef, broken
into large chunks
Splash of Worcestershire sauce
250ml beef stock
1 tbsp chopped parsley
Salt and pepper

Equipment
23cm metal pie plate

This double-crusted pie may have an old-fashioned thrifty feel, but it's ideal for a family supper, and very easy to put together. Use good-quality tinned corned beef for the best flavour and choose a reasonably waxy potato variety such as Desiree that will hold its shape, giving a good texture.

To make the pastry, put the flour into a bowl and mix in the salt. Add the butter and lard and rub into the flour with your fingertips until the mixture resembles fine breadcrumbs. Alternatively, do this in a food processor or mixer and then transfer to a bowl.

Now work in just enough cold water to bring the pastry together. When the dough begins to stick together, use your hands to gently knead it into a ball. Wrap the pastry in cling film and place in the fridge to rest while you make the filling.

Heat the oil in a large frying pan over a medium-low heat. Add the onion, carrot and celery and cook gently for 5–10 minutes until soft but not coloured. Add the potato and cook for another 5 minutes. Next, stir in the corned beef, making sure it's evenly distributed.

Add the Worcestershire sauce, pour over the stock and bring to the boil. Lower the heat and simmer, uncovered, for 20 minutes or so, until the carrot and potato are tender and most of the liquid has evaporated. Taste and add salt and pepper if necessary, then tip into a bowl and leave to cool completely.

Heat your oven to 200°C/gas 6. Have ready a 23cm metal pie plate.

Divide the pastry into two pieces: roughly two-thirds and one-third. Lightly flour your work surface and roll out the larger piece to a 2–3mm thickness. Use to line the pie plate. Roll out the remaining pasty ready to form the lid.

Stir the chopped parsley into the filling. Spoon the filling into the pastry-lined dish (if it's very wet, keep some of the liquid back to serve as gravy). Brush the edges of the pastry on the plate with a little beaten egg then cover the pie with the pastry lid. Crimp the edges together with a fork, or your fingers, then trim away the excess pastry neatly.

Brush the top of the pie with beaten egg and make a hole in the middle to let the steam out. Bake for 30–35 minutes until golden brown. Leave to rest for 15–20 minutes before slicing.

Thai chicken pie

SERVES 6
●●●●●●

For the shortcrust pastry

150g plain flour
Pinch of fine salt
40g cold unsalted butter, cut
into roughly 1cm dice
35g cold lard, cut into roughly
1cm dice
1 tsp lemon juice (optional)
3–4 tbsp very cold water
1 egg, beaten, to glaze

For the filling

2 skinless, boneless chicken
thighs, about 150g in total
2 skinless, boneless chicken
breasts, about 300g in total
2 tbsp vegetable oil
2 eschalions (banana shallots),
chopped
2 garlic cloves, finely chopped
1 red chilli, deseeded and finely
chopped
1 tsp finely grated root ginger
2 tsp Thai green curry paste
200ml coconut cream
150ml chicken stock
2 lime leaves
1 lemongrass stem, bruised
1 small sweet potato, about 175g,
peeled and cut into 1cm dice
1 tsp cornflour, mixed with
a splash of water
A splash of Thai fish sauce
Black pepper

Equipment

1.2 litre pie dish
Pastry lattice cutter

I love a good Thai chicken curry, fragrant with spices, chilli and ginger, and creamy with coconut milk. This is my pastry-topped tribute to that dish.

For the filling, cut all the chicken into 1.5cm chunks. Heat the oil in a sauté pan or wide saucepan over a medium-low heat. Add the shallots, garlic, chilli and ginger and fry gently for a few minutes until soft but not coloured.

Stir in the curry paste and cook for a minute or two. Add the chicken, increase the heat a little and cook, stirring, until it has lost its raw look. Add the coconut cream, chicken stock, lime leaves, lemongrass and sweet potato. Simmer for 12–15 minutes, until the sweet potato is tender.

Add the cornflour liquid, bring to a simmer and stir until the sauce begins to thicken, then take off the heat. Taste the sauce and season with pepper and a little fish sauce. Set aside to cool.

To make the pastry, put the flour and salt in a bowl. Add the diced butter and lard and rub in with your fingertips until the mixture looks like fine breadcrumbs. Alternatively, do this in a food processor or a mixer and then transfer to a bowl.

Now work in just enough cold water to bring the pastry together. When the dough begins to stick together, use your hands to gently knead it into a ball. Wrap the pastry in cling film and place in the fridge to rest for about 30 minutes.

Heat your oven to 200°C/gas 6.

Remove the lemongrass and lime leaves from the cooled pie filling if you prefer and transfer to a 1.2 litre pie dish.

Roll out the pastry on a lightly floured surface and cut a 2cm wide strip of pastry. Dampen the rim of the pie dish with water, press the pastry strip onto it and dampen this too. Use a pastry lattice cutter to cut a pattern in the remaining piece of pastry. Pull the pastry very gently to open up the lattice, then place over the pie. Press the edges down to seal, then trim away the excess pastry.

Brush the top of the pie with beaten egg then bake in the oven for about 30 minutes, until golden. Leave the pie to sit in the tin for 5 minutes before serving, with steamed or stir-fried greens.

Shallot, onion & chive tart

SERVES 4–6

●●●●●●●●●

For the shortcrust pastry

225g plain flour

Pinch of fine salt

60g cold unsalted butter,
cut into roughly 1cm dice

60g cold lard, cut into roughly
1cm dice

3–5 tbsp very cold water

For the filling

8 eschalions (banana shallots)

3 large onions, halved

25g unsalted butter

1 tbsp sunflower oil

4 medium eggs

2 medium egg yolks

200ml double cream

1½ tbsp wholegrain mustard

1 tbsp chopped chives

Salt and pepper

Equipment

23cm loose-based fluted tart
tin, 3.5cm deep

Three different alliums give this creamy tart a lovely range of savoury flavours, while the grainy mustard adds a note of sweetness. Like most savoury egg tarts, it is best eaten warm or at room temperature, rather than piping hot.

To make the pastry, put the flour into a bowl and mix in the salt. Add the butter and lard and rub into the flour with your fingertips until the mixture resembles fine breadcrumbs. Alternatively, do this in a food processor or mixer and then transfer to a bowl.

Now work in just enough cold water to bring the dough together. When it begins to stick together, gently knead it into a ball. Wrap in cling film and chill in the fridge for around 30 minutes.

Meanwhile, for the filling, thinly slice the shallots and onions. Heat the butter and oil in a large frying pan over a medium-low heat. Add the shallots and onions with a pinch of salt and cook slowly for at least 20 minutes, stirring occasionally, until they are very soft and golden. Season with pepper and more salt if needed. Leave to cool.

Heat your oven to 200°C/gas 6 and have ready a 23cm loose-based fluted tart tin, 3.5cm deep.

Roll out the pastry on a lightly floured surface to a 3mm thickness and use it to line the tart tin, leaving the excess hanging over the edge. Keep a little uncooked pastry back in case you need to patch any cracks later. Prick the pastry base with a fork. Line the pastry with baking parchment or foil and then fill with baking beans, or uncooked rice or lentils.

Bake blind for 15 minutes, then remove the parchment and baking beans and return the pastry to the oven for about 8 minutes or until it looks dry and faintly coloured. Trim away the excess pastry from the edge. Use a tiny bit of the reserved raw pastry to patch any cracks or holes if necessary. Turn the oven down to 180°C/gas 4.

For the filling, whisk the eggs, egg yolks and cream together, then whisk in the mustard and chives. Season with salt and white pepper.

Spoon the cooled onion mixture into the pastry case and spread it evenly, then carefully pour on the egg mixture. Bake in the oven for 30–35 minutes, until the filling is just set and golden. Leave in the tin for 5 minutes, then unmould. Serve warm or cold.

Step photographs overleaf

Shallot, onion & chive tart

Slicing the shallots and onions for the filling.

Setting aside the golden, softened slow-cooked shallots and onions to cool.

Whisking the eggs, egg yolks and cream together for the filling.

Spooning the cooled shallots and onions into the blind-baked pastry case.

Pouring the whisked egg, chive and mustard
mixture into the pastry case.

Bacon & egg pie

For the rich shortcrust pastry
275g plain flour
Pinch of fine salt
135g cold unsalted butter, diced
1 medium egg, beaten
1 tsp lemon juice
2–3 tbsp very cold water
1 egg, beaten, to glaze

For the filling
1 tbsp vegetable oil
1 large onion, finely chopped
1 garlic clove, crushed
200g unsmoked streaky bacon, diced
200g pork loin, cut into roughly 1.5cm dice
5 medium eggs
100g cream cheese
100g mature Cheddar, grated
1 tbsp chopped chives
Salt and pepper

Equipment
20cm loose-based sandwich tin, 4cm deep

This is a delicious savoury pie that really makes the most of a winning partnership. I love the way the whole eggs are hidden beneath the crust – if you get one when you cut into it, it's like gaining a prize. Serve this hot for supper or cold for lunch.

To make the pastry, put the flour and salt in a bowl. Add the diced butter and rub in with your fingertips until the mixture looks like fine breadcrumbs. Alternatively, do this in a food processor or a mixer and then transfer to a bowl.

Mix the egg with the lemon juice and 2 tbsp water. Make a well in the centre of the rubbed-in mixture and pour in the egg mix. Mix the liquid into the flour and fat mixture, using one hand; avoid overworking the dough. If it is too dry, add a splash more water. When the dough begins to stick together, use your hands to gently knead it into a ball. Wrap the pastry in cling film and place in the fridge to rest for about 30 minutes.

For the filling, heat the oil in a wide frying pan over a medium-low heat and add the onion and garlic. Cook gently for about 8 minutes, until soft. Add the bacon and pork, increase the heat a little, and cook for about 10 minutes, stirring from time to time, until any liquid from the meat has been driven off. Leave to cool completely.

Heat your oven to 200°C/gas 6 and have ready a 20cm loose-based sandwich cake tin, 4cm deep.

Beat two of the eggs with the cream cheese until smooth. Add the Cheddar and chives and season with salt and pepper. Stir in the cooled bacon mixture.

Roll out two-thirds of the pastry and use to line the cake tin. Roll out the remaining pastry ready to form the lid.

Put the filling mixture into the pastry case. Make 3 evenly spaced depressions in the filling and crack the remaining eggs into them.

Brush the rim of the pastry with water and place the lid on top. Press the edges to seal and trim off the excess neatly. Brush the top of the pie with beaten egg and make a steam hole in the centre.

Bake in the oven for 50–55 minutes, until golden brown. Leave the pie to settle for at least 15 minutes before cutting. It is delicious hot or cold.

Pork, apple & cider pie

SERVES 4
●●●●●●●

For the cider pastry

1 medium egg, beaten

125ml dry cider

125ml olive oil

1 tsp baking powder

Pinch of fine salt

350–400g plain flour

1 egg, beaten, to glaze

For the filling

1–2 tbsp vegetable oil

1 medium-large onion, chopped

2 celery sticks, de-stringed and chopped

500g pork shoulder, cut into 3–4cm pieces

2 tbsp plain flour

175ml dry cider

175ml chicken stock

1 cooking apple, about 150g, peeled, cored and sliced

2 eating apples, 225–250g in total, peeled, cored and sliced

6 large sage leaves, chopped

Salt and pepper

Equipment

1.2 litre pie dish

Pie funnel

This gorgeous pie plays on the wonderful affinity between pork and apples. The fruit gives a subtle sweetness to the cider-enriched gravy and sage lends an aromatic note.

First make the filling. Heat 1 tbsp oil in a large, wide pan over a medium-low heat. Add the onion and celery and cook gently for 8–10 minutes, until soft but not coloured. Remove the vegetables from the pan.

Add a little more oil if necessary, increase the heat to medium-high and add half the pork. Brown it well on all sides, remove from the pan and repeat with the remaining pork.

Turn the heat down a little. Return all the pork to the pan with the onion and celery. Sprinkle in the flour, stir and cook for 1 minute. Gradually add the cider and stock, stirring them in so the flour is absorbed. Add the apples and sage. Bring to the boil, reduce the heat and simmer for about 45 minutes, until the pork is tender. Taste the sauce and season with salt and pepper. Leave to cool.

To make the pastry, beat the egg in a large bowl with the cider, olive oil, baking powder and salt. Slowly mix in the flour until you have a soft dough. You may not need all the flour. Wrap the dough in cling film and leave to rest in the fridge for 30 minutes.

Heat your oven to 200°C/gas 6.

Position a pie funnel in the middle of a 1.2 litre pie dish and spoon the filling into the dish.

On a lightly floured surface, roll out the pastry to a 3mm thickness. Cut a 2cm wide strip from the pastry. Dampen the rim of the pie dish with water. Press the pastry strip onto the rim and dampen this too. Lift the pastry sheet over the pie and press down the edges to seal. Trim off the excess pastry and make a steam hole in the centre of the pie, exposing the funnel. Crimp the edges. Cut leaves and shape little berries from the pastry trimmings to decorate the pie.

Brush the pastry lid with beaten egg. Arrange the pastry leaves and berries on top of the pie and brush these with egg too. Bake for 35–40 minutes until the pastry is crisp and golden.

Let stand for 10–15 minutes before serving, with mash and greens.

Step photographs overleaf

Spooning the pork and apple filling into the pie
dish around the pie funnel.

Pressing the edges of the positioned pie lid onto the pastry strip to seal the pie.

Pressing the strip of pastry onto the dampened rim of the pie dish.

Trimming off the excess pastry from the edge of the pie.

Crimping the edges of the pastry by pinching between your thumbs and forefingers.

Smoked haddock & watercress tart

SERVES 4–6
●●●●●●●●●●

For the black pepper pastry

200g plain flour

Pinch of fine salt

½ tsp coarsely ground black pepper

50g cold unsalted butter, cut into roughly 1cm dice

50g cold lard, cut into roughly 1cm dice

1 tsp lemon juice (optional)

3–5 tbsp very cold water

For the filling

250g smoked haddock fillet

200ml whole milk

1 bay leaf

25g unsalted butter

25g plain flour

2 medium eggs, beaten

Small bunch of spring onions, finely sliced

30g watercress, stalks removed

25g fine white breadcrumbs

25g finely grated Parmesan

Finely grated zest of 1 lemon

Equipment

36 x 12cm loose-based fluted tart tin, 3cm deep, or a 23cm round tart tin

Savoury tarts need a punchy, well-flavoured filling. Smoked fish and peppery watercress fit the bill nicely and a crunchy, golden crumb topping is a lovely contrast to the creamy sauce beneath.

To make the pastry, mix the flour with the salt and pepper in a large bowl. Add the butter and lard and rub in with your fingertips until the mixture resembles fine breadcrumbs. Alternatively, do this in a food processor or mixer and then transfer to a bowl.

Mix the lemon juice, if using, with 3 tbsp water. Using one hand, work the liquid into the flour, adding a little more water if needed, just until the pastry clumps together. Gently knead into a ball, wrap in cling film and rest in the fridge for about 30 minutes.

Heat your oven to 200°C/gas 6 and have ready a 36 x 12cm loose-based fluted tart tin, 3cm deep, or a 23cm round tart tin.

Roll out the pastry on a lightly floured surface to a 3mm thickness and use to line the tart tin, leaving the excess overhanging the edge. Keep a little uncooked pastry back to patch any cracks later. Prick the pastry base with a fork. Line the pastry with baking parchment or foil then fill with baking beans, or uncooked rice or lentils.

Bake blind for 15 minutes, then remove the paper and beans and return the pastry to the oven for about 8 minutes or until it looks dry and faintly coloured. Trim away the excess pastry from the edge and patch any cracks or holes with raw pastry if necessary.

Meanwhile, for the filling, put the fish in a saucepan, pour on the milk and add the bay leaf. Bring to a simmer, turn the fish over and simmer gently for about 2 minutes, until it is just cooked. Lift out the fish and set aside. Discard the bay leaf. Pour the milk into a jug.

In the same pan, melt the butter over a low heat and stir in the flour. Cook, stirring, for 2 minutes, then take off the heat. Gradually beat in the warm milk until you have a smooth, thick sauce. Return to the heat and cook gently for 2–3 minutes, stirring often. Let cool for a few minutes. Stir in the beaten eggs, then the spring onions.

Flake the fish into bite-sized chunks, discarding any skin and bones. Scatter the fish in the pastry case, top with the watercress and pour over the sauce. Mix the breadcrumbs with the Parmesan and lemon zest and scatter over the filling. Bake for 20 minutes until the crust is golden brown. Let cool slightly in the tin, then serve with a salad.

Cheese, potato & onion pie

SERVES 6
●●●●●●

For the cheese pastry
200g plain flour
75g cold unsalted butter,
cut into roughly 1cm dice
75g white vegetable fat,
cut into small pieces
25g Parmesan, finely grated
25g mature Cheddar,
finely grated
2–3 tbsp very cold water
1 egg, beaten, to glaze

For the filling
1kg Desiree potatoes
1 medium onion, finely diced
375g mature Cheddar, grated
50ml milk
2 tbsp chopped chives
Salt and white pepper

Equipment
24 x 20cm metal baking dish,
5cm deep

I used to buy pies like this in my local chip shop, as a lad. Based on potatoes with lots of full-flavoured cheese, it's warming and filling – real comfort food. The rich pastry is very tender and almost melts into the filling beneath. Serve as a meat-free main course, with some steamed greens or a big bowl of salad.

To make the pastry, put the flour into a bowl. Add the butter and vegetable fat and rub them in with your fingertips until the mixture looks like coarse breadcrumbs (this dough is richer and stickier than a standard pastry). Alternatively, rub in the fat using a food processor or a mixer and then transfer to a bowl.

Add the cheeses to the flour and fat and mix well. Now, using one hand, work in just enough cold water to bring the pastry together into a dough. When the dough begins to stick together, gently knead it into a ball. Wrap in cling film and place in the fridge to chill while you make the filling.

Heat your oven to 200°C/gas 6 and have ready a metal baking dish, about 24 x 20cm and 5cm deep.

For the filling, peel the potatoes and cut them into large chunks. Place in a saucepan, cover with water, add a little salt and bring to the boil. Reduce to a simmer and cook until the potatoes are tender enough to mash – probably 12–15 minutes. Drain the potatoes well and put them through a ricer into a large bowl (this will give you smooth, lump-free mash but you can use a standard potato masher).

Add the onion, cheese, some salt and a good pinch of white pepper. Beat with a wooden spoon so the cheese is well incorporated. Add the milk and chives and give the mix a good stir.

Put the cheesy mash mixture into the tin and spread it out with the back of a spoon until smooth and even.

On a lightly floured surface, roll out the pastry so it will just fit on top of the mash. It should be 8–10mm thick. Place it on top of the mash, trim the edges neatly and mark the pastry into 6 portions by scoring with a knife.

Brush the pastry with beaten egg and bake for 20–25 minutes until the crust is golden. Let the pie stand for 15 minutes before cutting and serving.

Rabbit & pancetta pot pies

SERVES 4
●●●●●●●●

For the flaky pastry

175g plain flour

Pinch of fine salt

65g cold unsalted butter,
cut into 5mm–1cm dice

65g cold lard, cut into
5mm–1cm dice

1 tsp lemon juice

130ml very cold water

1 egg, beaten, to glaze

For the filling

1 tbsp sunflower oil

25g unsalted butter

2 rabbits (1.5–2kg total), jointed

175g diced pancetta

1 onion, sliced

1 garlic clove, sliced

1 fennel bulb, trimmed
and sliced

175ml white wine

600ml chicken stock

1 bay leaf

300ml double cream

2 tbsp chopped parsley

Salt and black pepper

Equipment

4 individual pie dishes

I kept rabbits as a child and was so distraught when a fox got them that I didn't eat rabbit until my thirties! I've since found it makes a great pie filling, with a little pancetta to balance its leanness. Make this warming, hearty dish during autumn and winter when you'll really appreciate it and rabbit is at its best.

Make the pastry following the recipe on page 24. Wrap the dough in cling film and chill in the fridge while you make the filling.

Heat a large sauté pan over a high heat and add the oil and butter. Working in batches, brown the rabbit well all over (include the liver and kidneys, if you have them, for extra flavour). Remove from the pan and set aside. Add the pancetta to the pan, reduce the heat a little and cook for 4 minutes or until golden and beginning to crisp around the edges. Add to the rabbit.

Turn the heat to low. Add the onion, garlic and fennel to the pan and cook gently for 2–3 minutes. Add the wine, increase the heat and let it bubble for a couple of minutes, scraping the base of the pan with a spatula to release any caramelised bits. Return the rabbit and pancetta to the pan. Add the stock and bay leaf, bring to a simmer, cover and simmer gently for 1½ hours, until the rabbit is tender.

Remove the rabbit from the pan and leave until cool enough to handle, then strip the meat from the bones and put into a large bowl.

Bring the contents of the pan to the boil, and boil to reduce the liquid by half. Stir in the cream and bring back to the boil. Add the parsley, taste the sauce and season with salt and pepper as required. Return the rabbit meat to the pan and turn to coat in the sauce. Divide the filling between 4 individual pie dishes. Leave to cool.

Heat your oven to 200°C/gas 6.

On a lightly floured surface, roll out the pastry to a 5mm thickness and cut lids for the pies, using the dishes as guides. Brush the rim of each dish with beaten egg and position the pie lids. Press the edges to seal and trim off the excess. Crimp the edges. Make a slit in the top of each pie lid and brush the pastry with beaten egg.

Bake for 20–30 minutes until the pastry is golden brown and the filling bubbling. Leave to settle for 10 minutes or so, then serve, with plain boiled potatoes, carrots and a green vegetable.

Step photographs overleaf

Rabbit & pancetta pot pies

Browning the rabbit joints for the filling.

Adding the wine to the softened onion, garlic and fennel and letting it bubble away.

Stripping the rabbit from the bones.

Adding the cream to the sauce for the filling.

Cutting the lids for the pies, using the dishes as a guide and allowing excess all round.

Positioning the pie lids over the filling.

Crimping the edges decoratively with the thumb and forefinger.

Cutting a slit in the top of the pie to allow steam to escape.

Buffalo & ale pie

SERVES 4–6
●●●●●●●●●

For the flaky pastry

175g plain flour

Pinch of fine salt

65g cold unsalted butter,
cut into 5mm–1cm dice

65g cold lard, cut into
5mm–1cm dice

1 tsp lemon juice

130ml very cold water

1 egg, beaten, to glaze

For the filling

2 tbsp plain flour

1kg buffalo stewing steak,
cut into 4–5cm cubes

1–2 tbsp vegetable oil

25g unsalted butter

12 shallots, peeled but left
whole

2 large carrots, peeled and
cut into 2cm slices

2 tsp mushroom ketchup

1 tbsp tomato purée

300ml ale or stout

300ml beef stock

Few thyme sprigs

1 tsp soft dark brown sugar

Salt and pepper

Equipment

1.5 litre pie dish

Pie funnel

Water buffalo are now farmed in this country. Their meat makes a delicious alternative to beef: it's lean and cooks to a lovely tenderness, with a rich flavour. If you can't get hold of buffalo, you can use good stewing beef such as braising or chuck steak (simmer it for about twice as long before putting in the pie).

Make the flaky pastry following the recipe on page 24. Wrap in cling film and chill in the fridge while you make the filling.

Put the flour in a large bowl and season it well with salt and pepper. Toss the meat in the flour until evenly coated.

Heat 1 tbsp oil and the butter in a flameproof casserole over a medium-high heat. Working in batches, brown the meat well all over, adding a dash more oil if you need to. Transfer the browned meat to a dish.

Lower the heat under the pan, add a little more oil if necessary and add the shallots and carrots. Sauté for a couple of minutes, until the shallots are just starting to soften. Return all the meat to the pan. Add the mushroom ketchup and tomato purée and cook for another 2 minutes.

Pour in the ale and stock, then add the thyme and sugar. Bring to the boil, then reduce the heat, cover with a lid and simmer gently for 1 hour or until the meat is very tender. Leave to cool completely.

Position a pie funnel in the middle of a 1.5 litre pie dish and spoon the filling into the dish. (If there is a lot of liquid, keep some of it back to serve as gravy.)

Heat your oven to 200°C/gas 6.

On a lightly floured surface, roll out the pastry to a 3mm thickness. Cut a 2cm wide strip of pastry. Dampen the rim of the pie dish with water and press the pastry strip onto the rim; dampen this too. Cut the remaining pastry a little larger than the pie dish. Position the lid over the filling, press the edges to seal and crimp them. Trim away the excess pastry.

Brush the pastry with beaten egg and make a steam hole in the middle, exposing the funnel. Bake for 35–40 minutes until the pastry is crisp and golden. Leave to settle for 10–15 minutes before serving.

Sausage plait

For the puff pastry
100g strong white bread flour
100g plain flour
Pinch of fine salt
75–100ml cold water
165g cold unsalted butter
1 egg, beaten, to glaze

For the filling
300g chestnut mushrooms, trimmed
2 tbsp thyme leaves
1 tbsp sunflower oil
25g unsalted butter
2 red onions, thinly sliced
2 tsp soft brown sugar
1 tbsp sherry vinegar
300g good-quality sausagemeat (or skinned butcher's sausages)
100g black pudding, cut into 1–2cm pieces
1 tbsp sesame seeds
Salt and pepper

Equipment
Large baking sheet (lipped)

This is either a poor man's Wellington, or a posh sausage roll, depending on how you look at it. It's certainly good enough for a special meal. The sausage filling is spiked with black pudding, enhanced with a savoury mushroom base and topped with caramelised onions. Wrapped in crisp, buttery 'plaited' pastry, it looks really impressive yet it's easy to make.

Make the puff pastry following the recipe on page 28. Wrap in cling film and chill in the fridge while you prepare the filling.

Put the mushrooms in a food processor, season with salt and pepper and pulse until reduced to a rough paste. Add the thyme and give the mix a final pulse. Transfer to a dry frying pan and cook over a medium-high heat, stirring often, until all the liquid has evaporated from the mushrooms. Remove from the pan and set aside to cool.

Heat the oil and butter in a wide frying pan on a medium-low heat. Add the onions with the sugar and cook slowly until soft and lightly caramelised. This will take at least 20 minutes. Stir in the sherry vinegar and set aside to cool.

Heat your oven to 200°C/gas 6. Line a large lipped baking sheet with baking parchment (some butter may leak out of the pastry).

Roll out the pastry to a rectangle, about 26 x 30cm. Spread the mushroom paste down the middle third of the pastry, leaving a 5cm gap at the top and bottom.

Mix the sausagemeat with the black pudding, mould into a long sausage shape that will fit on top of the mushroom paste and place it on the paste. Spread the caramelised onions on top of it.

Cut slits on the diagonal all the way down the pastry on each side of the filling at 2cm intervals. Brush lightly with egg. Take one strip over the filling from one side, then one from the other and so on, crossing the strips over to form a plaited effect. Tuck the ends of the pastry under the plait, trimming off excess if necessary. Using a large palette knife, carefully lift onto the prepared baking sheet.

Brush the plait with beaten egg and sprinkle with sesame seeds. Bake for 30 minutes or until the pastry is golden brown. Leave to settle for 10 minutes or so, then serve hot or cold. This is delicious with a dollop of apple sauce on the side.

Step photographs overleaf

Spreading the mushroom paste down the middle of the pastry.

Positioning the sausagemeat and black pudding mixture on the mushroom paste.

Cutting slits in the sides of the pastry, on the diagonal, at 2cm intervals.

Brushing the pastry on either side of the filling lightly with beaten egg.

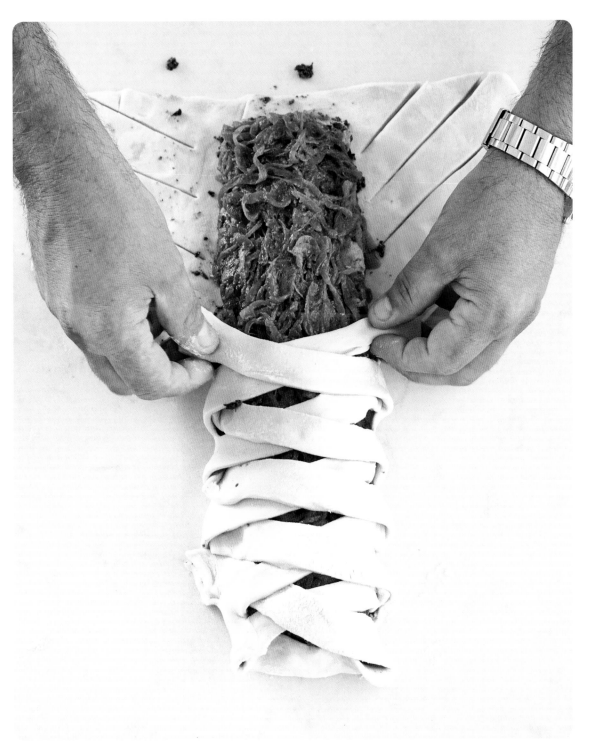

Crossing the strips of pastry over the filling to give a plaited effect.

Hollywood's temptation

SERVES 4–6
●●●●●●●●●●

75g unsalted butter

1 large onion, thinly sliced

800g waxy potatoes, such
as Maris Peer, peeled and
thinly sliced

About 500ml whole milk

4 large sheets of filo pastry
(about 25 x 40cm each)

400g hot-smoked salmon
fillet, flaked

100ml double cream

Salt and pepper

Equipment

20cm springform cake tin,
7cm deep

Baking sheet (lipped)

This recipe is based on a Swedish gratin-style dish called Janssen's Temptation, which pairs potatoes with sprats or anchovies. I like to use hot-smoked Scottish salmon instead, combining it with thinly sliced potatoes, sweet onion and cream, then encasing the whole lot in crisp filo pastry to give a contrasting texture.

Heat 25g of the butter in a large frying pan. Add the onion and sweat gently over a low heat for around 20 minutes, stirring often, until very soft and golden. Season with a little salt and pepper and set aside.

Put the sliced potatoes in a large saucepan and pour on enough milk to cover. Bring to the boil, lower the heat and simmer for about 5 minutes until the potatoes are just tender but not cooked through. Drain the potatoes, reserving 100ml of the milk.

Heat your oven to 200°C/gas 6 and put in a lipped baking sheet (as the pie may leak a little butter) to heat up. Use a little of the butter to grease a 20cm springform cake tin, about 7cm deep.

Melt the remaining butter. Brush a sheet of filo pastry with melted butter and place, butter-side up, in the cake tin, leaving the excess hanging over the side. Turn the cake tin slightly, then lay another sheet of filo in the tin at an angle to the first sheet and brush it with melted butter. Repeat to use the rest of the filo sheets, brushing with butter as you layer them in the tin.

Put one-third of the potatoes into the pastry-lined tin and season with a little salt and pepper. Follow with half the onions and then half the flaked fish. Repeat these layers, then finish off with the final third of potato.

Mix the reserved milk with the cream and pour over the filling.

Fold the overhanging pastry back over the filling to enclose it, and brush the top of the pie with melted butter. Place the pie on the hot baking sheet in the oven and bake for 30–35 minutes until the filo is crisp and golden.

Leave the pie to stand for 30 minutes or so – it's best eaten warm or at room temperature – then transfer to a large plate before slicing.

Step photographs overleaf

Hollywood's temptation

Brushing the first sheet of filo with melted butter and laying in the prepared cake tin.

Layering the sheets of filo in the tin, to line it fully and evenly.

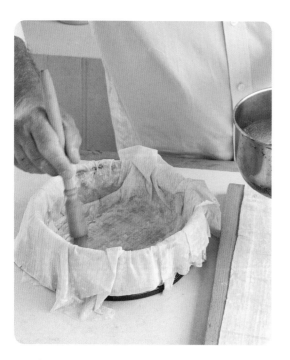

Brushing the layers of filo with melted butter as they are layered in the tin.

Scattering half the golden, softened onions over the potato layer in the bottom of the filo case.

Layering half of the flaked salmon over the onion layer.

Adding the second layer of sliced potatoes.

Folding the overhanging filo over the top of the filling to seal the pie.

Brushing the top of the pie with melted butter before baking.

Raised game pie

SERVES 8
●●●●●●●●

For the hot water crust pastry

100g lard, plus extra for
greasing
450g plain flour
100g strong white bread flour
75g cold unsalted butter,
cut into roughly 1cm dice
200ml water
½ tsp salt
1 egg yolk, beaten, to glaze

For the filling

2 eschalions (banana shallots),
finely chopped
2 garlic cloves, crushed
700g mixed, boned, diced
game meat, such as venison,
rabbit, pheasant, pigeon
and/or boar
200g minced pork belly
200g back bacon, rind
removed, diced
2 tbsp Madeira
½ tsp ground mace
½ tsp ground allspice
2 tbsp chopped parsley
2 tbsp chopped thyme
Salt and white pepper

Equipment

20cm springform cake tin,
about 7cm deep

A game pie makes a spectacular centrepiece and this handsome example is amazingly straightforward – especially if you buy mixed game meat ready-prepared from a good butcher. Don't be daunted by the idea of using hot water crust pastry either – the pie is moulded in a tin, which makes it very easy to put together.

Heat your oven to 200°C/gas 6. Grease a 20cm springform cake tin, about 7cm deep, with lard.

First make the filling. Put the shallots and garlic into a large bowl. Add the game, pork belly mince, diced bacon, Madeira, spices and herbs. Season with salt and a little white pepper. Using your hands, mix all the ingredients thoroughly together. Put in the fridge while you prepare the pastry.

To make the pastry, combine the flours in a bowl, add the butter and rub in with your fingertips. Heat the water, salt and lard in a pan until just boiling. Pour the mixture onto the flour and mix together with a wooden spoon. Once cool enough to handle, tip onto a lightly floured surface and knead to a smooth dough.

Work as quickly as you can now (as the pastry will become more crumbly as it cools). Cut off two-thirds of the pastry, roll it out and use to line the prepared tin, leaving any excess hanging over the side. Check there are no cracks or holes in the pastry. Roll out the remaining pastry for the lid and leave to one side.

Spoon the filling into the pastry-lined tin. Press it down and level the surface.

Brush the edge of the pastry in the tin with beaten egg yolk and place the pastry lid on top. Press the edges together to seal and trim off the excess pastry neatly. Crimp the edges decoratively. Make a couple of slits in the top of the pie to allow steam to escape and brush the pastry with egg yolk.

Stand the tin on a baking tray and bake the pie for 30 minutes. Then turn the oven down to 160°C/gas 3 and bake for a further 1¾ hours.

Leave the pie to cool completely in the tin before removing. Slice on a plate to catch any juices. Serve at room temperature.

Step photographs overleaf

Raised game pie

Lifting the rolled two-thirds portion of pastry into the cake tin to line the base and sides.

Pressing the pastry into the sides of the tin, making sure there are no cracks or holes.

Spooning the filling into the pastry-lined tin.

Positioning the pie lid over the filling.

Pressing the edges of the pastry together to seal the pie.

Trimming away the excess pastry from the edge of the tin.

Crimping the edges decoratively using the thumb and forefinger.

Cutting slits in the top of the pie to allow steam to escape.

Raised pork & egg pie

SERVES 8
●●●●●●●●

For the hot water crust pastry
100g lard, plus extra for
greasing
450g plain flour
100g strong white bread flour
75g cold unsalted butter,
cut into roughly 1cm dice
200ml water
½ tsp salt
1 egg yolk, beaten, to glaze

For the filling
300g good-quality
sausagemeat (or skinned
butcher's sausages)
300g minced pork
150g cooked ham hock, cut
into roughly 1.5cm pieces
2 eschalions (banana shallots),
finely chopped
3 tbsp chopped parsley
4 hard-boiled eggs, shelled
Salt and white pepper

Equipment
1kg loaf tin (about 10 x 20cm
base measurement)

I love pies that have the treat of whole eggs hidden inside. This is a picnic classic and a slice would be great in a lunchbox too.

Heat your oven to 200°C/gas 6. Grease a 1kg loaf tin (measuring about 10 x 20cm across the base) with lard, then strip-line it with baking parchment (i.e. cut one long strip of parchment, the width of the tin, and place it in the tin so that there's an overhang of parchment at each end, which will help you remove the pie later).

First make the filling. Put all the ingredients, except the hard-boiled eggs, into a large bowl, seasoning lightly. Mix together thoroughly (the easiest way to do this is with your hands). Cook a little nugget of the mixture in a frying pan and taste it to check the seasoning. Put the mix in the fridge while you make the pastry.

To make the pastry, combine the flours in a bowl, add the butter and rub in lightly with your fingertips. Heat the water, salt and lard in a saucepan until just boiling. Pour the mixture onto the flour and mix together with a wooden spoon. Once cool enough to handle, tip onto a lightly floured surface and knead to a smooth dough.

Working quickly (the pastry will become crumbly and more difficult to handle as it cools), roll out two-thirds of the pastry and use it to line the prepared tin, leaving the excess hanging over the edges.

Press half the meat filling into the pastry-lined tin. Take a thin slice off the top and bottom of each boiled egg (this helps them sit next to each other and makes slicing the pie easier), then place the eggs lengthways down the middle of the pie. Add the remaining meat filling and pat it down.

Brush the overhanging pastry edge with egg yolk. Roll out the remaining pastry to make a lid, place over the pie and trim away the excess. Pinch the pastry edges together to seal and crimp neatly. Cut leaves from the pastry trimmings to decorate the pie.

Brush the pastry lid with beaten egg and make a couple of steam holes in the centre. Arrange the pastry decorations on top of the pie and brush these with egg too.

Bake for 30 minutes then reduce the heat to 180°C/gas 4 and bake for a further hour. Leave to cool completely in the tin. To remove the pie, turn the tin on its side and use the parchment paper to slide out the pie. Serve in thick slices.

Lamb & kidney suet pudding with rosemary

SERVES 4–6

●●●●●●●●

For the suet pastry
Butter for greasing
285g self-raising flour
125g shredded suet
1 tsp baking powder
1 tbsp finely chopped rosemary
About 225ml very cold water

For the filling
30g unsalted butter
2–3 tbsp vegetable oil
2 eschalions (banana shallots), sliced
2 garlic cloves, sliced
1 tbsp plain flour
1 tbsp finely chopped rosemary
500g lamb shoulder, trimmed and diced into bite-sized pieces
3 lamb's kidneys, halved, tough white core removed, cut into bite-sized pieces
150ml red wine
150ml rich beef stock
Salt and pepper

Equipment
1.2 litre pudding basin

When it comes to comfort food, you just can't beat a traditional steamed suet pudding like this one. It takes a little while to cook but is very simple to put together. Here I am using flavour-rich shoulder of lamb for the filling, with aromatic rosemary, shallots and garlic. If you would prefer a classic steak and kidney pud, see the variation (overleaf).

First make the filling. Melt the butter with 1 tbsp oil in a large, wide heavy-based saucepan over a medium-low heat. When it is foaming, add the shallots and garlic and cook for a few minutes until they begin to soften, but not colour.

Meanwhile, in a large bowl, mix the 1 tbsp flour with the chopped rosemary and some salt and pepper. Add the lamb and kidneys and toss them thoroughly in the seasoned flour.

Transfer the softened shallots and garlic to a large bowl and set to one side. Add a little more oil to the pan and increase the heat. Add a third of the lamb and kidneys and cook until browned all over. Set aside with the shallots and repeat with the remaining meat, adding more oil if needed. Return all the meat and the shallots to the pan.

Add the wine to the pan and let it bubble and reduce for a couple of minutes, scraping the base of the pan with a spatula to help release any caramelised bits. Add the stock and simmer for 5 minutes. If the sauce looks too thick, add a little water. Taste the sauce and season with salt and pepper. Set aside to cool completely.

When you are ready to cook the pudding, first generously butter a 1.2 litre pudding basin.

To make the suet pastry, mix the flour, suet, baking powder and rosemary together in a bowl and season with salt and pepper. Add most of the water and mix to a soft, slightly sticky dough with one hand, adding more water as necessary. Divide the dough into two pieces – roughly three-quarters and one-quarter.

Dust your work surface with flour and roll out the larger piece of dough into a circle, roughly 30cm in diameter. Use this to line the pudding basin, leaving the excess pastry hanging over the edge.

Continued overleaf

Lamb & kidney suet pudding

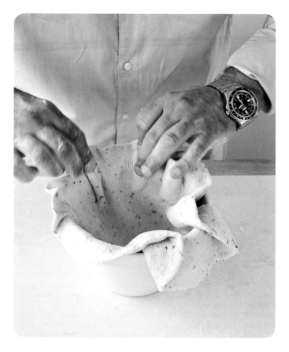

Lifting the rolled three-quarters portion of suet pastry into the greased pudding basin to line it.

Gently pressing the pastry against the sides of the basin, allowing the excess to overhang.

The pastry-lined pudding basin, ready to fill.

Spooning in the cooled filling.

Step photographs continued overleaf

Roll out the small piece of dough to a circle, large enough to form a lid for the basin. Spoon the cooled filling into the pastry-lined basin. Dampen the edge of the pastry in the bowl with water and position the pastry lid. Press the edges together and trim away the excess pastry neatly. Crimp the edges to ensure a good seal.

Place a large piece of baking parchment on a sheet of foil on your work surface and make a large pleat in the middle, folding both sheets together (this allows for the pudding's expansion as it cooks). Lay the parchment and foil over the top of the pudding basin, foil side up, and secure with string, looping the end of the string over the top of the pudding and tying it to form a handle that will enable you to lift the pudding in and out of the saucepan.

Stand the pudding basin in a large pan, and pour in enough boiling water to come halfway up the side of the basin. Put a tight-fitting lid on the pan and bring to a simmer. Lower the heat to maintain a simmer and steam the pudding for 2–2½ hours. Top up the boiling water during steaming if necessary so the pan doesn't boil dry.

Lift the pudding basin out of the pan, remove the foil and parchment and leave to rest for 5 minutes. Then run the tip of a small, sharp knife around the side of the pudding to release it from the basin. Invert a large, deep plate over the pudding and turn the plate and pudding over, so the pudding comes out onto the plate.

Serve straight away, with mashed potato and a green vegetable such as broccoli or leafy greens.

Variation: Steak & kidney pudding

Instead of the lamb, use 500g chuck (or braising) steak and 3 calf's kidneys, cut into bite-sized pieces. Dust the steak and kidneys with seasoned flour. Melt 30g butter with 1 tbsp oil in a heavy-based pan and gently cook 1 sliced large onion until beginning to soften but not colour. Remove from the pan and set aside. Add a little more oil to the pan and increase the heat. Brown the beef and kidneys all over in batches. Once it is all browned, return all the meat and the onion to the pan and pour in 150ml red wine. Let it bubble to reduce a little, then add 150ml rich beef stock. Taste the sauce and season as required. Leave the filling to go cold. Make the suet pastry and continue as above.

Positioning the pastry lid.

Pressing the edges of the pastry lid onto the dampened rim of the lining pastry to seal.

Trimming away the excess pastry.

The crimped, sealed pudding, ready for steaming.

Covering a pudding for steaming

Laying the pleated foil and parchment on top of the pudding.

Securing the foil and parchment in position with string.

Tying the string under the rim, leaving a length to loop over the basin and tie to create a handle.

The covered pudding ready for steaming.

Meat & potato pie

For the suet crust

375g self-raising flour

175g shredded beef suet

About 250ml very cold water

For the filling

2 large onions, chopped

700g chuck steak (braising steak), cut into 4–5cm chunks

400g waxy potatoes, such as Estima or Maris Peer, peeled and cut into 4cm chunks

400g floury potatoes, such as King Edward, peeled and cut into 4cm chunks

Salt and pepper

Equipment

1.2 litre pie dish

This no-nonsense recipe is one of my favourite pies. I use chuck steak (often sold as braising steak) which has lots of flavour, and two types of potato: a floury variety, which falls apart and thickens the gravy, and a waxier type that holds its shape to provide texture.

First make the filling. Put the onions and steak in a large pan. Add enough water to just cover them and bring to a simmer. Cover with a lid, reduce the heat and simmer very gently for 1½ hours.

Add the potatoes to the pan, along with some salt and pepper, and cook for a further 30–35 minutes or until the potatoes are soft and the meat is tender. The gravy should be nicely thickened by the potatoes. Check the seasoning.

Pour off 300–600ml of liquid from the pan – enough to leave the filling nicely moist but not swimming in liquid – and save this to serve as gravy with the pie. Transfer the filling to a 1.2 litre pie dish and leave to cool completely.

Heat your oven to 200°C/gas 6.

To make the suet pastry, combine the flour and suet in a large bowl with some salt and pepper. Add most of the water and mix to a soft, slightly sticky dough with one hand, adding more water as needed. Leave to stand for 5 minutes.

On a lightly floured surface, roll out the dough to around a 7–8mm thickness. Cut a 2cm wide strip of pastry. Dampen the rim of the pie dish with water. Stick the pastry strip onto the rim and dampen this too. Lay the sheet of pastry on top. Press down the edges to seal and crimp or flute them, trimming off the excess pastry.

Bake the pie for 30–40 minutes until the pastry is golden brown. Leave to stand for 10–15 minutes before serving.

Chilli beef cornbread pies

SERVES 4–6
●●●●●●●●●

For the filling

About 2 tbsp sunflower oil

500g shin of beef, trimmed
and cut into 1cm cubes

1 large onion, diced

2 garlic cloves, crushed

1 red chilli, finely chopped

1 tsp dried oregano

½ tsp cocoa powder

1 tbsp tomato purée

400g tin chopped tomatoes

200ml rich beef stock

400g tin kidney beans, drained
and rinsed

3 large roasted red peppers
from a jar, roughly chopped

Good pinch of chilli powder
(optional)

Salt and black pepper

For the cornbread topping

125g plain flour

125g cornmeal

½ tsp salt

115g unsalted butter, melted
and slightly cooled

2 medium eggs, beaten

250ml buttermilk

1 green chilli, deseeded and
very finely chopped

½ tsp baking powder

120g strong Cheddar, grated

Equipment

4–6 individual pie dishes

Freshly baked cornbread is a great accompaniment to stews and chilli and this recipe combines the two elements in one golden, bubbling dish. Shin of beef is a very economical cut – it needs a good, long cook to make it tender, but you'll be rewarded with a fantastic depth of flavour.

To make the filling (which you can do ahead of time), first heat your oven to 170°C/gas 3.

Heat about 1 tbsp oil in a flameproof casserole over a medium-high heat. Add half the beef and brown it well. Remove and set aside in a dish. Add the remaining meat, and a little more oil if necessary, brown it and remove from the pan.

Reduce the heat to medium-low and add a little more oil to the pan. Add the onion and garlic and cook for 5–8 minutes, until softened.

Add the chilli, oregano, cocoa powder and tomato purée to the onions and stir to mix. Return the meat to the pan, along with any juices that have seeped from it, and cook for a few minutes. Season with salt and pepper.

Add the tomatoes and beef stock, bring to a simmer, then cover and cook in the oven for 1 hour. Add the kidney beans and peppers and return to the oven for a further hour or until the meat is tender.

Check the seasoning (if it's not hot enough for you, you can spice it up with a little chilli powder) then spoon the mixture into 4–6 deep, individual pie dishes, leaving about 2cm below the rim.

Turn the oven up to 180°C/gas 4.

To make the cornbread batter, mix the flour, cornmeal and salt in a large bowl. Combine the melted butter, eggs, buttermilk, green chilli and baking powder in a jug. Add to the dry ingredients and mix just until combined. Don't overmix.

Top the chilli beef with the cornbread batter, then sprinkle cheese over each dish. Bake for about 30 minutes, until golden. If you like, you can finish the pies under the grill for a few minutes to get a really nice golden brown top. Serve straight away.

Luxury fish pie

SERVES 6
●●●●●●

For the poaching stock
600ml fish stock
600ml water
50ml Pernod
1 small onion, roughly chopped
1 small fennel bulb, roughly chopped
2 celery sticks, roughly chopped
1 bay leaf
Few parsley sprigs

For the filling
500g haddock fillet (or other white fish of your choice), skinned
250g salmon fillet, skinned
250g smoked langoustine tails

For the saffron mash
1.5kg floury potatoes, such as King Edward, peeled and cut into large chunks
100ml double cream
Good pinch of saffron strands
50g unsalted butter

For the sauce
40g unsalted butter
40g plain flour
300ml reserved poaching stock
100ml double cream
2 tbsp chopped tarragon
Salt and pepper

Equipment
1.5-2 litre ovenproof dish

A good fish pie, I think, always needs some smoked fish – or shellfish – to give it a real depth of flavour and what could be more luxurious than smoked Scottish langoustines? If you can't get hold of any, use giant tiger prawns instead, and replace half the plain haddock with smoked haddock.

Heat your oven to 200°C/gas 6. Have ready a large ovenproof dish, 1.5-2 litres capacity.

Place all the ingredients for the poaching stock in a large pan and bring to the boil. Reduce the heat to a simmer and add the haddock and salmon. Poach the fish for a few minutes, until it is just cooked. Strain the mixture, reserving all the liquid. Pick out and discard the stock vegetables. Leave the fish to cool.

Put the poaching liquid into a clean pan. Bring to the boil, and boil until the liquid has reduced by half. You will need 400ml of this reduced liquor. Set aside.

For the saffron mash, put the potatoes in a large saucepan, cover with cold water, add a little salt and bring to the boil. Lower the heat and simmer for 15-20 minutes, until tender.

Meanwhile, to make the sauce, melt the butter in a pan. Stir in the flour to form a roux. Let this cook over a medium heat, stirring often, for 2-3 minutes. Turn the heat down very low and gradually add the reduced poaching liquid, a ladleful at a time, beating well after each addition to create a smooth sauce. Return to the heat and cook, stirring often, for about 5 minutes. Stir in the cream, tarragon and some salt and pepper.

Drain the potatoes well. Heat the cream, saffron and butter gently in the potato pan, until the butter has melted, then take off the heat and pass the potatoes through a ricer into the pan (or just tip them in and mash). Season well with salt and pepper and stir to combine.

Flake the cooked fish evenly over the base of your ovenproof dish, checking for any bones as you go. Scatter over the langoustines. Pour over the sauce. Top with the mash, spread it evenly and then mark decoratively with a fork.

Bake for 25-30 minutes until golden brown on top and bubbling all the way through. If your assembled pie has cooled down, it may take longer. Serve with buttered peas.

Goat-herd pie

SERVES 4
●●●●●●●

For the filling
1–2 tbsp olive oil
2 medium onions, finely diced
2 celery sticks, de-stringed and diced
125g butternut squash, peeled and diced
2 garlic cloves, peeled
½ tsp coarse sea salt
4 anchovy fillets in oil, drained
500g goat mince
1 tbsp tomato purée
1 tbsp plain flour
1 tbsp roughly chopped green olives
150ml red wine
150ml beef stock
1 tbsp chopped rosemary
½ tsp ground cinnamon
Salt and pepper

For the topping
1kg floury potatoes, such as King Edward, peeled and cut into chunks
50g unsalted butter
25g crumbly goat's cheese, crumbled
25g Parmesan, finely grated

To finish (optional)
Extra grated Parmesan

Equipment
1.2 litre ovenproof dish

We've all heard of shepherd's pie. It's a dish thought to have originated in the sheep-farming country of northern England and, though the title itself is not recorded until Queen Victoria's time, the dish probably dates back much further. Some early versions were doubtless very basic but it's a recipe that's been embellished and perfected by generations of cooks. This recipe uses goat meat instead of lamb, which is a leaner meat and very tasty indeed. You can, of course, still use lamb if you prefer.

To make the filling, heat 1 tbsp olive oil in a wide frying pan over a medium-low heat. Add the onions, celery and squash and cook gently for about 10 minutes, until the onions begin to soften.

Using a pestle and mortar, crush the garlic with the salt to a paste. Add the anchovies and bash to form a rough paste, then add this mixture to the pan of vegetables. Cook gently for about 5 minutes, stirring, so the anchovies begin to 'melt' into the vegetables. Spoon the contents of the pan into a bowl, leaving any oil behind.

Increase the heat under the pan. Add a little more oil if necessary, and half the mince. Cook, stirring, until it is browned, then add it to the vegetables. Repeat with the remaining mince, then return all the meat and vegetables to the pan.

Stir in the tomato purée and flour and cook gently for 2–3 minutes. Add the olives and pour in the wine and stock. Bring to the boil, then lower the heat and simmer for 15 minutes. Add the rosemary and cinnamon and season with pepper, and a little salt if needed (the anchovies are already quite salty).

Transfer the filling to an ovenproof dish, about 1.2 litre capacity.

Heat your oven to 190°C/gas 5.

For the topping, put the potatoes in a saucepan, cover with water, add a little salt and bring to the boil. Lower the heat and simmer for 15–20 minutes, until the potatoes are tender. Drain well, mash or rice them back into the hot pan and stir in the butter.

Spread the mash over the meat in the dish. Combine the crumbled goat's cheese and Parmesan and sprinkle over the potato. Bake for 25–30 minutes until the top is golden and crusty and the filling is bubbling. Leave to stand for 10–15 minutes before serving, sprinkled with a little extra Parmesan if you like. Serve with a green vegetable.

Spinach, feta & pine nut parcels

MAKES 4
●●●●●●●

For the dough
250g strong white bread flour
1 tsp fine salt
1 tsp fast-action dried yeast
2 tbsp olive oil, plus extra for kneading
125–150ml water

For the filling
1 tbsp olive oil
2 garlic cloves, crushed
500g frozen whole-leaf (not chopped) spinach
125g Yorkshire Fettle cheese, or feta, crumbled
2 tbsp pine nuts, lightly toasted
3 tbsp chopped mint
Salt and black pepper

Equipment
Baking tray
18cm plate

These triangular pasties are based on a Lebanese speciality called *fatayer* and use soft bread dough, rather than pastry, to enclose the filling. I prefer frozen spinach for this recipe – it's very easy to use and actually produces a less watery mixture.

To make the dough, put the flour into a large bowl and add the salt to one side and the yeast to the other. Add the olive oil and pour in 125ml of the water. Start to mix with the fingers of one hand, adding a little more water as you go, gradually incorporating all the flour from the side of the bowl until you have a rough dough. It should be soft and slightly sticky. You may not need to add all the water or you may need a bit more (depending on the absorbency of the flour).

Trickle a little olive oil onto your work surface and knead the dough on it for a good 5 minutes until it becomes smooth and is no longer sticky. Return to the bowl and cover with cling film. Leave it in a warm place for about an hour until doubled in size and puffy.

Meanwhile, make the filling. Heat the olive oil in a wide frying pan over a low heat, add the garlic and cook gently for a minute or until just starting to colour. Transfer to a large bowl. Now add the frozen spinach to the pan and turn the heat up high. Cook, stirring often, until the spinach is soft and all the liquid released has evaporated. Add to the bowl with the garlic and season with pepper and a pinch of salt (remember that the cheese will be very salty). Leave to cool, then add the cheese, pine nuts and mint. Mix thoroughly.

When you are ready to assemble the parcels, heat your oven to 220°C/gas 7 and line a baking tray with baking parchment.

Transfer the risen dough to a lightly floured surface and deflate it gently, then roll it out to a 5mm thickness. Using a plate as a guide, cut out 4 circles, 18cm in diameter.

Divide the filling between the circles, forming it into a pyramid shape in the centre. Dampen the pastry margin with water. Bring the dough up over each side of the triangle of filling, forming a pyramid shape. Pinch the edges of the dough together with your fingers to seal. Trim off any excess and press together again.

Put the spinach parcels on the prepared baking tray and bake for 12–15 minutes until golden. Eat hot, warm or cold.

Step photographs overleaf

Spinach, feta & pine nut parcels

The risen dough, ready for rolling out.

Rolling and smoothing out the deflated dough to a 5mm thickness.

Using a plate as a template to cut out 18cm dough circles.

Removing the pastry trimmings.

Dividing the filling between the circles and forming it into a pyramid shape.

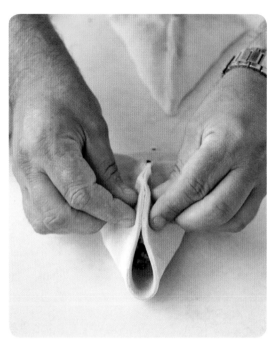

Bringing the dough up over two sides of the triangle of filling to join over the top.

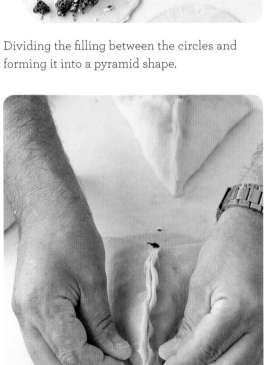

Pinching the edges together between thumbs and forefingers to seal.

The triangular parcel ready to bake, with the third side of dough sealed over the filling.

Chicken & chorizo empanadas

MAKES 10
●●●●●●●

For the empanada dough
150g unsalted butter
300g plain flour
Large pinch of fine salt
1 medium egg, lightly beaten
3–5 tbsp water

For the filling
4 chicken thighs, on the bone and skin on
1 tbsp olive oil
1 medium onion, finely chopped
1 garlic clove, crushed
100g cured chorizo sausage (ready-to-eat), finely diced
½ tsp cumin seeds
50g raisins
Salt and pepper

To finish
1 egg, beaten, to glaze

Equipment
Large baking sheet
12cm cutter or bowl

Traditional in Spain, Portugal and Latin America, empanadas are little pastry pockets with an intensely flavoured savoury filling. They are great eaten any time but make a particularly good tapas-style snack with a cold beer.

Heat your oven to 180°C/gas 4. For the filling, put the chicken thighs in a small roasting dish, season well all over with salt and pepper and roast for about 45 minutes until cooked through. Set aside to cool a little.

Meanwhile, make the pastry. Melt the butter and leave it to cool slightly. Put the flour into a large bowl and mix in the salt. Pour in the butter and egg. Start mixing, adding the water as you go, until you have a soft dough. Turn out onto your work surface and knead gently for a couple of minutes, until smooth. Return the dough to its bowl, cover and set aside to rest while you prepare the filling.

Heat the olive oil in a frying pan over a medium-low heat. Add the onion and cook for 10–12 minutes, until soft. Add the garlic, chorizo, cumin seeds and raisins. Cook over a medium heat for 5–8 minutes, stirring often, until the chorizo is cooked. Remove from the heat.

Once the chicken thighs are cool enough to handle, remove the skin. Pull all the meat from the bones and chop it roughly. Add to the chorizo mixture. Taste and add salt and pepper if needed (the chorizo is already quite salty), then leave to cool completely.

Turn the oven up to 200°C/gas 6 and line a large baking sheet with baking parchment.

Lightly flour your work surface and roll out the dough to a 3–4mm thickness. Using a 12cm cutter, or a small bowl as a guide, cut out 10 discs. You will probably need to re-roll the offcuts once to get this many. Divide the filling between the discs. Dampen the edges of the dough with water, then fold over one half of each disc to make a semi-circular parcel. Press the edges together firmly, then crimp or press the edges with a fork.

Put the empanadas on the baking sheet and brush with beaten egg. Bake for 15–20 minutes, until golden. Eat them warm, on their own or with a chilli sauce.

Savoury choux buns with creamy mushrooms

SERVES 6
●●●●●●●

For the choux buns

100g unsalted butter, cut into roughly 1cm cubes

Pinch of fine salt

300ml water

130g strong white bread flour

1 tbsp chopped thyme

4 medium eggs, beaten

25g Parmesan, finely grated

For the filling

25g unsalted butter

1 tbsp olive oil

1 large eschalion (banana shallot), sliced

600g mixed mushrooms, roughly chopped

2 garlic cloves, chopped

1 tsp thyme leaves

2 tbsp dry sherry

200g crème fraîche

Juice of ½ lemon

1 tbsp chopped flat-leaf parsley

Salt and pepper

Equipment

Baking tray

This recipe has a retro feel about it, and it's none the worse for that. The deliciously savoury flavours here, and the beautifully crisp choux pastry, will always go down a storm.

Heat your oven to 220°C/gas 7 and line a baking tray with baking parchment.

To make the choux buns, put the butter, salt and water into a large saucepan. Heat gently until the butter has melted then bring to the boil. Immediately remove from the heat and tip in the flour and thyme. Beat with a wooden spoon to form a smooth ball of dough that should leave the sides of the pan.

Now vigorously beat the beaten eggs into the hot dough, a little at a time. This takes some elbow grease! As you do so, the dough will become stiff and glossy. Stop adding the egg if the dough starts to become loose – but you should use up all or most of it.

Spoon the dough into 6 large blobs, each about 7cm in diameter, on the prepared baking tray. (Alternatively, you can pipe the choux onto the tray.) Sprinkle the Parmesan evenly on top of them.

Bake in the centre of the oven for 10 minutes until the choux buns are well risen and golden. Then turn the oven down to 190°C/gas 5 and bake for a further 30 minutes to ensure the centres are cooked. The buns should be crisp and dry. On removing from the oven, split one side of each bun open to allow the steam to escape. Transfer to a wire rack to cool.

For the filling, melt the butter with the oil in a large, wide frying pan. Add the shallot and cook for a few minutes until soft but not coloured. Add the mushrooms, garlic and thyme. Cook over a high heat for about 10 minutes, stirring often, until the mushrooms are buttery, soft and reduced in volume by about half, and their liquid has been driven off.

Add the sherry and crème fraîche and allow to bubble gently for about 10 minutes to reduce the sauce. Stir in the lemon juice and parsley and season with salt and plenty of black pepper.

Cut each choux bun fully in half. Fill with the warm mushroom mixture and serve, with a green salad.

Scotch pies

MAKES 8
●●●●●●●●

For the hot water crust pastry
720g plain flour
320ml water
1 tsp fine salt
240g lard
1 egg yolk, beaten, to glaze

For the filling
1.2kg minced mutton
½ tsp ground mace
½ tsp freshly grated nutmeg
150ml gravy or stock
Salt and white pepper

Equipment
Large baking tray
18cm plate
10cm saucer

Also known as mutton pies, these have a long history. In the Middle Ages, they were viewed as luxurious, decadent English-style food and frowned upon by the Scottish church. As time moved on, they proved to be convenient, sustaining snacks for working people, who would buy them hot from pie-men or pie-wives in the city streets. The space in the top of the pie, created by the raised crust, would sometimes be filled with gravy, beans or mashed potato.

Line a large baking tray with baking parchment.

First make the filling. Mix the ingredients together, seasoning well and working the liquid into the meat. Divide into 8 portions and mould each into a ball. Refrigerate while you make the pastry.

Have ready 8 strips of baking parchment, about 5cm deep and 25cm long, to wrap around the pies, and 8 lengths of string to secure them.

For the pastry, put the flour into a bowl. Heat the water, salt and lard in a saucepan until just boiling. Pour the mixture onto the flour and mix together with a wooden spoon. Once cool enough to handle, tip onto a lightly floured surface and knead to a smooth dough.

Working quickly, cut off a quarter of the pastry and set aside. Roll out the remaining dough to a 5mm thickness and cut out 8 circles, 18cm in diameter, using a plate as a guide. Roll out the remaining pastry and cut out 8 lids, 10cm in diameter, using a saucer as a guide.

Place a ball of filling on each large pastry circle. Gather the pastry around the meat and bring up the sides to form the shape of a pork pie, stretching the pastry so it comes above the meat by about 2cm.

Dampen the edges of the pies with water and press the lids on top of the filling. Seal the edges together with your fingers. Wrap a strip of parchment around the pie and secure with string, to make sure the pie holds its shape when cooked. You will find this easier to do if you have someone to help you. Repeat until you have 8 pies.

Put the pies on the baking tray and cut a steam hole in the centre of each. Brush with egg yolk. Leave to rest in the fridge for 30 minutes.

Meanwhile, heat your oven to 200°C/gas 6. Bake the pies for 35–40 minutes until golden brown. Serve hot.

Step photographs overleaf

Scotch pies

Quickly rolling out the pastry, while it is still warm and pliable.

Cutting out 18cm circles, using a plate as a guide.

Placing a ball of filling in the centre of each pastry circle.

Bringing the pastry up around the filling.

Positioning the pie lids.

Tying a band of parchment around each pie to ensure it holds its shape on baking.

Cutting a steam vent in the middle of each pie.

Brushing the tops of the pies with beaten egg yolk to glaze.

Bedfordshire clangers

For the suet pastry

300g self-raising flour

1 tsp fine salt

100g beef suet

50g cold unsalted butter,
cut into roughly 1cm dice

About 200ml very cold water

1 egg, beaten, to glaze

For the savoury filling

1 tbsp vegetable oil

25g unsalted butter

1 small leek, trimmed,
quartered lengthways and
thinly sliced

1 large potato, about 250g,
peeled and cut into 5mm dice

175g uncooked gammon, cut
into 1cm cubes

1 tsp English mustard

Salt and pepper

For the sweet filling

50g soft brown sugar

1 small cooking apple, about
150g, peeled, cored and diced

1 pear, about 150g, peeled,
cored and diced

50g sultanas

½ tsp ground cinnamon

15g unsalted butter, cut into
4 pieces

Equipment

Large baking sheet (lipped)

These pies have a savoury filling at one end and a sweet one at the other. They used to function as complete, portable meals for farm labourers – the savoury portion would be marked by three steam holes and the sweet with two, so everyone knew which end to eat first. The name may come from an old Midlands word 'clanging', which means 'eating with great relish'.

First make the savoury filling. Heat the oil and butter in a frying pan over a medium heat. Add the leek and potato and cook gently for about 5 minutes, until the leek is soft. Add the gammon and cook for another 5 minutes, until it is just cooked. Take off the heat and stir in the mustard and some salt and pepper. Leave to cool.

To make the sweet filling, just mix all the ingredients, except the butter, together in a bowl.

Heat your oven to 220°C/gas 7. Line a large lipped baking sheet with baking parchment.

For the pastry, mix the flour, salt and suet in a bowl. Add the butter and rub in lightly with your fingertips until the mix resembles breadcrumbs. Stir in just enough cold water to form a soft dough.

To assemble, lightly dust a work surface with flour and roll out the dough to about 60 x 25cm. Now cut across into 4 rectangles, about 25 x 15cm. Trim the edges so they are neat and straight, then roll the trimmings from each portion of dough into a little sausage.

Brush a line of beaten egg across the middle of each piece of pastry and lay the pastry sausage on it. Pinch to form a 'dam' which will keep the fillings separate. Put one quarter of the savoury filling on one half of each piece of pastry and one quarter of the sweet on the other. Top the sweet filling with a dot of butter.

Brush the pastry edges with beaten egg. Fold the pastry over the fillings to form a long sausage roll shape. Press either side of the central pastry 'dam' and press the edges together to seal. Make three diagonal slashes on the savoury ends and two on the sweet. Transfer to the baking sheet, seam side down, and brush with egg.

Bake for 15 minutes, then turn the oven down to 180°C/gas 4 and bake for a further 20 minutes. Serve the clangers hot or cold.

Step photographs overleaf

Bedfordshire clangers

Cutting the pastry into 4 rectangles, each about 25 x 15cm.

Trimming the pastry edges to ensure they are straight and neat.

Positioning a pastry 'sausage' along the middle of each pastry rectangle.

Pinching the pastry sausage to form a ridge that will keep the savoury and sweet fillings separate.

Brushing the edges of the pastry around the fillings with beaten egg.

Folding the pastry over the fillings to enclose them and form a long sausage roll shape.

Pressing either side of the central pastry divider towards the middle to ensure a good seal.

Cutting three slashes on the savoury ends and two on the sweet ends (to identify them).

SWEET

PUDDINGS MAY BE INDULGENT but that doesn't mean we shouldn't enjoy them. I'm a firm believer that a little of what you fancy does you good. I would rather skip the starter than miss out on pudding. In fact, I am one of those pud lovers who looks at the dessert menu first in a restaurant, so I can decide how much room I need to leave!

I've seen traditional puddings like the ones in this book make a real comeback in recent years, not that they ever really went away – they have been on the menu of every 5-star hotel I've ever worked in. But more and more home cooks are looking for recipes like these, the kind of timeless comfort puds that take us all back to our childhoods. It makes sense: if you can turn out a beautiful steamed sponge or a classic treacle tart, you're on to a winner. They are what I call class-breakers: everyone likes them, no matter their background.

Baked puddings have always been a big part of my life. My Nan was a great pudding cook and I have fond memories of her fruit pies and tapioca puds. She even used to make little chocolate puds similar to my chocolate volcanoes (page 176), though she cooked them for a little bit longer so the filling was not so molten. The nostalgic appeal of these dishes partly explains their popularity, but there's more to them than that. They are, or at least they can be, truly delicious. They've become classics for a reason.

These recipes are straightforward: good, simple baking. To start with, you may find it helpful to refer back to my step-by-step guides to the individual pastries in the Pastry chapter (pages 14–43) when you are making one of the tarts or pies. In time, they will become second nature.

The secret to success is to use the very best ingredients you can. I think cooks can sometimes be a bit blasé about 'basic' items like flour, sugar and butter, but these are the absolute mainstay of most puddings and the quality is crucial. Start out with good ingredients, weigh and measure with care, and you can expect great results.

Apple & Wensleydale pie

For the shortcrust pastry
350g plain flour
175g cold unsalted butter,
cut into roughly 1cm dice,
plus extra for greasing
About 75ml very cold water

For the filling
500g cooking apples
500g eating apples
100g caster sugar
125g Wensleydale cheese,
crumbled

To finish
A little milk
About 1 tbsp granulated sugar

Equipment
26 x 20cm baking tin, about
4cm deep

There's a saying in Yorkshire that 'apple pie without cheese is like a kiss without a squeeze'. I couldn't agree more – tangy, salty cheese and sweet apple go beautifully together. I like to use a mixture of cooking and eating apples in this pie, in order to create a varied, interesting texture.

To make the pastry, put the flour in a bowl. Add the diced butter and rub it in with your fingertips until the mixture looks like fine breadcrumbs. Alternatively, do this in a food processor or a mixer and then transfer to a bowl.

Now work in just enough cold water to bring the pastry together, using one hand. When the dough begins to stick together, gently knead it into a ball. Wrap the pastry in cling film and rest in the fridge for about 30 minutes.

Heat your oven to 200°C/gas 6. Lightly butter a baking tin, about 26 x 20cm and about 4cm deep.

For the filling, peel, quarter and core all of the apples. Slice them into a large bowl and toss together.

Once the dough has rested, cut it into two pieces, roughly one-third and two-thirds. Lightly dust your work surface with flour. Roll out the larger piece of pastry so it's a good 6cm larger all round than the base of the tin. Line the base and sides of the tin with the pastry, leaving the excess hanging over the sides.

Lay a third of the apple slices in the pastry-lined tin and sprinkle with a third of the sugar. Repeat with the remaining apple and sugar. Now scatter the crumbled cheese evenly over the fruit.

Roll out the remaining pastry to make a lid. Brush the edges of the pastry in the tin with milk, then put the pastry lid on top. Seal the edges with your fingertips and crimp them; trim off the excess pastry neatly. Brush the pastry with milk and sprinkle with sugar. Make two slits in the top to allow steam to escape.

Bake for 30–35 minutes or until the crust is golden brown. Leave to stand for at least 15 minutes before slicing. The pie is delicious hot or cold and needs no accompaniment.

French-style apple tart

SERVES 6
●●●●●●●●

For the sweet shortcrust

200g plain flour
2 tbsp icing sugar
100g cold unsalted butter,
cut into roughly 1cm dice
1 medium egg, lightly beaten
1 tsp lemon juice
2 tbsp very cold water

For the frangipane

100g unsalted butter, softened
100g caster sugar
2 medium eggs
50g plain flour
75g ground almonds
2-3 drops of almond extract

For the apples

3 medium eating apples
15g cold butter, cut into small
pieces
1½ tbsp caster sugar
4 tbsp sieved apricot jam,
to finish

Equipment

25cm loose-based fluted tart
tin, 3cm deep

Inspired by the wonderful *tarte aux pommes* of Normandy, this is a beautiful way to show off the flavours of our home-grown apples too. The apples – tender and caramelised but holding their shape – are cushioned on a soft, almondy frangipane layer and finished with an apricot glaze.

To make the pastry, mix the flour and icing sugar together in a bowl. Add the diced butter and rub it in with your fingertips until the mixture looks like fine breadcrumbs. Alternatively, do this in a food processor or a mixer and then transfer to a bowl.

Mix the egg with the lemon juice and water. Make a well in the centre of the flour mixture and pour in the egg mix. Using one hand, work the liquid into the flour to bring the pastry together. If it seems too dry, add a splash more water. When the dough begins to stick together, gently knead it into a ball. Wrap in cling film and rest in the fridge for at least 15 minutes.

Heat your oven to 200°C/gas 6 and put a baking tray in to heat up. Have ready a 25cm loose-based fluted tart tin, 3cm deep.

Roll out the pastry on a lightly floured surface to about a 3mm thickness and use it to line the tart tin. Trim the edge neatly and prick the base of the pastry with a fork.

To make the frangipane, cream the butter and sugar together until soft and fluffy. Beat in the eggs, one at a time, then mix in the flour, ground almonds and almond extract. Spread the frangipane over the pastry base, smoothing it out evenly.

Peel, core and thinly slice the apples. Starting at the edge and working towards the centre, lay them, overlapping, on top of the frangipane. Dot with the 15g cold butter. Place on the hot tray in the oven and bake for 15 minutes. The tart will be starting to brown.

Sprinkle the sugar over the apples, then return to the oven for 10–15 minutes, until the sugar has melted and caramelised.

While still warm, heat the apricot jam very gently with a splash of water, to make a glaze, and brush it over the apples. Leave the tart to cool completely, then serve with crème fraîche, or whipped or clotted cream.

Step photographs overleaf

French-style apple tart

Combining the ingredients for the frangipane.

Spreading the frangipane evenly over the base of the pastry case with the back of a spoon.

Thinly slicing the apples for the filling.

Arranging the apple slices in a circular pattern over the frangipane.

Glazing the warm tart with sieved apricot jam after baking.

Cobnut, pear & sticky toffee tart

SERVES 8

●●●●●●●●

For the sweet shortcrust

200g plain flour

2 tbsp icing sugar

100g cold unsalted butter,
cut into roughly 1cm dice

1 medium egg, lightly beaten

1 tsp lemon juice

2 tbsp very cold water

For the filling

200g stoned dates, roughly
chopped

150ml whole milk

3 ripe medium pears, about
500g in total

50g unsalted butter, softened

1 tsp vanilla extract

100g plain flour

1 tsp bicarbonate of soda

50g ground almonds

2 large eggs

100g light muscovado sugar

2 tbsp treacle

100g shelled cobnuts or
hazelnuts, roughly chopped

For the toffee sauce

200g light muscovado sugar

50g unsalted butter

250ml double cream

Equipment

25cm loose-based fluted tart
tin, 3.5cm deep

Kentish cobs are cultivated hazelnuts, often larger than the wild variety, and easier to gather. Crunchy and sweet, they partner apples and pears perfectly in this autumnal, nutty, treacly tart.

To make the pastry, mix the flour and icing sugar together in a bowl. Add the diced butter and rub it in with your fingertips until the mixture looks like fine breadcrumbs. Alternatively, do this in a food processor or a mixer and then transfer to a bowl.

Mix the egg with the lemon juice and water. Make a well in the centre of the flour mixture and pour in the egg mix. Using one hand, work the liquid into the flour to bring the pastry together. If it seems too dry, add a splash more water. When the dough begins to stick together, gently knead it into a ball. Wrap in cling film and rest in the fridge for at least 15 minutes.

For the filling, put the chopped dates and milk in a pan. Bring to the boil, and then set aside for 30 minutes to soak.

To make the toffee sauce, heat the sugar, butter and cream together in a pan over a low heat until melted and smooth, then bring to a simmer and let bubble for 5 minutes to thicken. Leave to cool.

Heat your oven to 180°C/gas 4 and put in a baking tray to warm up. Have ready a 25cm loose-based fluted tart tin, 3.5cm deep.

Roll out the pastry on a lightly floured surface and use it to line the tart tin. Prick the base with a fork. Peel, quarter and core the pears; slice each quarter in two. Arrange in a circular pattern in the tart case. Drizzle over 4 tbsp of the toffee sauce and place in the fridge while you prepare the rest of the filling.

Mash the date mixture to a coarse purée with a potato masher. Tip it into a bowl with the softened butter, vanilla, flour, bicarbonate of soda, ground almonds, eggs, sugar and treacle. Whisk together with an electric whisk until just combined. Stir in the chopped nuts.

Spoon the date and nut mixture over the pears in the pastry case, spreading it out evenly. Bake the tart on the hot baking tray for 40-45 minutes, until the filling is well risen and browned. Leave to stand for 10 minutes before removing from the tin.

Serve the tart warm, with clotted cream or ice cream and the rest of the toffee sauce.

Yorkshire curd tart

SERVES 6

For the sweet shortcrust

150g plain flour

2 tbsp icing sugar

75g cold unsalted butter, cut into roughly 1cm dice

1 egg yolk

½ tsp lemon juice

1 tbsp very cold water

For the filling

50g caster sugar

225g curd cheese

2 medium eggs

2 medium egg yolks

Finely grated zest of 1 lemon

1 tsp rosewater

25g unsalted butter, melted

50g currants

½ tsp freshly grated nutmeg

Equipment

20cm loose-based sandwich cake tin, 2–3cm deep

Curd tarts were traditionally baked for Whitsuntide, when many Yorkshire villages held feasts and fair days. The filling was originally made from 'beestings', the first, very rich milk from newly calved cows, though nowadays it's easier (and just as good) to use curd cheese. Rosewater is a classic flavouring.

For the pastry, mix the flour and icing sugar together in a bowl. Add the diced butter and rub it in with your fingertips until the mixture looks like fine breadcrumbs. Alternatively, do this in a food processor or a mixer and then transfer to a bowl.

Mix the egg yolk with the lemon juice and water. Make a well in the centre of the flour mixture and pour in the egg mix. Using one hand, work the liquid into the flour to bring the pastry together. If it seems too dry, add a splash more water. When the dough begins to stick together, gently knead it into a ball. Wrap in cling film and rest in the fridge for at least 15 minutes.

Heat your oven to 200°C/gas 6 and have ready a 20cm loose-based sandwich cake tin, 2–3cm deep.

Roll out the pastry on a lightly floured surface to about a 3mm thickness and use it to line the tart tin, leaving the excess pastry hanging over the edge. Keep a little uncooked pastry back in case you need to patch any cracks later. Prick the base with a fork.

Line the pastry case with baking parchment or foil, then fill with baking beans, or uncooked rice or lentils. Bake blind for 15 minutes, then remove the parchment and baking beans and return to the oven for about 8 minutes or until the pastry looks dry and faintly coloured. Use a small, sharp knife to trim away the excess pastry from the edge. Use a tiny bit of the reserved raw pastry to patch any cracks or holes if necessary. Turn the oven down to 180°C/gas 4.

To make the filling, beat the sugar and curd cheese together until smooth, then beat in the eggs and egg yolks, lemon zest, rosewater and melted butter. Stir in the currants.

Pour the filling into the pastry case and grate a little nutmeg over the surface. Bake for about 20 minutes, until the filling is just set. Leave to cool completely in the tin before slicing.

Cumberland rum nicky

SERVES 6–8

For the sweet shortcrust

200g plain flour

2 tbsp icing sugar

100g cold unsalted butter,
cut into roughly 1cm dice

1 medium egg, lightly beaten

1 tsp lemon juice

2 tbsp very cold water

For the filling

225g dates, coarsely chopped

100g dried apricots, coarsely
chopped

50g stem ginger in syrup,
drained and finely chopped

50ml dark rum

50g soft dark brown sugar

50g unsalted butter, cut into
1–2cm cubes

For the rum butter

100g unsalted butter, softened

225g soft light brown sugar

75ml dark rum

Equipment

20cm metal pie plate, about
3cm deep

This traditional northern treat is a real favourite of mine. It's stuffed with sticky dates and treacly brown sugar and laced with ginger and rum – ingredients that came to Cumberland via the merchant ships that docked along the coastline. The name may stem from the original technique of covering the filling with a whole piece of pastry then making slashes or 'nicks' in it.

Start by mixing all the filling ingredients, except the butter, together in a bowl. Set aside to soak while you make the pastry.

For the pastry, mix the flour and icing sugar together in a bowl. Add the diced butter and rub it in with your fingertips until the mixture looks like fine breadcrumbs. Alternatively, do this in a food processor or a mixer and then transfer to a bowl.

Mix the egg with the lemon juice and water. Make a well in the centre of the flour mixture and pour in the egg mix. Using one hand, work the liquid into the flour to bring the pastry together. If it seems too dry, add a splash more water. When the dough begins to stick together, gently knead it into a ball. Wrap in cling film and rest in the fridge for at least 15 minutes.

Heat your oven to 180°C/gas 4 and have ready a 20cm metal pie plate, about 3cm deep.

Once the dough has rested, cut it into two pieces, roughly one-third and two-thirds. Roll out the larger piece on a lightly floured surface and use to line the pie dish, leaving the excess pastry hanging over the edge. Spread the filling in the pastry case and dot with the butter.

Roll out the remaining pastry and cut into 12–14 long strips, about 1cm wide. On a board covered with a sheet of parchment, use the pastry strips to create a lattice with 6–7 strips going each way, passing them under and over each other. Dampen the rim of the pastry in the tin with water then invert the lattice from the paper onto the tart. Press the ends of the strips to the pastry rim to secure and crimp the edges.

Bake for 15 minutes, then turn the oven down to 160°C/gas 3 and cook for a further 20 minutes. Meanwhile, for the rum butter, beat together the butter and sugar, then gradually beat in the rum.

Serve the tart warm or cold, with a spoonful of rum butter.

Step photographs overleaf

Cumberland rum nicky

Spooning the dried fruit filling into the pastry-lined pie plate.

Dotting the butter over the filling.

Rolling out the remaining pastry for the lattice top.

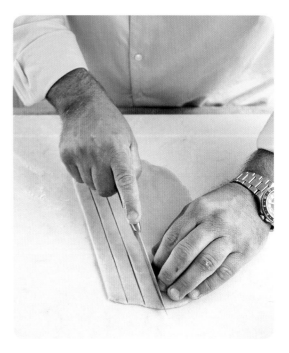

Cutting the pastry into strips for the lattice.

Weaving the strips of pastry on a piece of baking parchment to form a neat lattice.

The finished lattice, ready to go on the pie.

Inverting the lattice on top of the pie.

The finished pie, with the lattice neatly trimmed and the pastry edge crimped, ready to bake.

Sweet beetroot pie

SERVES 6–8
●●●●●●●●●●

For the sweet shortcrust
200g plain flour
2 tbsp icing sugar
100g cold unsalted butter,
cut into roughly 1cm dice
1 medium egg, lightly beaten
1 tsp lemon juice
2 tbsp very cold water

For the filling
350g cooked peeled beetroot
(vacuum-packed is fine, but not
beetroot in vinegar)
125ml double cream
2 large eggs
175g dark muscovado sugar
1 tsp ground cinnamon
½ tsp ground ginger
Finely grated zest of 1 lemon

Equipment
23cm loose-based tart tin,
3cm deep

This recipe is based on the sweet, spicy American pumpkin pie but uses very British beetroot, which gives it an amazing, deep colour and flavour.

For the pastry, mix the flour and icing sugar together in a bowl. Add the diced butter and rub it in with your fingertips until the mixture looks like fine breadcrumbs. Alternatively, do this in a food processor or a mixer and then transfer to a bowl.

Mix the egg with the lemon juice and water. Make a well in the centre of the flour mixture and pour in the egg mix. Using one hand, work the liquid into the flour to bring the pastry together. If it seems too dry, add a splash more water. When the dough begins to stick together, gently knead it into a ball. Wrap in cling film and rest in the fridge for at least 15 minutes.

Heat your oven to 200°C/gas 6 and have ready a 23cm loose-based tart tin, 3cm deep.

Roll out the pastry on a lightly floured surface to about a 3mm thickness and use it to line the tart tin, leaving excess pastry hanging over the edge. Keep a little uncooked pastry back in case you need to patch any cracks later. Prick the base with a fork.

Line the pastry case with baking parchment or foil, then fill with baking beans, or uncooked rice or lentils. Bake blind for 15 minutes, then remove the parchment and baking beans and return to the oven for about 8 minutes or until the pastry looks dry and faintly coloured. Using a small, sharp knife, trim away the excess pastry from the edge. Use a tiny bit of the reserved raw pastry to patch any cracks or holes if necessary.

Turn the oven down to 180°C/gas 4.

For the filling, if you're using pre-packed beetroot, drain off any excess liquid, then roughly chop the beetroot and put into a food processor with the cream. Blend to a thick purée.

Whisk the eggs and sugar together thoroughly. Add the beetroot purée, spices and lemon zest and mix well.

Pour the mixture into the pastry case and bake for 30–40 minutes until the filling is set with a slight wobble in the middle. Leave to cool completely before serving, with crème fraîche.

Treacle tart

SERVES 6

●●●●●●●●

For the sweet shortcrust

150g plain flour

2 tbsp icing sugar

75g cold unsalted butter,
cut into roughly 1cm dice

1 egg yolk

½ tsp lemon juice

1 tbsp very cold water

For the filling

350g golden syrup

50g unsalted butter, melted

3 tbsp double cream

1 large egg

Pinch of salt

125g slightly stale white
breadcrumbs

Finely grated zest of 1 lemon

Equipment

20cm loose-based cake tin,
4cm deep

Gloriously sweet but nicely cut with a little lemon acidity, a treacle tart is a wonderful, simple treat. You might think that it ought really to be called a syrup tart, since that's what it's based on – but 'golden syrup' was originally a trade name for what was also known as 'pale treacle'.

For the pastry, mix the flour and icing sugar together in a bowl. Add the diced butter and rub it in with your fingertips until the mixture looks like fine breadcrumbs. Alternatively, do this in a food processor or a mixer and then transfer to a bowl.

Mix the egg yolk with the lemon juice and water. Make a well in the centre of the flour mixture and pour in the egg mix. Using one hand, work the liquid into the flour to bring the pastry together. If it seems too dry, add a splash more water. When the dough begins to stick together, gently knead it into a ball. Wrap in cling film and rest in the fridge for at least 15 minutes.

Heat your oven to 200°C/gas 6 and have ready a 20cm loose-based cake tin, 4cm deep.

Roll out the pastry on a lightly floured surface and use to line the cake tin, leaving excess pastry hanging over the edge. Keep a little uncooked pastry back in case you need to patch any cracks later. Prick the base with a fork.

Line the pastry with baking parchment or foil, then fill with baking beans, or uncooked rice or lentils. Bake blind for 15 minutes, then remove the parchment and baking beans and return to the oven for about 8 minutes or until it looks dry and faintly coloured. Use a small, sharp knife to trim away the excess pastry from the edge of the tin. If necessary, patch any cracks or holes with raw pastry. Turn the oven down to 160°C/gas 3.

To make the filling, put the golden syrup into a saucepan and warm gently over a low heat to make it more liquid. Take off the heat and stir in the melted butter. Beat the cream with the egg and mix into the syrup. Add the salt, breadcrumbs and lemon zest and stir until combined. Pour into the pastry case.

Bake for 40–45 minutes or until the filling is coloured and just set. Remove from the oven and leave to cool completely in the tin. Slice and serve with whipped or clotted cream.

Gypsy tart

SERVES 6

●●●●●●●●

For the sweet shortcrust
150g plain flour

2 tbsp icing sugar

75g cold unsalted butter,
cut into roughly 1cm dice

1 egg yolk

½ tsp lemon juice

1 tbsp very cold water

For the filling
230ml condensed milk

170g tin evaporated milk

175g light muscovado sugar

Equipment
20cm loose-based tart tin,
about 4.5cm deep

Muscovado sugar lends a rich caramel flavour to this unique, very sweet tart. The recipe comes from Kent but its history is uncertain. The story goes that the tart was first cooked by a kindly Kentish woman to feed some hungry gypsy children.

To make the pastry, mix the flour and icing sugar together in a bowl. Add the diced butter and rub it in with your fingertips until the mixture looks like fine breadcrumbs. Alternatively, do this in a food processor or a mixer and then transfer to a bowl.

Mix the egg yolk with the lemon juice and water. Make a well in the centre of the flour mixture and pour in the egg mix. Using one hand, work the liquid into the flour to bring the pastry together. If it seems too dry, add a splash more water. When the dough begins to stick together, gently knead it into a ball. Wrap in cling film and rest in the fridge for at least 15 minutes.

Heat your oven to 200°C/gas 6 and have ready a 20cm loose-based tart tin, about 4.5cm deep.

Roll out the pastry on a lightly floured surface to about a 3mm thickness and use it to line the tart tin, leaving excess pastry hanging over the edge. Keep a little uncooked pastry back in case you need to patch any cracks later. Prick the base with a fork.

Line the pastry case with baking parchment or foil, then fill with baking beans, or uncooked rice or lentils. Bake blind for 15 minutes, then remove the parchment and baking beans and return the pastry to the oven for about 8 minutes or until it looks dry and faintly coloured. Using a small, sharp knife, trim away the excess pastry from the edge. Use a tiny bit of the reserved raw pastry to patch any cracks or holes if necessary. Turn the oven down to 190°C/gas 5.

For the filling, put both milks and the sugar in a large bowl or the bowl of a mixer. Beat together with an electric whisk, starting off slowly then increasing the speed, for around 10 minutes until the mixture is increased in volume, light and bubbly.

Pour the mixture into the pastry case. Bake for about 20 minutes, until just set and still a bit wobbly in the centre. Remove from the oven and leave to cool in the tin before slicing and serving. A little crème fraîche or plain yoghurt balances the sweetness nicely.

Pecan pie

SERVES 6–8

●●●●●●●●●●

For the sweet shortcrust

200g plain flour

2 tbsp icing sugar

100g cold unsalted butter,
cut into roughly 1cm dice

1 medium egg, lightly beaten

1 tsp lemon juice

2 tbsp very cold water

For the filling

100g unsalted butter

150g golden syrup

125g dark muscovado sugar

200g pecan halves

3 medium eggs, beaten

Equipment

23cm loose-based tart tin,
3.5cm deep

I like this classic American recipe – it's very simple and really makes the most of the delicious affinity between nuts and toffee. The rich, dark, sticky filling is perfectly set off by a spoonful of lightly whipped cream.

To make the pastry, mix the flour and icing sugar together in a bowl. Add the diced butter and rub it in with your fingertips until the mixture looks like fine breadcrumbs. Alternatively, do this in a food processor or a mixer and then transfer to a bowl.

Mix the egg with the lemon juice and water. Make a well in the centre of the flour mixture and pour in the egg mix. Using one hand, work the liquid into the flour to bring the pastry together. If it seems too dry, add a splash more water. When the dough begins to stick together, gently knead it into a ball. Wrap in cling film and rest in the fridge for at least 15 minutes.

Heat your oven to 180°C/gas 4 and put in a baking tray to heat up. Have ready a 23cm loose-based tart tin, 3.5cm deep.

Roll out the pastry on a lightly floured surface and use it to line the tin. Prick the base with a fork. Put it in the fridge while you make the filling.

Put the butter, syrup and sugar in a saucepan and melt gently over a low heat. Once the butter has melted, remove from the heat and leave to cool for 10 minutes.

Arrange the pecans over the base of the pastry case. Mix the beaten eggs into the cooled syrup mixture and pour over the pecans.

Bake for 35–40 minutes or until the filling is almost set but still a bit wobbly. It will firm up as it cools. Leave to cool completely in the tin before serving, with whipped cream.

Individual fruit pies

MAKES 12
●●●●●●●●●

For the sweet shortcrust
200g plain flour
2 tbsp icing sugar
100g cold unsalted butter,
cut into roughly 1cm dice
1 medium egg, lightly beaten
1 tsp lemon juice
2 tbsp very cold water

For the apple filling
7 medium eating apples (1kg)
25g unsalted butter
75g caster sugar
Finely grated zest of 1 lemon
50ml Calvados
2 tbsp mascarpone

For the pear filling
7 medium pears (about 1kg)
25g unsalted butter
75g caster sugar
Finely grated zest of 1 lemon
50ml perry
2 tbsp mascarpone

For the apricot filling
9 apricots (about 500g)
25g unsalted butter
75g caster sugar
50ml Amaretto

To finish
Beaten egg or milk for brushing
Granulated sugar for sprinkling

Equipment
12-hole bun tray
8.5cm, 6cm and 6.5-7cm cutters

With their luscious fruity filling, these little pies remind me of the ones my Nan used to make. They are a real treat, especially when served warm with whipped cream. I've given you three fillings to choose from; each uses the full quantity of pastry.

To make the pastry, mix the flour and icing sugar together in a bowl. Add the diced butter and rub it in with your fingertips until the mixture looks like fine breadcrumbs. Alternatively, do this in a food processor or a mixer and then transfer to a bowl.

Mix the egg with the lemon juice and water. Make a well in the centre of the flour mixture and pour in the egg mix. Using one hand, work the liquid into the flour to bring the pastry together. If it seems too dry, add a splash more water. When the dough begins to stick together, gently knead it into a ball. Wrap in cling film and rest in the fridge for at least 15 minutes.

To make any of the fillings, first prepare the fruit. Peel, quarter and core apples or pears; halve and stone apricots. Cut the fruit into 1cm pieces. Melt the butter in a wide pan over a medium heat. Add the fruit, sugar, lemon zest (if applicable) and the alcohol. Simmer for about 10 minutes, stirring from time to time, until the fruit is tender and most of the liquid has evaporated. Leave to cool completely, then mix in the mascarpone (if included) and chill the mixture.

Heat your oven to 200°C/gas 6.

On a lightly floured surface, roll out the pastry until 2–3mm thick. Using an 8.5cm plain cutter, cut out 12 circles and use them to line a bun tray (the kind you use for fairy cakes, not a deep muffin tray). Re-roll the pastry as necessary and cut out 6cm circles, for the lids.

Spoon the filling into the pastry cases, taking care not to overfill them. Dampen the rim of the pastry with water and top each pie with a lid. Press a 6.5–7cm cutter over the pie to seal the edge and trim away any excess pastry. Make a small steam hole in the top of each pie. Brush with a little beaten egg or milk and sprinkle with sugar. Bake for 25–30 minutes until the pastry is crisp and golden.

Leave to cool in the tin for 5 minutes before removing. Serve warm or at room temperature, within 24 hours of baking, or they'll start to lose their crispness.

Step photographs overleaf

Individual fruit pies

Using an 8.5cm cutter to stamp out circles from the pastry.

Lining a 12-hole bun tin with the circles, pressing the pastry well into the corners.

Spooning the apple filling into the pastry cases.

Cutting out smaller circles, 6cm in diameter, for the lids.

Positioning the pastry lids.

Pressing a smaller cutter over the pie to seal the edge and trim away excess pastry.

Brushing the tops of the pies with beaten egg.

The sugar-dusted pies, ready for the oven.

Chocolate & prune tart

SERVES 6
●●●●●●●

For the chocolate pastry

175g plain flour

2 tbsp icing sugar

2 tbsp cocoa powder

100g cold unsalted butter,
cut into roughly 1cm dice

1 egg yolk

1 tsp lemon juice

2 tbsp very cold water

For the filling

150g ready-to-eat prunes
(ideally d'Agen), cut into
quarters

1 tbsp brandy

1 tsp vanilla extract

50ml boiling water

75g dark chocolate, broken
into small pieces

125ml double cream

200g mascarpone

2 medium eggs, beaten

Equipment

23cm loose-based tart tin,
3.5cm deep

The combination of prunes, chocolate and brandy rarely fails to please and this deliciously dark and sophisticated tart uses cocoa pastry for an extra chocolate hit.

For the filling, put the prunes, brandy and vanilla in a bowl. Pour on the boiling water and leave to soak for several hours or overnight.

To make the pastry, sift the flour, icing sugar and cocoa together. Add the diced butter and rub it in with your fingertips until the mixture looks like fine breadcrumbs. Alternatively, do this in a food processor or a mixer and then transfer to a bowl.

Mix the egg yolk with the lemon juice and water. Make a well in the centre of the flour mixture and pour in the egg mix. Using one hand, work the liquid into the flour to bring the pastry together. If it seems too dry, add a splash more water. When the dough begins to stick together, gently knead it into a ball. Wrap the pastry in cling film and put in the fridge to rest for at least 15 minutes.

Heat your oven to 200°C/gas 6.

Roll out the pastry on a lightly floured surface and use to line a 23cm loose-based tart tin, 3.5cm deep, leaving excess pastry hanging over the edge. Keep a little uncooked pastry back in case you need to patch any cracks later. Prick the base with a fork.

Line the pastry with baking parchment or foil, then fill with baking beans, or uncooked rice or lentils. Bake blind for 15 minutes, then remove the parchment and baking beans and return to the oven for about 8 minutes or until the pastry looks dry. Use a small, sharp knife to trim away the excess pastry from the edge. Use a tiny bit of the reserved raw pastry to patch any cracks or holes if necessary. Turn the oven down to 180°C/gas 4.

To make the filling, put the chocolate and cream in a heatproof bowl over a pan of simmering water and leave until the chocolate has just melted, stirring from time to time. Take off the heat and leave to cool for 3 minutes, then beat in the mascarpone and eggs with a balloon whisk to keep it smooth. Stir in the prunes and any soaking juices.

Pour the chocolate and prune mixture into the tart case. Bake for 20–25 minutes until almost set, with a bit of wobble still in the centre. Leave in the tin to cool completely. Serve the tart at room temperature, with a spoonful of cream if you like.

Spiced plum pizza

SERVES 6–8

●●●●●●●●●●●

For the pizza dough
250g strong white bread flour

5g fine salt

20g caster sugar

5g fast-action dried yeast

30g unsalted butter, cut into
small cubes

180ml water

For the plum topping
100g dark muscovado sugar

1 tsp ground cinnamon

1 tsp ground star anise

Finely grated zest of 1 orange

2 tbsp semolina

1kg firm, slightly under-ripe
plums, stoned and halved,
or quartered if large

15g unsalted butter, cut into
small pieces

Equipment
30cm pizza pan or tart tin,
about 2cm deep

**With its generous filling encased in a lightly sweetened and
enriched dough, this gorgeous fruit pizza makes an impressive
centrepiece. Make it in August or September when our plums
are at their juicy best.**

To make the pizza dough, put the flour in a bowl and add the salt
and sugar to one side and the yeast to the other. Combine them,
then add the butter and rub it into the flour with your fingertips.
Add 150ml of the water and start mixing with your fingers,
gradually incorporating all the flour from the edges of the bowl,
and adding more water a little at a time, until you have a rough
dough. You may not need to add all the water (or you may need
a little more) but the dough should be very soft and sticky.

Tip the dough out onto a lightly floured surface and knead it for
5–10 minutes until it is smooth and elastic. Shape into a ball and
place in a lightly oiled bowl. Cover and leave in a fairly warm place
for about 1½ hours until tripled in size.

Heat your oven to 220°C/gas 7. Have ready a 30cm pizza pan or
a similar-sized tart tin, about 2cm deep.

Shortly before you're ready to bake the pizza, for the topping,
mix the muscovado sugar, cinnamon, star anise and orange zest
together in a large bowl.

Tip the risen dough onto a lightly floured work surface. Gently
knock the air out of the dough, then roll it out to a circle, about
35cm in diameter. Lift the dough into the pizza pan and press well
into the corners of the tin and onto the base, leaving the excess
dough hanging over the edge. Sprinkle the semolina over the base.

Scatter the plums into the lined pizza pan, sprinkle with the spiced
sugar mixture and dot with the butter.

Bake for 30 minutes, until the dough is a dark golden colour and
the plums are tender but still holding their shape. Leave to cool
slightly for 5 minutes before serving on a large wooden board
dusted with icing sugar.

Step photographs overleaf

Spiced plum pizza

Kneading the pizza dough on a lightly floured surface until smooth and elastic.

Shaping the dough into a ball, ready to place in a bowl and leave in a warm place to rise.

The risen pizza dough, ready to pummel and knock back.

Rolling out the dough on a lightly floured surface to a large round.

Carefully lifting the thinly rolled dough into the pizza pan.

Pressing the dough into the corners of the pan.

Pressing the dough onto the base of the pan.

Sprinkling the spiced sugar mixture over the plums in the pizza case.

Chocolate orange pond pudding

SERVES 4–6
●●●●●●●●●●

150g unsalted butter, cut into
1–2cm cubes, plus extra for
greasing

185g self-raising flour

15g cocoa powder

20g caster sugar

125g shredded suet

1 orange

150–175ml whole milk

150g soft dark brown sugar

25g dark chocolate, chopped
into small pieces

Equipment

1.2 litre pudding basin

This is my take on Sussex pond pudding – the classic suet pud boiled with a whole lemon inside. I use a whole orange instead and add chocolate. The juice from the fruit combines with the melted chocolate, butter and sugar to create an irresistible sauce that floods out as the pudding is cut – hence the name.

Grease a 1.2 litre pudding basin with butter.

Mix the flour, cocoa, caster sugar and suet together in a large bowl. Finely grate the zest of the orange and mix this in too. Gradually work in enough milk to form a soft, slightly sticky dough.

Take a third of the pastry. Roll out on a lightly floured surface to a circle slightly bigger than the basin. Invert the basin onto the pastry and cut around it to form a lid. Add the offcuts to the remaining pastry and roll out to a circle, about 30cm in diameter. Use this to line the pudding basin. Make sure there are no cracks in the pastry.

Put half the butter, brown sugar and chocolate in the lined basin. Pierce the zested orange all over with a skewer and sit it on top. Add the remaining butter, sugar and chocolate.

Dampen the pastry edges with milk or water and put the pastry lid on top. Press the edges together to seal and trim off the excess.

Place a piece of baking parchment on a sheet of foil and make a large pleat in the middle, folding both sheets together. Put the parchment and foil on top of the pudding, foil side up, and secure with string, looping the end of the string over the top of the pudding and tying it to form a handle (as shown on page 91).

Stand the pudding basin in a large pan and pour in enough boiling water to come halfway up the side of the basin. Put a tight-fitting lid on the pan and bring to a simmer. Lower the heat to maintain a simmer and steam the pudding for 2¼ hours. Top up the boiling water during this time if necessary so the pan doesn't boil dry.

Lift the pudding basin from the pan. Remove the paper and foil and run the tip of a small, sharp knife around the edge of the pudding, to help release it, if necessary. Invert a large plate or deep dish over the top of the basin and turn both over to unmould the pudding.

Serve at once, cutting into the pudding carefully as the juices flood out (the orange isn't intended to be eaten). Serve with cold cream.

Gooseberry & elderflower crumble

SERVES 4–6

For the filling

500g fresh gooseberries,
topped and tailed

1 large cooking apple (about
225g), peeled, cored and diced

50ml elderflower cordial

100g soft light brown sugar

For the crumble topping

100g plain wholemeal flour

75g porridge oats

100g soft dark brown sugar

75g cold unsalted butter,
cut into roughly 1cm dice

25g sunflower seeds

15g pumpkin seeds

Equipment

25 x 20cm baking dish

Gooseberry and elderflower is a classic combination, but this crumble is a little different to most. I make the topping with wholemeal flour, brown sugar and crushed seeds, to give it extra colour and flavour.

Heat your oven to 180°C/gas 4 and have ready a baking dish, about 25 x 20cm.

To make the filling, put the gooseberries, apple, elderflower cordial and sugar in a pan. Cook over a medium heat for about 10 minutes, stirring from time to time, until the sugar has dissolved and the fruit is just beginning to collapse. Taste and add more sugar if required then transfer the mixture to the baking dish and set aside.

To make the crumble topping, combine the flour, oats and sugar in a bowl. Add the butter and rub in lightly with your fingertips until the mixture resembles coarse crumbs.

Using a pestle and mortar or a small processor, crush the sunflower and pumpkin seeds so they break down a little. Do not reduce them to a fine powder. Stir the crushed seeds into the crumble mixture.

Spoon the crumble mixture over the gooseberry filling. Bake for 35–40 minutes until golden brown and bubbling. Leave to settle for about 10 minutes, then serve with custard, cream or ice cream.

Apricot, peach & almond cobbler

SERVES 6
● ● ● ● ● ● ●

For the filling

350g apricots

350g peaches

3 tbsp honey

75g good-quality ready-made
marzipan, chilled

For the cobbler topping

175g plain flour

2½ tsp baking powder

2 tbsp caster sugar

75g cold unsalted butter,
cut into roughly 1cm dice

125ml single cream

1 egg white

2 tbsp demerara sugar

Equipment

1.3 litre ovenproof dish

With its scrumptious, golden scone-like topping, a cobbler lies somewhere between a crumble and a pie. You can use all sorts of fruit, depending on what's in season – this recipe is ideal for late summer. The almond element comes from sweet marzipan, which is grated onto the fruit, enhancing the apricots and peaches beautifully.

Heat your oven to 190°C/gas 5.

For the filling, cut the apricots and peaches into quarters and prise out the stones. Cut the peach quarters in two if they are large. Combine the fruit in a 1.3 litre ovenproof dish. Drizzle over the honey, then coarsely grate the marzipan over the fruit.

To make the cobbler dough, put the flour, baking powder and caster sugar into a large bowl and mix well. Add the butter and rub it in lightly with your fingers until the mixture resembles breadcrumbs. Stir in the cream, a little at a time, bringing the mixture together into a soft dough; you may not need all the cream.

With floured hands, divide the cobbler mixture into 10 pieces. Roll each portion into a ball and flatten slightly with the heel of your hand to make a 'cobble'. Carefully place the cobbles on top of the fruit and marzipan.

Brush the cobbles with egg white and sprinkle with demerara sugar. Bake the cobbler for 40 minutes or until the topping is risen and golden brown and the fruit is bubbling. Serve warm, with cream.

Apple & blackberry charlottes

SERVES 4

●●●●●●●

125g unsalted butter

500g cooking apples, peeled, cored and chopped

75g caster sugar

250g blackberries

About 400g slightly stale white bread, cut into 7–8mm slices, crusts removed

Equipment

4 individual pudding moulds, 175ml capacity

In these puddings, crisp, buttery bread takes the place of pastry. Apple is the classic filling, and recipes for apple charlottes date back over 200 years, but adding blackberries makes them all the more delicious. No one knows exactly how the name came about but it is often thought to be a tribute to Queen Charlotte, wife of George III.

Heat your oven to 200°C/gas 6.

Melt 25g of the butter in a large saucepan. Add the apples and sugar and cook gently for about 5 minutes, until the apples begin to soften, but are not cooked through. You may need to add a splash of water. Remove the apples from the heat. Stir in the blackberries, then taste for sweetness and add more sugar if required. The filling should be quite sweet as there is no sugar in the bread cases.

Melt the remaining butter and use some of it to grease 4 individual pudding moulds, 175ml capacity.

Cut 4 bread discs to fit in the bases of the moulds and 4 larger discs to fit the tops. Cut the remaining bread into 3–4cm strips. Brush one side of each piece of bread with melted butter. Put the smaller discs in the base of the moulds, butter side down. Line the sides with the bread strips, butter side outwards. Cut extra pieces of bread to fill any gaps so the bread lining is snug.

Divide the apple and blackberry filling between the lined moulds. Top with the bread lids. Fold any excess bread from the sides over the lid to help keep it in place.

Stand the pudding moulds on a baking tray and bake in the oven for 30–35 minutes until the bread is golden brown. Leave to stand for 5–10 minutes, then turn out into shallow bowls and serve warm, with ice cream or custard.

Step photographs overleaf

Apple & blackberry charlottes

Lining the sides of the moulds with the bread strips, butter side outwards.

Spooning the fruit filling into the bread-lined moulds.

Cutting out bread discs to fit the tops of the moulds.

Positioning the bread lids over the filling.

Folding the ends of the bread strips over the top
of the pastry lid and pressing down gently.

Chocolate bread & butter pudding

SERVES 6
●●●●●●●●

25g unsalted butter, softened

About 500g come-again cake (see page 210) or other leftover cake

50g sultanas

100ml whole milk

325ml double cream

150g dark chocolate, finely chopped

2 large eggs

25g caster sugar

1 tbsp demerara sugar

Equipment

18 x 23cm ovenproof dish

I've given a twist to this classic dish by using cake instead of leftover bread. My come-again cake on page 210 works a treat (you'll need about two-thirds of it), but any decent cake will do.

Use the butter to grease an ovenproof dish, about 18 x 23cm.

Cut the cake into roughly 1.5cm slices and cut each into quarters. Arrange one-third of the cake slices in the buttered dish. Sprinkle over one-third of the sultanas. Repeat twice, using up all the cake and sultanas.

In a saucepan, heat the milk and cream until almost boiling. Take off the heat and tip in the chopped chocolate. Whisk until all the chocolate has melted. You can heat the mixture gently again if you need to, to get it completely smooth, but don't let it boil.

Whisk the eggs and caster sugar together in a large bowl or jug. Gradually pour on the chocolate cream, whisking until all the cream is incorporated and you have a smooth chocolate custard.

Pour the custard over the cake in the dish then leave to stand for 30 minutes so the cake can absorb some of the custard.

Heat your oven to 180°C/gas 4.

Sprinkle the demerara sugar over the surface of the pudding and bake for 30–40 minutes, until the custard has set. Leave to stand for 15 minutes or so before serving, with cold cream.

Cherry croissant pudding

Butter for greasing
300ml double cream
300ml whole milk
75g caster sugar
4 large egg yolks
2 tbsp Kirsch
6 medium or 4 large croissants
5–6 tbsp cherry conserve
or jam
100g cherries, stoned and
halved

Equipment
1.2 litre ovenproof dish

This takes the classic bread and butter pud idea and raises it to new heights. The croissants soak up the Kirsch-scented custard beautifully, but go deliciously crisp on top.

Grease a 1.2 litre ovenproof dish.

Pour the cream and milk into a saucepan and heat just to the boil, then remove from the heat. Beat the sugar and egg yolks together in a large bowl, then pour on the hot milk and beat thoroughly. Stir in the Kirsch.

Halve each croissant and spread with the cherry conserve. Arrange in the ovenproof dish. Scatter over the cherries and pour over the custard. Leave to stand for about 30 minutes to allow the custard to soak into the croissants.

Meanwhile, heat your oven to 160°C/gas 3. Bake the pudding for 40–45 minutes, until the custard is set. If the top seems to be browning too quickly, cover the pudding with foil. Serve warm.

Queen of puddings

SERVES 4
●●●●●●●●

For the puddings
Butter for greasing
75g slightly stale white
breadcrumbs
100g raspberry jam

For the custard
600ml whole milk
1 vanilla pod
50g caster sugar
1 large egg
2 large egg yolks

For the meringue topping
4 large egg whites
150g caster sugar

Equipment
4 individual heatproof dishes,
about 10cm in diameter
Roasting tray

This nursery pud is a classic, and a great way to turn some leftover slices of bread and a few storecupboard staples into a spectacular little treat.

Heat your oven to 180°C/gas 4. Butter 4 individual heatproof glass dishes, about 10cm in diameter. Divide the breadcrumbs between them, scattering them evenly.

To make the custard, pour the milk into a saucepan. Split open the vanilla pod with a small, sharp knife and scrape out the seeds with the tip of the knife. Add both the seeds and the pod to the saucepan. Slowly bring the milk just to the boil, then take off the heat.

Whisk the sugar, egg and egg yolks together in a bowl. Pour on the hot milk and whisk well. Strain this back into the pan or into a jug.

Pour the custard into the prepared dishes, dividing it equally.

Stand the dishes in a roasting tray and pour in enough hot water to come about halfway up the sides of the dishes. Bake in the oven for 25–30 minutes, or until the custards are set. Remove the dishes from the roasting tray and allow to cool.

If your jam is very stiff, beat it to soften, or heat it slightly. When the custards are cool, spread the jam over them. Return the dishes to the emptied-out roasting tin.

For the meringue topping, whisk the egg whites with an electric whisk, or using a mixer with a whisk attachment, until they hold stiff peaks. Whisk in the sugar a spoonful at a time, until you have a fluffy meringue that holds stiff peaks.

Spoon the meringue into a piping bag fitted with a 1cm nozzle and pipe it on top of the jam-topped custards, or simply spoon it on top and swirl decoratively. Bake for 10–15 minutes, until the meringue is golden, then serve straight away.

Step photographs overleaf

Queen of puddings

Whisking the sugar, egg and egg yolks together for the custard.

Whisking the vanilla-infused hot milk into the egg and sugar mixture.

Pouring the warm custard over the breadcrumbs in the dishes.

Pouring hot water into the roasting tray to make a bain marie for the custards to gently cook in.

Spooning the raspberry jam on top of the cooled custards.

Whisking the egg whites for the meringue until forming stiff peaks.

Whisking the sugar into the whisked egg whites to make a stiff, glossy meringue.

Piping the meringue onto the jam-topped custards, ready to bake.

Steamed liquorice sponges

●●●●●●●

100g unsalted butter, softened, plus extra for greasing

4 liquorice spirals or Pontefract cakes

100g caster sugar

3 medium eggs

100g self-raising flour

1 tsp baking powder

1 tsp liquorice extract

Equipment

4 dariole moulds or individual pudding moulds, 175ml capacity

With these light and fluffy puddings, I've created a dish that carries the memory of some of the sweet-shop flavours of my childhood. Liquorice was the obvious choice – it has a lovely fruity tang that enhances the sponge beautifully.

Butter 4 dariole moulds or individual pudding basins, about 175ml capacity, and line the base of each with a disc of baking parchment.

Place a liquorice spiral or Pontefract cake in the base of each prepared mould.

Put all the remaining ingredients in a large bowl and beat together using an electric whisk. Start off slowly, then increase the speed and mix for 2 minutes until all the ingredients are well combined.

Divide the mixture between the moulds. Tap each mould on the work surface to remove any air pockets and level out the mixture.

Create a lid for each pudding by placing a small piece of baking parchment over a small piece of foil and making a pleat in the middle, folding both sheets together (to allow for the puddings' expansion as they cook). Put the lids on top of the pudding moulds, foil side up, and secure with string.

Stand the moulds in a steamer. Alternatively, put them in a large saucepan and pour in enough boiling water to come halfway up the sides of the moulds. Put the lid on the pan and bring to a simmer. Either way, steam the puddings for 45 minutes.

Uncover the puddings and run the tip of a small, sharp knife around the edge of each, to help release them. Invert them onto warmed plates and serve straight away, with custard.

Heather honey sponge

SERVES 4
● ● ● ● ● ● ● ●

100g unsalted butter, softened,
plus extra for greasing
130g heather honey
100g caster sugar
3 medium eggs
110g self-raising flour
1 tsp baking powder

Equipment
1 litre pudding basin

There's nothing to compare to the light, fluffy texture of a steamed sponge pudding. Golden syrup is a classic addition, of course, but I love this version, which makes the most of the fragrant flavour of Scottish heather honey. Any other well-flavoured honey will work too.

Butter a 1 litre pudding basin. Put 2 tbsp of the honey into the prepared basin (if the honey is very thick, warm it gently first to make it more liquid).

Put the remaining honey and all the other ingredients into a large bowl and beat together using an electric whisk. Start off slowly, then increase the speed and mix for 2 minutes until all the ingredients are well combined.

Spoon the mixture into the pudding basin, on top of the honey.

Place a piece of baking parchment on a sheet of foil and make a large pleat in the middle, folding both sheets together (this allows for the pudding's expansion as it cooks). Put the parchment and foil on top of the pudding, foil side up, and secure with string, looping the end of the string over the top of the pudding and tying it to form a handle that will enable you to lift the pudding in and out of the pan (as shown on page 91).

Stand the pudding basin in a large pan and pour in enough boiling water to come halfway up the side of the basin. Put a tight-fitting lid on the pan and bring to a simmer. Lower the heat to maintain a simmer and steam the pudding for 1¼ hours or until risen and springy to the touch. Top up the boiling water during this time if necessary so the pan doesn't boil dry.

Carefully lift the pudding basin from the pan, remove the foil and parchment and run the tip of a small, sharp knife around the edge of the pudding to help release it. Turn out onto a warmed large plate and serve piping hot, with custard or cream.

Sticky toffee pudding

SERVES 9–12

For the pudding
75g unsalted butter, softened, plus extra for greasing

175g stoned dates, chopped

200ml boiling water

1 tsp bicarbonate of soda

150g soft dark brown sugar

2 medium eggs, beaten

175g self-raising flour

½ tsp baking powder

2 tbsp fudge pieces

75g macadamia nuts, coarsely chopped

For the sticky toffee sauce
100g unsalted butter, cut into chunks

150g soft dark brown sugar

150ml double cream

Equipment
24 x 26cm baking tin, 4–5cm deep

Puddings don't get more gloriously indulgent than this one. Its origins are shrouded in mystery, but it is believed to have been invented at The Sharrow Bay Hotel in the Lake District in the seventies. I love the fact that it is not just about sweetness; there are lots of rich and nutty flavours in there too, making it the perfect pud after Sunday lunch on a cold winter's day.

Heat your oven to 180°C/gas 4 and butter a 24 x 26cm baking tin, 4–5cm deep.

Put the dates in a bowl, pour on the boiling water and stir in the bicarbonate of soda.

Cream the butter and sugar together in a large bowl until light and fluffy. Gradually add the beaten egg, beating well after each addition. Sift the flour and baking powder together over the mixture and fold in. Stir in the dates and their soaking water, then fold in the fudge pieces and 50g of the macadamia nuts.

Transfer the mixture to the prepared tin, spreading it evenly. Bake for 25–30 minutes, until firm and springy to the touch.

Meanwhile, to make the toffee sauce, melt together the butter, sugar and cream in a saucepan over a low heat. Bring to the boil and let bubble for 3–4 minutes, until the sauce is thick enough to coat the back of a wooden spoon.

Preheat your grill to high. Make holes all over the cooked pudding with a skewer. Pour half the sauce over the pudding and place under the hot grill. Grill for 2–3 minutes until the sauce is bubbling. Keep your eye on it as it can burn easily.

Cut the hot pudding into portions and serve with the remaining warm toffee sauce, sprinkled with the rest of the chopped nuts, and ice cream or cream.

Chocolate volcanoes

MAKES 4
●●●●●●●

165g unsalted butter, cut into
small pieces, plus extra for
greasing
165g dark chocolate, about
70% cocoa solids, chopped
into small pieces
3 medium eggs
3 medium egg yolks
85g caster sugar
2 tbsp plain flour

Equipment
4 individual pudding moulds or
dariole moulds, 175ml capacity

This is my version of the classic chocolate fondant – but I like this name better. These little hot chocolate puddings really do remind me of volcanoes as they release their soft, silky river of chocolate. Achieving the molten centre is all about timing. Don't let the puddings bake to the point that their surface begins to crack, as this means the centres are starting to cook.

Grease 4 individual pudding moulds, about 175ml capacity, with a little butter.

Put the butter and chocolate into a heatproof bowl over a pan of gently simmering water (bain marie). Remove the pan from the heat and leave to melt, stirring once or twice.

Using an electric whisk, whisk the eggs, egg yolks and sugar together for several minutes until thick, pale and moussey.

Carefully fold the chocolate mixture into the egg and sugar mix, using a spatula or large metal spoon. Sift in the flour and fold this in carefully too.

Divide the chocolate mixture between the prepared moulds. Place in the fridge for at least 2 hours until firm. (You can make the puddings up to 24 hours in advance and leave them in the fridge until you are ready to cook and serve them.)

When you are ready to cook, heat the oven to 200°C/gas 6. Stand the moulds on a baking tray and bake for 12–14 minutes, or until the puddings are risen but not cracked.

Turn the puddings out onto individual plates and serve at once, with pouring cream.

Step photographs overleaf

Chocolate volcanoes

Melting the butter and chocolate together, over a bain marie.

Whisking the eggs, egg yolks and sugar together, using a handheld electric whisk.

Whisked until pale and moussey, the egg and sugar mixture is thick enough to leave a trail.

Adding the melted chocolate mix to the whisked mixture and starting to fold it in with a spatula.

Continuing to fold the two mixtures together to combine evenly.

Carefully folding in the flour, using a cutting and folding action to avoid knocking out air.

Spooning the chocolate mixture into the prepared pudding moulds.

Standing the pudding moulds on a baking tray, ready to chill before baking.

Traditional rice pudding

SERVES 4

●●●●●●●

60g pudding rice
600ml whole milk
1 tbsp skimmed milk powder
2 tbsp caster sugar
1 thinly pared strip of lemon zest
Freshly grated nutmeg, to taste
15g unsalted butter, cut into
small dice

Equipment
1 litre baking dish

An oldie but a goodie, this is one of the best and simplest of all puds. You just need to serve it with a blob of jam for sheer comfort food heaven. The little bit of milk powder in the mix is an old trick that makes the pudding especially creamy.

Heat your oven to 150°C/gas 2.

Wash the rice and drain in a sieve, then put it into a wide baking dish, at least 1 litre capacity. Pour on the milk. Add the milk powder, caster sugar and lemon zest and stir together. Grate some nutmeg over the top and dot with the butter.

Bake in the oven for 2–2½ hours, until the pudding has a golden brown skin and the rice is tender and creamy (the longer you give it, the thicker and stickier it will become).

Serve warm, with a blob of your favourite jam on top.

Coffee crème caramels

MAKES 4
●●●●●●●●

For the custard

1 tbsp instant coffee granules
75g caster sugar
600ml whole milk
3 medium eggs
3 medium egg yolks

For the caramel

125g caster sugar
50ml water

Equipment

4 ramekins or individual
pudding moulds, 175ml
capacity
Roasting tray

These are very sophisticated puds, the sweetness of the custard balancing the flavour of the coffee, with a touch of bitterness from the caramel. You need to make them a day in advance so they can sit in the fridge, where the caramel will gradually melt into the coffee custard.

Heat your oven to 150°C/gas 2. Have ready 4 ramekins or individual pudding moulds, about 175ml capacity.

For the custard, put the coffee, sugar and milk in a saucepan and bring slowly up to simmering point, stirring occasionally to dissolve the coffee. Do not boil. Remove from the heat and set aside while you make the caramel.

Put the sugar and water for the caramel in a heavy-based saucepan. Heat gently until the sugar has dissolved, then bring to the boil. Boil steadily for a few minutes until the syrup has turned to a dark golden caramel.

As soon as the caramel has reached the right colour, pour it into the moulds. Tilt and rotate the moulds to swirl the caramel and coat partway up the sides; take care because it will be extremely hot. Leave to set (but do not refrigerate) while you make the custard.

Beat the eggs and egg yolks together in a large bowl. Gently pour on the coffee-flavoured milk, whisking as you do so until well combined. Strain the custard into a jug, then pour into the moulds.

Stand the moulds in a roasting tray and pour enough hot water into the tray to come about three-quarters of the way up the sides of the moulds. Cover the tray with foil and place in the oven. Bake for 40–45 minutes, or until the custards are just set but still have a slight wobble.

Remove the moulds from the roasting tray and leave the custards to cool completely, then refrigerate for 24 hours.

To turn out the puddings, first run a thin-bladed knife around the outside of the custard, then invert a deep plate over the top and turn the mould and plate over, so the custard and its lovely caramel slide out onto the plate. Serve straight away.

Step photographs overleaf

Coffee crème caramels

Boiling the sugar syrup steadily to a dark golden caramel.

Carefully pouring the very hot caramel into the individual moulds.

Tilting and rotating the moulds to swirl the caramel partway up the sides.

Pouring the strained custard over the caramel in the moulds.

Pouring hot water into the roasting tray to make
a bain marie for the custards to gently cook in.

Lemon & lavender posset with lavender biscuits

SERVES 4–6

For the posset

600ml double cream

150g caster sugar

1 tbsp lavender (fresh buds and leaves or edible dried lavender)

Juice of 2 lemons, strained

For the lavender biscuits

100g unsalted butter, softened

2 tsp lavender (fresh buds and leaves or edible dried lavender)

50g caster sugar

175g plain flour

Equipment

4 glass tumblers or small dishes, or 6 espresso cups

A posset is a very simple pudding that dates back to the Middle Ages. It was originally made by adding lemon juice or wine to milk but modern versions rely on cream. Here I've used lemon juice and fragrant lavender to cut the richness of the cream. You can buy edible dried lavender from baking suppliers and some supermarkets. Alternatively, if you have lavender in your garden, you can use fresh buds and leaves, finely chopped.

To make the posset, put the cream, sugar and lavender in a pan. Slowly bring to the boil, stirring all the time to dissolve the sugar. Reduce the heat a little and simmer for 2-3 minutes, stirring often so the cream doesn't stick and burn.

Remove the pan from the heat and stir in the lemon juice. Leave to cool for 5 minutes, then pour into 4 glass tumblers or small dishes, or 6 espresso cups. Leave to cool completely then cover with cling film and chill in the fridge for at least 3 hours, until set. Remove from the fridge 20 minutes before serving.

To make the biscuits, beat the butter and lavender together in a bowl; this helps release the flavour of the lavender. Add the sugar and beat until pale and fluffy. Work in the flour with a fork or wooden spoon. Don't worry if it seems like there is too much flour at this point – it is supposed to be a fairly dry mix. Use your hands to bring the mixture together into a smooth dough.

Form the mixture into a cylinder, about 4cm in diameter and 18cm long, and wrap in greaseproof paper or cling film. Put in the fridge for at least a couple of hours, until firm.

When you are ready to bake the biscuits, heat your oven to 160°C/ gas 3 and line a large baking tray with baking parchment.

Unwrap the dough and use a sharp, serrated knife to cut 5mm thick discs from the cylinder. Place these discs on the lined tray, allowing room for the biscuits to spread a little. (You'll need to cook them in batches.) Bake for about 15 minutes, until the edges of the biscuits are just starting to turn golden. Transfer to a wire rack to cool.

Serve the lemon posset with the lavender biscuits. Any leftover biscuits will keep in an airtight container for a few days.

Baked custards with pistachio shards

SERVES 6

●●●●●●●●

For the custards

1 vanilla pod

500ml double cream

100ml whole milk

6 large egg yolks

50g caster sugar

For the pistachio shards

75g unsalted, shelled
pistachio nuts

125g caster sugar

50ml water

Equipment

6 ramekins

Roasting tray

This is a variation on the classic crème brûlée, which normally calls for a super-thin, burnt-sugar topping. Getting that just right can be a bit tricky; making the caramel separately is a handy shortcut that many chefs use. I like to add some nuts to the caramel too, so you get a praline flavour to enhance the simple custard. This is a great pud to make in advance.

Heat your oven to 150°C/gas 2.

To make the custards, split the vanilla pod in half and scrape out the seeds with the tip of a small, sharp knife. Pour the cream and milk into a saucepan and add the vanilla seeds. Heat until just below boiling, then remove from the heat.

In a bowl, whisk the egg yolks and sugar together until thoroughly combined. Pour on the hot vanilla cream and whisk until smooth. Ladle into 6 ramekins.

Stand the ramekins in a roasting tray and pour in enough hot water to come halfway up the side of the dishes. Cover the tin with foil and bake for 30–40 minutes or until the custards are just set. There should be a slight wobble in the centre of the set custards.

Remove the ramekins from the roasting tray and allow to cool, then cover and put in the fridge to chill for about 3 hours.

To make the pistachio shards, first toast the pistachio nuts in a dry frying pan over a medium heat for a few minutes, until lightly coloured and fragrant. Tip them out onto a board and chop them roughly. Put to one side.

Lay a large piece of baking parchment on a baking tray. Put the sugar and water in a heavy-based pan. Heat gently until the sugar has dissolved, then bring to the boil and boil for a few minutes until the syrup has turned to a dark golden caramel. Immediately pour onto the lined baking tray and sprinkle with the pistachios. Leave the praline to set hard (not in the fridge).

If you are not serving straight away, put the pistachio praline in an airtight container as soon as it has set and cooled, to keep it crisp and brittle.

When you are ready to serve, break the praline into rough shards. Serve the chilled custards topped with the shards.

Hazelnut meringue roulade

SERVES 8

For the meringue

4 medium egg whites

225g caster sugar

75g toasted, skinned hazelnuts, finely chopped

For the filling

350ml double cream

3 tbsp chocolate hazelnut spread

25g dark chocolate, finely grated

25g toasted, skinned hazelnuts, finely chopped

Equipment

25 x 38cm shallow baking tin

This is a wonderful dessert – it looks impressive and tastes really sophisticated but it is pretty simple to make. I love the praline flavour created by the combination of sweet meringue and hazelnuts.

Heat your oven to 180°C/gas 4 and line a 25 x 38cm shallow baking tin with baking parchment.

For the meringue, whisk the egg whites with an electric whisk or using a mixer with a whisk attachment, until they form firm peaks. Now whisk in half the sugar, a spoonful at a time, whisking well between each addition to make sure the sugar is fully incorporated. Lightly fold in the remaining sugar to make a stiff, glossy meringue.

Spread the meringue evenly in the prepared tin and sprinkle over the chopped hazelnuts. Bake for 15–20 minutes until risen, lightly golden and set. Have ready a large piece of baking parchment.

Carefully invert the meringue onto the paper, nut side down. Peel away the lining paper and leave to cool completely.

For the filling, whip the cream until it holds soft peaks. Beat the chocolate spread in another bowl until it is soft and fold it lightly into the whipped cream.

Spread the chocolate cream on top of the cooled meringue, leaving a 1cm margin at each edge. Sprinkle the grated chocolate over the cream, followed by the chopped hazelnuts.

Using a palette knife, make an indentation across the width of the meringue, about 1.5cm in from one of the short ends (this makes it easier to start rolling). Now, using the greaseproof paper to help you, roll up the roulade from that short end. Don't worry if it cracks a little – that's all part of its charm.

Carefully transfer the roulade to a rectangular serving plate or board and serve straight away.

Step photographs overleaf

Hazelnut meringue roulade

Spreading the stiff, glossy meringue in the prepared baking tin.

Sprinkling the chopped toasted hazelnuts evenly over the surface of the meringue.

Inverting the cooked meringue onto greaseproof paper and peeling away the lining paper.

Spreading the chocolate cream on top of the cooled meringue.

Making an indentation across the width of the meringue, about 1.5cm in from one edge.

Starting to roll up the meringue from the indented edge, using the greaseproof paper.

Continuing to roll up the roulade firmly and evenly, using the paper to help.

Removing the paper, ready to transfer the roulade to a serving plate or board.

Black Forest trifle

SERVES 8

For the cherry blondies

225g unsalted butter,
cut into cubes

225g white chocolate, broken
into small pieces

225g caster sugar

4 medium eggs

½ tsp vanilla extract

175g self-raising flour

100g dark chocolate, chopped

100g glacé cherries, halved

For the chocolate custard

150ml double cream

150ml whole milk

4 medium egg yolks

100g caster sugar

30g plain flour

100g dark chocolate,
finely chopped

To assemble

3 tbsp Kirsch

2 x 470g jars morello cherries
in syrup, drained

1 x 340g jar cherry conserve
or jam

200g mascarpone

200ml double cream

To finish

25g dark chocolate, grated
Dark chocolate curls, pared
with a veg peeler (optional)

Equipment

20 x 26cm brownie tin
Large trifle bowl

Black Forest gâteau, with its blend of chocolate, cream, cherries and Kirsch, is a seventies classic that is still universally popular. This trifle uses the same combination of flavours to even more spectacular effect. If you don't have time to make the cherry blondies, buy a good ready-made sponge for the base instead.

Begin by making the blondies. Preheat your oven to 180°C/gas 4 and line a 20 x 26cm brownie tin with parchment.

Melt the butter and white chocolate together in a bowl over a pan of barely simmering water, stirring once or twice. Let cool slightly.

Whisk the sugar, eggs and vanilla together in a large bowl with an electric whisk or using a mixer for several minutes until pale, mousse-like and increased in volume. Slowly pour the melted chocolate mixture onto the eggs and fold in gently.

Add the flour and fold in lightly, then fold in the chopped dark chocolate. Pour into the lined tin and scatter over the glacé cherries.

Bake for about 30 minutes or until a skewer inserted into the centre comes out almost clean. Leave to cool in the tin.

To make the custard, put the cream and milk in a pan and heat until almost boiling. Take off the heat. Whisk the egg yolks, sugar and flour together, then pour on the hot milk and cream, whisking as you do so. Pour back into the pan and add the chocolate. Stir over a low heat until the chocolate has melted and the custard is well thickened. Strain into a jug and cover the surface of the custard with cling film (to prevent a skin forming). Leave to cool completely.

To assemble the trifle, cut about a third of the blondies into 2–3cm cubes and use to line the base of a large trifle bowl. (You won't need the rest here, but they will keep in an airtight tin for several days or you could use them for my chocolate bread and butter pudding on page 162.) Trickle over the Kirsch, so it soaks into the blondies. Scatter over the drained cherries, then spread over the cherry jam.

Spoon the cooled chocolate custard over the cherries then put into the fridge for several hours to allow the custard to set.

Whip the mascarpone with the cream until holding soft peaks, then swirl over the custard. Sprinkle with grated chocolate and decorate with chocolate curls, if using.

Cranachan cheesecake

SERVES 8

For the base

125g unsalted butter, melted,
plus extra for greasing
250g fine-milled oatcakes
3 tbsp honey

For the filling

60g pinhead (coarse) oatmeal
100g caster sugar
350g crowdie or ricotta
350g full-fat cream cheese
4 medium eggs
200g raspberries

For the raspberry coulis

500g raspberries
50g icing sugar

To finish

Handful of raspberries

Equipment

Deep 23cm springform cake tin

The classic Scottish dessert cranachan is a delicious blend of toasted oatmeal, raspberries, honey and crowdie – a type of soft, mild cheese. I've used those ingredients as the inspiration for this gorgeous cheesecake – make it in summer or early autumn when British raspberries are at their best. If you can't get hold of any crowdie, ricotta works equally well.

Butter a deep 23cm springform cake tin.

To make the base, put the oatcakes in a food processor and blitz until finely ground. Add the melted butter and honey and process briefly again until thoroughly combined. Press this mixture evenly into the base of the prepared tin. Chill in the fridge to set while you make the filling.

Heat your oven to 180°C/gas 4.

Heat a small frying pan over a medium heat. Add the oatmeal and 1 tsp of the sugar and toast, tossing frequently, until golden. Tip onto a plate to cool.

Put the crowdie or ricotta, cream cheese, eggs and remaining sugar in a food processor and blend until smooth. Stir in the cooled toasted oatmeal. Pour the mixture over the chilled oat base and scatter over the raspberries.

Bake for 35–40 minutes or until the cheesecake is set around the edges but still a bit wobbly in the middle. Turn off the oven and leave the cheesecake inside with the door ajar until it is cool. (Allowing it to cool slowly this way helps prevent it from cracking.)

Meanwhile, to make the raspberry coulis, purée the raspberries and icing sugar together in a blender, or using a handheld stick blender. Push the purée through a sieve into a jug to remove the pips.

Carefully unmould the cheesecake onto a large plate or board and cut into slices. Serve with fresh berries and the raspberry coulis.

Arctic roll

SERVES 8
● ● ● ● ● ● ● ●

For the Swiss roll

A little sunflower oil for oiling

3 medium eggs

100g caster sugar, plus extra
for dusting

100g self-raising flour

1 tbsp warm water

For the filling

500ml good-quality vanilla
ice cream

200g raspberry jam

Equipment

22 x 32cm Swiss roll tin

This wonderfully retro pud dates back to the 1950s and is a fun way to round off a dinner party. Serve it just as it is or with fresh raspberries or strawberries on the side.

Heat your oven to 200°C/gas 6 and line a Swiss roll tin, 22 x 32cm or thereabouts, with baking parchment, and oil this very lightly.

For the filling, put the ice cream in a large bowl and beat it with the end of a rolling pin or something similar until just soft enough to mould. Scoop it onto a sheet of baking parchment and quickly shape into a sausage, 25–30cm long and about 5cm in diameter. Wrap in the parchment and place in the freezer to firm up.

To make the Swiss roll, use an electric whisk or a mixer with a whisk attachment to whisk the eggs and sugar together for several minutes until pale, moussey and almost tripled in volume. The mixture should be thick enough to hold a trail on the surface when the whisk is lifted. Sift the flour over the mixture and fold it in carefully. Fold in the warm water.

Pour the mixture into the prepared tin and smooth it out gently so it reaches into the corners. Bake for 10–12 minutes until golden and just firm to the touch.

Cut a sheet of baking parchment slightly larger than the Swiss roll tin, lay it on your work surface and sprinkle with sugar. Invert the cooked sponge onto the parchment and carefully peel away the lining paper from the sponge. Leave to cool completely.

To assemble the roll, first trim the two long sides of the sponge into neat, straight lines. Spread the jam over the sponge, leaving a 2cm margin along the edges.

Unwrap the ice cream and place it lengthways across the sponge, close to one edge. Use the parchment to help you roll the sponge around the ice cream. Use a bread knife to neatly trim each end of the roll.

Place the Arctic roll on a plate and serve straight away, cut into thick slices. You can wrap any of the roll that isn't eaten and return it to the freezer. Take it out and let it stand for a few minutes so the sponge can soften slightly, before slicing to serve.

Step photographs overleaf

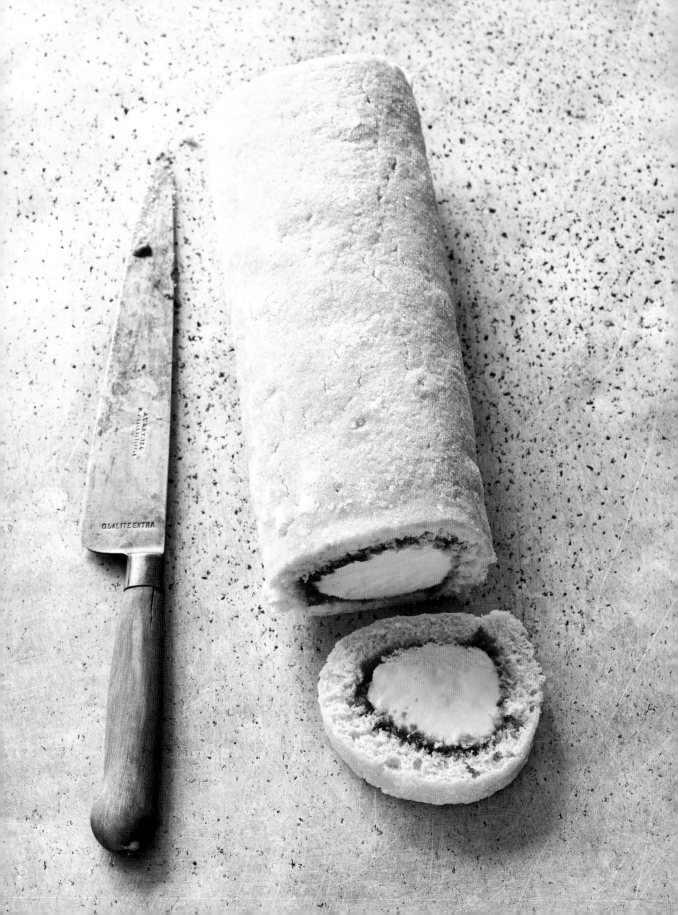

Arctic roll

Shaping the ice cream into a roll in baking parchment and twisting the ends to secure.

Whisking the eggs and sugar together until the mixture is pale and thick enough to leave a trail.

Folding the flour into the whisked mixture, using a cutting and folding action.

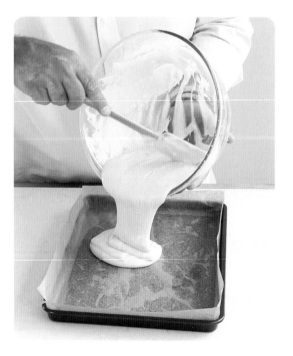

Pouring the sponge mixture into the prepared Swiss roll tin.

Peeling the lining paper away from the sponge.

Positioning the frozen ice cream roll on the jam-topped sponge.

Rolling the sponge around the ice cream to enclose it.

Trimming off the ends of the Arctic roll.

Strawberry mousse cake

SERVES 8

For the genoise sponge base

15g unsalted butter, melted, plus extra for greasing

2 medium eggs

50g caster sugar

50g plain flour, sifted

For the mousse layer

135g packet strawberry jelly

1 tbsp water

200g strawberries

2 x 170g cans evaporated milk

250g strawberries, hulled and cut in half top-to-toe (or sliced into 3 if large)

To finish

50g dark chocolate, chopped

50g white chocolate, chopped

6–8 strawberries, hulled

Equipment

23cm springform cake tin

2 small greaseproof paper piping bags

This is a really pretty gâteau, perfect to serve as a dessert for a summer party or special meal.

First make the sponge. Heat your oven to 180°C/gas 4. Butter and base-line a 23cm springform cake tin.

Put the eggs and sugar in a heatproof bowl over a pan of simmering water and whisk together using a handheld electric whisk until thick, pale and moussey, and doubled in volume. The mixture should hold a trail on the surface when you lift the whisk. Take off the heat and gently fold in the melted butter, then the flour.

Pour the mixture into the prepared tin and bake for 15–20 minutes until cooked and lightly golden. Leave to cool completely, then remove the sponge from the tin and peel off the paper.

Line the sides of the same tin with baking parchment, first snipping a line of parallel cuts along the base of the paper so it will fit snugly against the base. Put the sponge base back into the tin.

To make the mousse, break up the jelly and put it into a small pan with the water. Melt gently over a low heat until smooth. Take off the heat and set aside. Purée the 200g strawberries in a blender until smooth and pass through a sieve to remove the seeds.

Using an electric whisk or a mixer with a whisk attachment, whisk the evaporated milk for at least 5 minutes until it is thick, bubbly and doubled in volume. Gently fold in the liquid jelly, then fold in the strawberry purée.

Arrange the strawberry slices around the edge of the lined tin, cut side against the tin. Scatter any extra strawberries over the sponge. Pour the strawberry mousse into the tin and gently level the surface. It doesn't matter if the mousse doesn't quite cover the strawberries. Place in the fridge for at least 2 hours to set.

Carefully unmould the mousse cake onto a plate. To finish, melt the dark and white chocolate separately in bowls over hot water. Dip the strawberries into the melted dark chocolate to coat and place on parchment to set. Put the rest of the dark chocolate and the white chocolate into separate greaseproof paper piping bags, snip off the tip and drizzle lines of dark and white chocolate over the top of the mousse. Top with the chocolate-dipped strawberries and serve.

Step photographs overleaf

Strawberry mousse cake

Spooning the genoise mixture into the prepared springform tin.

Peeling away the lining paper from the base of the cooked sponge.

Fitting the cooled sponge into the base of the re-lined tin.

Adding the liquid jelly to the whisked evaporated milk.

Adding the strawberry purée to the evaporated milk and jelly mixture.

Positioning the strawberry slices around the edge of the cake tin, cut side outwards.

Carefully pouring the strawberry mousse mixture into the tin.

Drizzling melted chocolate decoratively over the surface of the set mousse.

Marmalade & almond cake

SERVES 8
● ● ● ● ● ● ● ●

200g unsalted butter, softened,
plus extra for greasing
150g semolina
75g ground almonds
½ tsp baking powder
200g caster sugar
3 tbsp fine-cut marmalade
2 medium eggs
Finely grated zest of 2 oranges
50ml orange juice

For the cream cheese frosting
175g cream cheese
25g unsalted butter, softened
100g icing sugar

To finish
Finely pared orange zest

Equipment
20cm springform cake tin

This is based on a classic orange polenta cake, though I prefer to use semolina rather than polenta, which can lead to a slight grittiness. Semolina gives the cake a lovely, fine texture but you can opt for polenta or fine cornmeal instead if you'd like to keep the cake wheat-free.

Heat your oven to 180°C/gas 4. Grease a 20cm springform cake tin with butter and line the base with baking parchment.

Combine the semolina, ground almonds and baking powder in a bowl, mix thoroughly and set aside.

Beat the butter and sugar together in a large bowl until pale and fluffy. Beat in the marmalade, then beat in the eggs, one at a time.

Add the semolina and almond mixture, along with the orange zest, and fold in gently. Finally, incorporate the orange juice to give a soft dropping consistency.

Spoon the mixture into the prepared cake tin and gently smooth the surface with the back of a spoon.

Bake for 35 minutes, or until the cake is golden brown. Leave in the tin to cool for 5 minutes, then remove and transfer to a wire rack to cool completely.

To make the frosting, beat the cream cheese and butter together. Sift in the icing sugar and beat until smooth. Use a palette knife to spread the frosting on top of the cake. Chill before serving, to allow the frosting to set.

Before serving, scatter fine shreds of orange zest on top of the cake for a decorative finish.

Lemon & lavender loaf

SERVES 8
●●●●●●●●

For the cake

250g plain flour

½ tsp baking powder

½ tsp bicarbonate of soda

125g caster sugar

1½ tbsp lavender (fresh buds and leaves or edible dried lavender)

Finely grated zest of 2 lemons

2 large eggs

200g full-fat plain yoghurt

100g unsalted butter, melted

For the lemon drizzle

Juice of 2 lemons, strained

2 tbsp icing sugar

For the topping

1 tbsp granulated sugar

2 tsp edible dried lavender

Equipment

1kg loaf tin, about 10 x 20cm base measurement

This simple variation on the classic lemon drizzle works a treat. It has a wonderful, light texture, a very fresh taste and it looks incredibly pretty – perfect with a cuppa on a sunny afternoon. For advice on sourcing edible lavender, see page 187.

Heat your oven to 180°C/gas 4. Line a 1kg loaf tin (about 10 x 20cm base measurement) with baking parchment.

In a bowl, combine the flour, baking powder, bicarbonate of soda, sugar, lavender and lemon zest.

In a jug, beat the eggs with the yoghurt and melted butter until evenly blended. Pour this onto the dry ingredients and, using a spatula, stir until just combined.

Pour the mixture into the prepared tin and bake for 40 minutes or until a skewer inserted into the centre of the cake comes out clean.

Just before the cake is cooked, mix the ingredients for the drizzle together. Remove the cake from the oven and prick it deeply all over with a cocktail stick. Pour the lemon drizzle over the hot cake, then sprinkle over the granulated sugar followed by the lavender. Leave to cool completely in the tin before slicing.

Come-again cake

SERVES 8–10
● ● ● ● ● ● ● ● ● ●

200g unsalted butter, softened

150g caster sugar

200g self-raising flour

2 tbsp cocoa powder

2 medium eggs, beaten

2 tbsp golden syrup

200g mixed dried fruit

Finely grated zest and juice
of ½ lemon

Equipment

1kg loaf tin, about 10 x 20cm
base measurement

This lovely, fruity, lightly chocolatey cake is based on an old Yorkshire recipe. Its texture improves on keeping, hence the name. It will keep for up to a month, and is very good used in my chocolate bread and butter pudding (page 162).

Heat your oven to 160°C/gas 3. Line a 1kg loaf tin (about 10 x 20cm base measurement) with baking parchment.

Beat the butter and sugar together in a large bowl until pale and fluffy. Beat in 3 tbsp of the flour together with the cocoa powder, then gradually beat in the eggs. Fold in the remaining flour, then add the remaining ingredients and fold these in too.

Spread the mixture in the prepared tin and bake for 1½ hours or until a skewer inserted into the centre comes out clean. Leave to cool in the tin for 10 minutes, then turn out and cool on a rack. Store in an airtight tin.

Salted caramel & coffee éclairs

MAKES 8

●●●●●●●●

For the choux pastry

50g unsalted butter, cut into roughly 1cm dice

1 tsp caster sugar

Pinch of salt

150ml water

65g strong white bread flour

2 medium eggs, beaten

For the coffee filling

200g mascarpone

1 tbsp icing sugar

3 tbsp cold strong coffee (espresso is ideal)

250ml double cream

For the salted caramel icing

150g soft light brown sugar

75g unsalted butter, softened

Pinch of salt

50ml whole milk

125g icing sugar

Equipment

2 baking trays

Piping bag

1cm plain nozzle

If you think you couldn't turn out a batch of professional-looking and utterly irresistible éclairs, think again. These are very straightforward and will impress family and friends.

Heat your oven to 190°C/gas 5. Line two baking trays with baking parchment.

To make the choux pastry, put the butter, sugar, salt and water into a large saucepan. Heat gently until the butter has melted then bring to the boil. Immediately remove from the heat and tip in the flour. Beat with a wooden spoon to form a smooth ball of dough that leaves the sides of the pan.

Now vigorously beat the egg into the hot dough, a little at a time. This takes some elbow grease! As you add the egg, the dough will become stiff and glossy. Stop adding the egg if the dough starts to become loose – but you should use up all or most of it.

Spoon the choux paste into a piping bag fitted with a 1cm plain nozzle. Pipe eight 12cm lengths onto the baking trays, leaving plenty of space for spreading. Bake for 30 minutes, or until well risen and golden. Remove from the oven and split one side of each éclair to allow the steam to escape. Cool on a wire rack.

To make the filling, beat the mascarpone until smooth. Beat in the icing sugar and coffee. Whip the cream until it holds soft peaks and fold in. Spoon the mixture into a piping bag fitted with a 1cm plain nozzle and pipe into the éclairs.

To make the icing, put the sugar, butter and salt into a small pan and heat gently until the butter has melted and the mixture is smooth. Add the milk, bring to the boil and boil for 2 minutes, stirring occasionally. Remove from the heat and sift in the icing sugar. Stir until smooth.

Spread the icing on top of the éclairs. You'll need to work quickly before the icing sets but it can be reheated if it sets before you have finished. Serve the éclairs as soon as the icing is set.

Step photographs overleaf

Salted caramel & coffee éclairs

Spooning the choux paste into a piping bag.

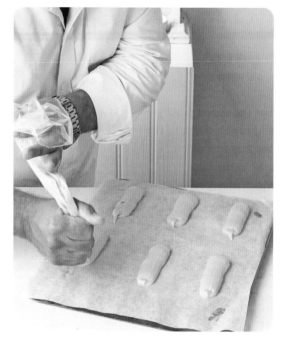

Piping the choux paste into 12cm lengths on the lined baking trays.

Splitting each cooked éclair along one side to release the steam from inside.

Piping the coffee filling into each éclair.

Spreading the salted caramel icing on top
of each éclair with a small palette knife.

Shortbread whisky dodgers

MAKES 12

For the biscuits
225g unsalted butter, softened
100g caster sugar, plus extra
for sprinkling
225g plain flour
100g fine semolina

For the whisky and white chocolate ganache
200g white chocolate,
broken into small pieces
100ml double cream
1½ tbsp whisky

Equipment
7.5cm cutter, plus small heart-
and/or star-shaped cutters
2 baking sheets

These are, of course, a sophisticated and delicious version of the classic jam-sandwich biscuit.

Beat the butter and sugar together in a large bowl until light and fluffy. Combine the flour and semolina, add to the butter mix and use a wooden spoon to start working in. When the mixture starts to form clumps, use your hands to bring it together into a smooth dough. Form it into a rough disc, wrap in cling film and chill for about an hour.

Heat your oven 170°C/gas 3. Line two baking sheets with baking parchment.

Tip the chilled dough onto a floured work surface and roll it out until about 3mm thick. Don't worry if it seems a little crumbly at first, just press it back together and re-roll.

Use a 7.5cm round cutter to cut out 24 discs of dough. Put these on the lined baking trays. Use a small star- and/or heart-shaped cutter to cut out shapes from the centre of half the discs.

Bake for 15 minutes, until the shortbread biscuits are just starting to turn golden at the edges. While still hot, sprinkle caster sugar over the biscuits with shapes cut out. Leave the biscuits on the trays to cool and firm up.

Meanwhile, to make the ganache filling, put the chocolate and double cream in a bowl. Heat over a pan of simmering water until the chocolate has melted, stirring from time to time to amalgamate the mixture. When completely smooth, stir in the whisky. Leave to cool, then cover and refrigerate for 2–3 hours, until firm.

To assemble the dodgers, spoon some ganache into the centre of each base biscuit (those that do not have shapes cut out) in a roughly circular shape, leaving a small gap around the edge. Alternatively, you can pipe the ganache onto the biscuits.

Sit the star or heart cut-out biscuits on top of the filling and press down very lightly. Repeat until all of the biscuits are sandwiched together. Serve as soon as they are assembled, as the biscuits will start to lose their crispness after a few hours.

Step photographs overleaf

Shortbread whisky dodgers

Stamping out discs of shortbread dough with a 7.5cm plain cutter.

Cutting out hearts or stars from the centre of half of the shortbread rounds.

Carefully lifting out the hearts and stars (these can be re-rolled to cut more biscuits).

Spreading the whisky and white chocolate ganache on the plain shortbread rounds.

Applying the star and heart cut-out biscuits
to sandwich the filling.

To Josh – my special boy

Acknowledgments

Thank you to everybody involved in this book at Bloomsbury, in particular my editor Natalie Hunt, for her unstinting dedication to the project; Nikki Duffy and Janet Illsley, for their excellent work on the text; Jude Drake, Ellen Williams, Amanda Shipp, Roísín Nield, Nikki Morgan, Marina Asenjo and Xa Shaw Stewart for their support and creativity.

This book would not have been possible without the talents and patience of the wonderful Claire Bassano and the creative vision of photographer Peter Cassidy, and designers Peter Dawson and Louise Evans.

Thank you to the production team behind the series at Spun Gold Television, Nick Bullen, Chris Kelly and Dunk Barnes, and to Gerard Melling and Damian Kavanagh at the BBC for making it happen.

Finally thanks to my agents Geraldine Woods and Anna Bruce who championed this from the outset... and have always had a soft spot for pies and puds!

• •

Bloomsbury Publishing Plc, 50 Bedford Square, London WC1B 3DP
Bloomsbury Publishing, London, New Delhi, New York and Sydney
www.bloomsbury.com

A CIP catalogue record for this book is available from the British Library.

ISBN 978 1 4088 6006 9

10 9 8 7 6 5 4 3 2 1

Project editor: Janet Illsley
Designers: Peter Dawson, Louise Evans www.gradedesign.com
Photographer: Peter Cassidy
Food editor: Nikki Duffy
Recipe development consultant: Claire Bassano
Food stylists: Claire Bassano and Nikki Morgan
Props stylist: Roísín Nield
Indexer: Hilary Bird

Printed and bound by Mohn Media, Germany

Innovative use of combined heat and power technology when printing this product reduced CO$_2$ emissions by up to 52% in comparison to conventional methods in Germany.